INSTITUTIONS AND THE RIGHT TO VOTE IN AMERICA

Elections, Voting, Technology

The series Elections, Voting, Technology examines the relationships between people, electoral processes and technologies, and democracy. Elections are a fundamental aspect of a free and democratic society and, at their core, they involve a citizenry making selections for who will represent them. This series examines the ways in which citizens select their candidates—the voting technologies used, the rules of the game that govern the process—and considers how changes in processes and technologies affect the voter and the democratic process.

Thad Hall is an associate professor of political science at the University of Utah and a research affiliate with the Caltech/MIT Voting Technology Project. He is the coauthor of several books on elections and voting, including *Point, Click, and Vote: The Future of Internet Voting* and *Electronic Elections: The Perils and Promise of Digital Democracy,* and coeditor of the book *Election Fraud.*

INSTITUTIONS AND THE RIGHT TO VOTE IN AMERICA

Martha E. Kropf

Martha E. Kropf
Department of Political Science
University of North Carolina at Charlotte
Charlotte, NC, USA

Elections, Voting, Technology

ISBN 978-1-137-30170-3   ISBN 978-1-137-30171-0 (eBook)
DOI 10.1007/978-1-137-30171-0

This Palgrave Macmillan imprint is published by Springer Nature
The registered company is Nature America Inc. New York

I dedicate this book to my family: my husband, Dr. John Szmer. He provided his unwavering support and constant love while I wrote this. My children, Gwendolyn and Zachary Szmer, provided plenty of distraction, snuggles, and love. I love you all.

I also dedicate this book to the memory of my former undergraduate student, Jessica Link. With fierce dedication, she completed her senior thesis under my direction. She had cystic fibrosis and missed a good bit of class while at the University of North Carolina at Charlotte, but I have never had any student before or since with as much determination to complete her work. We worked on her senior thesis in cooperation with Dr. Mark Hirsch of the Carolinas Medical Center examining how "typical" undergraduates compared in political knowledge to individuals with traumatic brain injury. We published the article in the *Election Law Journal*, and if the reader looks at the end of Chapter 5, I invoke our work to discuss some of the ideas of limitations on voting for those with cognitive capacity.

She earned her degree in political science in 2008.

I admire that woman's strength and passion for her education. She died in 2015 at age 28.

CONTENTS

Figures and Tables

Figures

Tables

CHAPTER 1

INTRODUCTION

IN THE UNITED STATES TODAY, if one asked the person on the street what the central meaning of citizenship is, many might respond it is the right to vote. This is a concept that starts rather early in our life—look, for example, at the US government website about the basics of government for various ages of children. "Ben's [Franklin's] Guide to U.S. Government for Kids" explains that many different people live in the United States, but that those who are not "citizens" "have some of the same freedoms and legal rights as U.S. citizens, but they cannot vote in elections."[1] Yet, there are still cases of citizens who want to vote, but whom the laws seem to have left behind. A man named Stephen L. wrote in a court brief:

> My name is Stephen. I am 20 years old. I am an American citizen. I also have a disability. Earlier this year, I was at risk of losing the right to vote. Just because I have a disability. With help from Dr. Nora Baladerian and attorney Tom Coleman, I was able to keep the right to vote. But other people with disabilities were not so lucky. They had their right to vote taken away by judges in the Los Angeles Superior Court. I hope that Attorney General Eric Holder makes the judges give the right to vote back to these Americans. Mr. Holder, if you read or learn about my statement, I am asking you to please help people with disabilities keep our right to vote. We want to participate in our democracy, not be excluded.[2]

In the summer of 2014, nearly 100 individuals under "limited conservatorships" (a form of adult guardianship) filed a federal lawsuit asking that their legal ability to vote not be blocked automatically when a judge places them under guardianship and/or they can't complete their own voter registration. The plaintiffs charge that is the same as a literacy test for voting.[3] It may seem easy for some to dismiss the example here—it's not anything like broad classes of individuals—women or African Americans or those aged 18–20 who long lacked suffrage in this country—but who should judge who can vote and who can't?

Perhaps some might argue that only those who are well informed and completely cognitively able should vote. But then who should decide who is cognitively able?

Determining voting eligibility and administering elections is a state responsibility. But what about cases where a person—such as Anna Nick—is cognitively able to vote, and probably more qualified to vote than many other US citizens? She is an elder of her Native American tribe in Alaska and had at one point had served as a pollworker. Because of the educational system in Alaska, Nick only had through a fifth-grade education. She is classified as a "limited English proficiency" (LEP) individual—for example, a ballot measure calling for English-only elections may be very confusing to her, causing her to vote (or not) in a way inconsistent with her self-interest. As a result, she was one of many LEP plaintiffs living near her in a lawsuit filed under the national Voting Rights Act against state election officials. The VRA was amended in 1975 to protect language minorities' ability to vote. The plaintiffs asked for election materials and translations in their native language. The state of Alaska settled the lawsuit. All in all, it took the federal government VRA to ensure Anna Nick's ability to vote as she wished.[4]

For the most part, we hold the voting piece of our citizenship very dear. People have fought and died for the right. Court cases are fought not just on obtaining the individual "right" to vote, but also to prevent our votes from being diluted or cancelled out. By 2014, some state officials vowed to protect this vote requiring "satisfactory evidence of United States citizenship" in order for new registrants to vote, as in the case of the state of Kansas.[5] The Kansas Secretary of State's website declares: "Elections are the cornerstone of democracy, and we are committed to protecting the sanctity of the democratic process." Clearly, the value of self-governance runs strong in those in this country, even though arguably, for the most part, our country is not "a democracy"—our country is a republic wherein we elect our representatives who make most formal decisions. Perhaps some might be more comfortable with calling the United States a representative democracy with constitutional limits! Nevertheless, the Constitution of the United States, our founding document, does not even directly articulate a right to vote.[6]

Some citizens in this country cannot or do not vote in elections; many argue it is not "rational" to bother with voting. Still others continue to fight despite the idea that it appears that most everyone now shares that "right"—not simply just in the form of arguing that proof of citizenship or requiring government-issued picture identification to vote potentially disenfranchises voters. As noted earlier, in July 2014, the Disability and Abuse Project of Spectrum Institute filed a lawsuit against the state of California as a result of a complex set of laws that essentially outlined that those who were living under guardianship lost their right to vote. "Stephen" wanted to vote and have a say in governance. Under what circumstances should someone with arguably diminished mental capacity be able to vote?

The bottom line is that rules matter. Way too much ink has been spilled discussing the infamous 2000 election, but however trite the statement might be, the 2000 election caused citizens and policymakers alike to see that the rules governing the complex administrative process of elections can vitally affect what many view as the heart of citizenship and what it means to be an American. However, it is not just the formal laws that are on the books, but also the informal values and norms that affect our ability to vote. Political scientist B. Guy Peters writes that

> an institution is created when a formal structure has meaning for the members, and when those members begin to believe that the structure is something more than a means to an end. The institution will, therefore, be able to motivate the members— through its logic of appropriateness—to a greater extent than would a simple, mechanical organization.
>
> (2012: 35)

Our election system is an institution whose stability is guarded not just by formal rules about structure and ability to vote, but also by a complex system of norms and values about the purpose of the "system" and our role in it. Individuals living in this country basically make an implicit daily choice—to live with the form of government and not rebel and, for the most part, live with the laws created by those elected to government. Most value our "membership" in democracy. The institutions— comprising both the formal and informal rules and structures—thus shape our vote choices and thus our very ability to change the institution. The institution governs whether Stephen can vote and whether he should have the right to vote.

Hence, this book is called *Institutions and the Right to Vote*. The key point is to understand that we are talking about a framework of rules created when 13 colonies declared independence and when the federal constitution was first written (well, perhaps more aptly, rewritten). There is an institution nested inside the structure, which enables the continued existence of the framework of rules known as our government. In other words, we arguably have an institution within an institution (rather than differing levels of rules nested within each other—see for example, Ostrom, 1990: 50–55). Using the establishment of the United States of America as the basis, the institution of elections enables the peaceful transfer of power over time.

Although the institution of elections is largely stable, the rules, to some extent, continue to be developed today. This book is not necessarily about *why* an institution changes over time per se, but the reader should observe that the struggle for power comes up over and over again when documenting *how* the institution has changed. The framework of rules outlined how the institution would be set up, accounted for an official allocation of resources and power, and specified how individual citizens would participate. Yet, the US Constitution did not specify who could vote, but rather, left that to the states, saying, "The Times, Places and Manner of holding Elections for Senators and Representatives, shall be prescribed in each State by the Legislature thereof; but the Congress may at any time by law make or alter such Regulations, except as to the Places of chusing Senators." (United States Constitution, Article I, Section 4). In other words, the founders left the power of elections with the states. However, part of institutional change has been the passage of constitutional amendments to ensure that certain groups had the right to vote and the passage of laws to enforce the amendments (various parts of the Voting Rights Act). This history has both constrained and enabled groups where voting is concerned.

An important early scholar of the effect of such institutions on voter turnout, political scientist Jerrold D. Rusk, wrote in 1970 about the history of the use of the Australian system of voting—also known as the "Australian ballot" (introduced in the United States the late 1870s) and its effects on turnout and split-ticket voting in order to make a bigger point about the effects of "institutions" on voting. The Australian ballot changes made printing ballots a government responsibility, not a political party one. Not only that, the ballots listed the candidates of all qualifying political parties rather than just the one that happened to print the ballots. Finally, the voter cast the ballot in private. Rusk defined "institutional properties" as follows:

> By "institutional properties" are meant those laws, customs, and norms that define and regulate the broader entity known as the electoral system. Such things as registration requirements, electoral qualification laws, voting systems (e.g., plurality, proportional representation systems), ballot and voting machine arrangements, and the like are the framework of the system. Introduction of new properties or changes in existing ones affect the voting setting and, in turn, the behavior and attitudes of people.
>
> (Rusk, 1970: 1237–1238)

Close to 50 years after these words were written, voters take for granted many of the electoral laws and customs, including the secret ballot published by a government rather than a political party. Dr. Rusk's point was that the rules written on a paper somewhere in a government archive affect our political behavior in the same way that attitudes such as partisanship do. The thesis of this book agrees with Rusk.

As our system of voting—the institution of elections—has grown and aged, the institution has changed and norms and expectations have grown up around the institution that shape and constrain our political behavior. When written rules (laws) change, then behavior, as well as norms (unwritten rules) surrounding the institutions, may change. Dr. Rusk examined how reforms in ballot secrecy and format changed choices surrounding partisan voting and split-ticket voting between 1876 and 1908.

> The presence of a secret vote gave further notice that the prevailing norms of the partisan world were capable of being broken at the polling station. In fact, the new system encouraged different norms more compatible with the changing milieu. Split ticket voting was on the rise because the opportunity clearly existed to be used. This did not mean that electorates immediately registered large split ticket tendencies overnight; voters had to adjust to the new ballot instrument and the new norms that the changing milieu created. Old habits had to be modified or broken to adjust to the new situation-habits that had been in existence for a long time.
>
> (Rusk, 1970: 1223)

In other words, the institution defines how we (as citizens) interact and make changes to the institution—but the institution constrains and shapes our ability to do so.

Institutions and the Right to Vote is about the interaction of the legal systems and the constraints over voting the laws create; however, unwritten rules or norms also govern our behavior within the institution of elections. A major theme here is how the institutions of democracy relate to the individual behavior within the institution. Political scientist B. Guy Peters explains various aspects of *new institutional theory* in the field of political science. He notes that "… there must be a mechanism through which the institution shapes the behavior of individuals, and there must be a mechanism through which individuals are able to form and reform institutions" (page 38). Thus, the central question is how have institutions shaped and constrained individual behavior, and how have individuals shaped and constrained institutions? Further, how do actors within the system operate within the system of rules in order to take advantage of the rules? American democracy, in its fits and starts of "rule by the people," is an excellent example of an institution wherein these processes operate. Thus, this book will outline various aspects of the formal, written "institution," including how elections are governed, descriptions of the history of the institutions that govern elections, and the development of the "right" to vote. This book will also discuss "informal" rules such as the norms of civic cooperation or feelings of duty regarding our vote. Why do some individuals choose not to take advantage of the ability to vote that they have? Who is still fighting for the right? Why do we call voting "a right" or a "privilege" … or both? The next section explains why formal and informal rules are so important.

THE PURPOSE OF VOTING AND ELECTIONS

There are many reasons one might hold an election, but ultimately, elections are about the legitimate (and hopefully peaceful) transfer of power. Elections allow us to aggregate the interests of citizens (who are eligible)[7] to have a say in the continuation or transfer of power. The vote is an act of communications, and the structure we use for that purpose is a system consisting of a vast, hyperdecentralized architecture of individuals who implement election law. The communication system includes polling places on Election Day (or in the case of early and absentee voting, the system allowing for the transfer of the ballot to the potential voter and back to a central counting location) and the counting mechanism for those ballots, as well as security protocols to enable that preference in the voter's mind to be, hopefully, accurately communicated in such a way so as to translate votes into representation.[8] We translate those votes using formal rules and formulas laid out in the US Constitution, federal and state law, and sometimes local law. (We have rules to, as many political scientists have said, "translate votes into seats.") The communication system includes a large volunteer force with relatively little training. The communication system requires some sort of positive step on the part of the communicator to enter into communication— he or she must determine how to register to communicate and how to maintain that registration; the communicator must get to the place wherein he or she will transfer his or her preference to those in charge of aggregating the interests of the democratic community. He or she must leave the mode of communication at one of those locations and hope that it makes its way through to a "place" where it might be added to others so there may be an election result.

Any individual communicator (or noncommunicator) should theoretically believe the results of the aggregation procedure are binding. That is, even if the citizen does not believe in the specific outputs the system is producing at some time, the citizen will still believe the outputs produced by the system are binding (Easton, 1965: 258).[9] Perception that an institution is "legitimate" is vital to the survival of any social compact—the US government included. If people do not believe in the legitimacy of decisions, we will not have a peaceful transfer of power.

Yale University professor Tom Tyler's research gives us a reason to expect that if elections run "fairly," then people will obey the law and our social compact that is the US government will continue to operate. Before discussing his argument, it is worth noting that complying with government and living under the laws of the country is simply a macro-level example of obeying the law on a daily basis. (In other words, we do not live in utter chaos because we respect laws concerning property rights, taxes, traffic, etc. We may not like some of the laws and even not obey some laws, but in general terms, our government stands as a large-level example of obeying the law.) He argues that procedural justice is an important reason why people obey the law. But it is not just that elections are fair; it is also that we have normative expectations about behavior in our society. He writes in *Why People Obey the Law*,

> [t]he key implication of the Chicago study is that normative issues matter. People obey the law because they believe that it is proper to do so, they react to their experiences by reevaluating their justice or injustice, and in evaluating the justice of their experiences they consider factors unrelated to outcome, such as whether they have had a chance to state their case and been treated with dignity and respect. On all these levels people's normative attitudes matter, influencing what they think and do.
>
> (page 178)

Tyler asserts that citizens comply with laws because they believe in the legitimacy of the government to create the laws.[10] One's personal morality matters as well. However, Tyler's research also shows that individuals may be influenced by social expectations for behavior—norms that dictate whether someone will comply with the law. He writes,

> Given that the regulation of behavior through social control is inefficient and may not be effective enough to allow a complex democratic society to survive, it is encouraging that social theorists have recognized other potential bases for securing public compliance with the law. Two such bases are commonly noted: social relations (friends, family, and peers) and normative values. Concerns about social relations reflect the influence of other people's judgments; normative values [reflect] a person's own ethical views.
>
> (page 23)

Thus, in analyzing the institution of elections, one must not just analyze the written rules governing elections, but also the unwritten rules that have their basis in our country's history and philosophy.

THE RIGHT TO VOTE AS INDIVIDUAL ACT AND COMMUNITY RIGHT

This book is about the right to vote, something that most individuals reading this probably think is really straightforward, but it is not. In fact, the purposes of elections mentioned earlier are essentially about the right to vote, but are primarily central to one particular conception of the right to vote. The idea of the legitimacy of the government to continue ruling and the peaceful transfer of power are structural goals—all citizens living under this social compact have an interest in such things that make for a healthy democracy: participation in elections, choice (competitive elections), and the acceptance of the transfer of power (legitimacy). What the idea of legitimacy suggests, however, is that the "right to vote" is structural in a sense, in that it benefits the community. Yet, the conception of the right to vote being an individual right fits how most Americans view it. Consider the interaction between the structural view and the individual view. Within legal scholarship, another view of "the right" has developed. Legal scholar Richard H. Pildes argues that when law protects an "individual" right, the law is protecting society more generally. He writes,

> [t]hat is because rights are better understood as means of realizing certain collective interests; their content is necessarily defined with reference to those interests. Rights do protect the interests of individual right claimants, but not only these interests. An intended and justifying consequence of rights is that through protecting the interests of specific plaintiffs, rights also realize the interests of others, including the construction of a political culture with a specific kind of character. In other words, the justification for many constitutional rights cannot be reduced to the atomistic interest of the right holder alone.
>
> (1998: 731)

Thus, put more simply, he would argue that when the courts make a decision about voting rights, the courts should consider rights as ones that advance collective interests, including stability and legitimacy of the government and the electoral institution embedded within the country. The "right" to vote, Pildes has argued, protects a variety of interests, including the individual and the individual's interest in a group.[11] Institutional theory gets to the heart of what it means to be a collective. Institutions comprise individuals, who together make something bigger than the individuals themselves.

Contrast this view with the idea that rights inhere within the individual. This should seem familiar; the idea of "one person, one vote" is often expressed in popular rhetoric.[12] As an American citizen of voting age, a person has the right to a say in what government does. By including the individual in voting, society "includes them in a circle of full and equal citizens. The harm of disenfranchisement thus cannot be reduced to its impact on election outcomes" (Fishkin, 2011: 1296). The ability to vote is an issue of human dignity and autonomy. Voting is also a way in which Americans express their membership in this country—it has expressive benefits. Similarly, legal scholars argue, it is an expressive harm when a person is denied the ability to vote.

Legal scholar James Fishkin sums up the argument in terms of the requirements for "full and equal citizenship," which are both written (e.g., the Fifteenth Amendment) and unwritten (individuals having to pass a literacy test in order to vote may be formally written as a requirement, which did in effect exclude African Americans from voting, which is unwritten). Fishkin writes, "[a] would-be voter could even be rendered something less than a full and equal citizen without her knowledge—for example, if election officials appear to allow her to cast a ballot, but as soon as her back is turned, secretly discard the ballot instead of aggregating it together with the others" (page 1337) In the so-called "first generation" of voting rights cases, courts decided many cases because individuals did not have the franchise. The right to vote was often denied due to the structure of the formally written institutions.

Return to the example of Stephen that I related at the beginning of the chapter. Under the individual view of the right to vote, Stephen should be accorded the dignity of making his choice, even if he has relatively diminished mental capacity. He is a part of a group fighting in court to rid the state of California of the blanket injunction that those who have guardians lose their right to vote.

So what this question has meant in effect is not just whether certain groups are able to vote (through, say, the Fifteenth Amendment), but also are able to elect a representative of their choice? Or, do electoral structures make it difficult, if not impossible, to do so? The idea of structuralism apparently had its growth in legal scholarship during the period of time in which most of the voting rights cases were structural in nature, which would include whether a city elected members on an at-large basis or via districts, which tend to influence the ability of minority groups to elect a representative of "their choice"; gerrymandering, which affected whether or not certain representatives, particularly minorities, were elected; and other issues, such as ballot access and campaign finance (Fishkin, 2011: 1289). As a result, the courts began to weigh the rights questions in bigger terms than simple individual rights. The question for contemporary election observers is: Should the right to vote be considered from a structural perspective or from an individual perspective? This idea will come up in later chapters in the discussion of voter fraud and particular types of elections (that is, differing ways of aggregating votes than simply "one person one vote").

CONCLUSION AND MOVING FORWARD

Scholars have been repeating this for at least the past 15 years, but Americans were surprised when the 2000 election revealed the true extent of the unwieldiness of US elections. Most Americans probably did not think much more about "the institution" except for the most high profile of factors in the system. Political scientist Jack Dennis wrote an article in the *American Political Science Review* in 1970 called "Support for the Institution of Elections by the Mass Public." In it he examined beliefs about core democratic principles, such as whether voting is a civic duty; but in terms of the process, he focused on campaigns and political parties—which are a part of the process, but not the whole thing.[13]

This book cannot encompass the "whole institution" either. However, the 2000 election established the idea that elections are an administrative process, created by the Constitution and by statutes and codes in all 50 states and US territories. The process included millions of volunteers, and the process was surprisingly different in all the states, and even in all the local election jurisdictions. A "volunteer army" had the discretion to implement your ability to vote. Yet, your ability to vote was affected not only by those volunteers, but also by the physical mechanism by which you cast your vote (did you use an electronic machine resembling an ATM, a 900-pound behemoth, a piece of paper, or a computer punch card?). A complex system of rules—both written and unwritten—governs the process. Relationships among levels of government, or even types of government on the local level, affect whether you are able to cast your vote, or whether individuals like you can cast their votes, and whether your group is represented. Every bit of the administrative process shapes whether or not the individual has a right to vote, from the biggest (the US Constitution) to the smallest (a hanging chad or, perhaps, Aunt Martha, the 100+ pound pollworker). The legal framework matters; but how the legal framework is created in the first place and how it affects the voter are affected by informal institutions, which include many of the factors related in this chapter and discussed throughout this book.

Almost 50 years of political science have provided excellent evidence that institutions have strong effects on turnout and other forms of political behavior (see for example, Wolfinger and Rosenstone, 1980; more recently see Leighley and Nagler, 2014). Earlier eras of scholars may very well have clashed over the relative effects of institutions and behavioral factors in determining political behavior (see Rusk, 1974, etc.). Not only do scholars now know that institutions in terms of legal structures do affect behavior, but we also know that informal rules are key to the maintenance and survival of institutions and that individuals and institutions interact. As political scientist Cox and historian Kousser note,

> In any era of institutional and behavioral instability, an explanation which treats as exogenous the behavioral causes of institutional changes or fails to trace the effects of such changes on the behavior of all actors—not just voters, but also politicians—cannot be comprehensive, but it is likely to be misleading.
>
> (1981: 662)

In other words, the change within institutions shapes behavior, which in turn shapes institutions. We can learn much by observing election institutions, in all their glory, and all their administrative everyday-ness.

This book will not examine which institutions of democracy perform "best" in terms of citizen satisfaction, or in terms of policy preferences, or even if "democracy works" (see, for example, Lijphart, 1999; Thomassen, 2014). However, one must understand that what we learn about the institution of elections is fundamental to the understanding of power, most particularly, the idea of "mobilization of bias" (Bachrach and Baratz, 1962; Schattschneider, 1960). Political scientists Peter Bachrach and Morton S. Baratz argue that the study of the power requires not just the study of decisions, but also the values, norms, and rules that help maintain power for those who have it. They write,

> can the researcher overlook the chance that some person or association could limit deci-sion-making to relatively non-controversial matters, by influencing community values and political procedures and rituals, notwithstanding that there are in the community serious but latent power conflicts?
>
> (page 949)

Once a scholar has analyzed the values, procedures, and rituals, the scholar may pro-ceed to understanding "which persons or groups, if any, gain from the existing bias and which, if any, are handicapped by it" (page 952). Thus, we begin to study the institutions, formal and informal, that maintain power, as well as how they have changed over time.

When I first started conducting research on ballot design, my co-author and I sub-mitted some of our scholarship to one major political science journal—one big cri-tique was that it was "not political science." It is relatively rare for a political scientist to say that these days, and some of my esteemed colleagues have made great strides in articulating why ballot design is key. Political scientists Paul S. Herrnson, Michael J. Hanmer, and Richard G. Niemi (2012: 716) wrote:

> Ballots constitute a front line of study for a number of reasons. First, the ballot is the means through which voters register their intentions, and it is the dominant feature voters observe once they begin the voting process. Symbolically, it is more meaningful. As Beard pointed out a century ago: "The point of contact between the average voter and his government is the ballot ... " (1909, 590). Second, varieties of ballot layouts, options, and tasks routinely affect the number of votes cast (undervoting), the expres-sion of voter attitudes (initiatives), and the relative advantage to candidates and parties (candidate order, straight-party options).

Their scholarship and that of many others is critical to understanding the proper func-tioning of our democratic system. *Institutions and the Right to Vote* will show that ballots are only one piece of a larger system—an institution of elections that is large, complex, and even in graphic design elements, political, and deserving of scholarly study.

Scholars have called states the "laboratories of democracy," and indeed, in the case of elections, some states will innovate programs and the programs will diffuse throughout other states (for example, Hale and McNeal, 2010). This "laboratory" nature of policy in the United States is "good" in that it allows scholars to analyze the programs; given differences in programs and differences in populations served by programs, what are the outcomes? How can we improve policy? The reader will observe quickly herein that not just states, but also localities and precincts, are some-times very different, providing variation scholars need to study and therefore improve elections. A social scientist might say that the variation within levels of administra-tion of the electoral institution improve "leverage" over problems in democracy, in particular, the nuts and bolts of election administration. Gary King, Robert O.

Keohane, and Sidney Verba (1994) provide research design guidelines for testing theory. They argue, "The more evidence we can find in varied contexts, the more powerful our explanation becomes and the more confidence we and others should have in our conclusions" (page 30). We gain leverage on theory by examining as many observable implications of theory as possible. In this context of this book, I propose theory that can help us understand many aspects of election administration, explore observable implications, and suggest further hypotheses to increase our confidence in the theory. But I have practical goals as well. Understanding the idea that those individuals who work in the local precinct have "roles"—both defined by the institution and defined by their own perceptions—is key to understanding how local officials can govern elections.

Overall, my goal with this book is to show that the election institution—the types of laws we make and the ways in which we as Americans act within that institution—affects our right to vote. A variety of individuals have roles to play within the system, from state chief election officers to the local precinct worker who checks in a voter. These roles are defined by the system, but the person within the role also defines it (Searing, 1991). The institution affects your right to vote. Formal rules affect your right to vote. Informal rules affect your right to vote. Norms and values within the system affect your right to vote. All in all, however, actors within the institution may attempt to change the formal or informal rules to gain power. Throughout this book, I challenge you to consider what the right to vote is. What does that really mean?

I have studied election administration for many years, considering such mundane issues as whether ballot design or differing types of voting equipment make it easy or hard for a voter to express his or her preference (Knack and Kropf, 2003; Kimball and Kropf, 2005). Isn't that about voting rights? I have studied local election officials and implementation of election laws, such as failsafe voting (provisional voting) (Kimball, Kropf, and Battles, 2006; Kropf, Vercellotti, and Kimball, 2013). I have studied how early voting may change the composition of the electorate, given competitive campaigning (Kropf, Parry, Barth, and Jones, 2008) and following the 2008 Obama victory (Kropf, 2012, 2013). I have also studied how social pressure affects a person's incentive to vote or give to organizations such as public broadcasting (Knack and Kropf, 1998; Kropf and Knack, 2003; Kropf, 2009). In my public policy studies I have read the scholarship of political scientist Elinor Ostrom and her many collaborators; I have studied the work of rational-choice sociologist James Coleman (1988, 1990). However, it was not until I taught a PhD-level theory course that I realized that election administration is new institutionalism.[14] Big theory perhaps, but I argue the theory makes scholars think about voting rights in differing ways, not just as legal barriers. I also argue the theory encourages us to consider how norms and expectations (including normative expectations for the jobs local officials do in elections) shape the implementation of election law, from voter turnout to the decisions made by precinct workers to the official heading up that local election authority. Interactions with precinct workers shape voter confidence (Hall, Monson, Patterson, 2009), but those precinct workers have a vision of what their role in the election is, which theoretically is shaped by the institution of elections, including both formal and informal rules. However, at its heart, this book is about election administration and thinking about ways to study it.

THE BOOK OUTLINE

In order to describe the institution and its effects, I first analyze some of the unwritten rules of elections—our widely shared understandings or informal rules. Chapter 2 illustrates some of the many values and norms that US citizens hold concerning the electoral institution. However, even with these informal rules for which there is "shared understanding," one must be aware that there is variation all over the country in terms of how strongly we hold these values and expectations. As a result, scholars have leverage in our studies of their effects on the operation of the institution.

Chapters 3 and 4 delve into the formal rules of the US institution of elections. I argue that these rules are best understood by thinking about a pyramid; voters form the basis of the pyramid. Voters vote in precincts, central locations, or their own homes, or even places in which they are stationed overseas. Local laws govern precincts and polling places, but county and town election officials cannot be at every polling place. The chief pollworker in a precinct is the final arbiter of rulers, and she or he is the face of the government whom most everyone who votes must face. This immense variation gives us leverage when studying questions about election administration because we can make many observations at once; for example, a volunteer army of precinct workers governs elections—they are really street-level bureaucrats because these volunteers represent the government to the Americans who choose to vote (Alvarez and Hall, 2006). Yet, scholars can and should study the jurisdictions at different points in time. Over the localities are systems of state laws. The pyramid grows smaller as one moves toward the top.

Thus, Chapter 4 shows the "top" of the pyramid—so illustrated because the number of federal laws governing elections is relatively small compared with the number of state and local laws governing elections, even though the US Supreme Court has had quite a bit to say about elections in our country. Generally speaking, the US government has worked to provide access to elections—what we might say is protecting the "right" to vote. Scholars obtain leverage in order to understand the federal laws by studying those laws over time.

Thus, Chapter 5 examines three case studies of voting history in the United States. Historians and scholars of American political development certainly spend much more time studying the history of the United States, but in examining their insights, one can see rather strong evidence that decisions about who "is allowed" to vote often seem to be determined by political considerations of one group or another gaining power. These are important lessons we learn by taking a careful view of history and not an idealistic one. Harvard historian Alexander Keyssar provides intellectual inspiration for the history chapters here, but so, too, do numerous historians who have examined how US democracy has grown and changed over time. A key theme in Chapter 5 reflects one of the main lessons from Keyssar: the right to vote is neither linear (developing over time in a straightforward manner) nor is the right to vote universal.

This research then takes a small turn to some of the individual actors involved in the system in Chapter 6. As noted previously, the basis for the electoral institution is the voter. As such, a discussion of the electoral institution must also include a review of the key reasons why individuals choose to vote at all. Certainly, entire books, or even entire careers, are devoted to various theories explaining voter turnout, but this chapter briefly covers economic, psychological, and sociological theories explaining turnout and, I hope, shows the value of interdisciplinary research. All these themes are arguably part and parcel of the *new institutionalism theory*.

I am especially conscious of developing the idea of voter motivations because Chapter 7 shows that it is not just formal rules that matter to outcomes, but also voter motivations. Chapter 7 shows where and when individuals can vote. In particular, a great deal of scholarship recently has examined early voting, vote centers, and voting by mail. Furthermore, cost cutting in election administration has meant consolidation of precincts. Given our norms and values surrounding the electoral institutions, what are the long-term implications of these location changes? This chapter shows how formal and informal rules interact.

Chapters 8 asserts that the right to vote is not a straightforward concept. This chapter considers the voter in the voting booth. Presumably, that voter has won the right to vote. Yet by utilizing a paper ballot (by mail or in person) or voting on a machine, the voter may lose the right to vote and not even know it. By utilizing a failsafe (provisional ballot), a voter who may otherwise lose the right to vote may gain it, but also may not. This chapter explores some of the trade-offs policymakers must make to make voting as available and usable as possible.

There are still other conceptions of the right to vote—considering it a structural, as opposed to an individual, right is a key part of court precedent and legal scholarship. Part of the ideas generated by the structural view is that policymakers also consider whether or not a voter can elect the representative of his or her choice. Once that person is in office, is that person really a representative? Chapter 9 considers this idea while discussing redistricting and gerrymandering. Some policymakers and advocates would like to use "value-free" methods of districting (e.g., computers), but as with voting equipment, somebody must make decisions to purchase and program these devices, and such decisions are not value free.

Chapter 10 concludes by asking the following questions: Where does the right to vote stand today? What does it all mean? What are some possible arenas for future study? As I outline election administration issues to you, I hope you find it as interesting as I do. There is a lot beyond the ballot that voters don't think about. I want you to think.

INSTITUTIONS AND THE NORMS THAT HELP MAINTAIN STABILITY

USUALLY WHEN THERE IS AN ELECTION, local and state newspapers also have an editorial encouraging citizens to vote. One does not always receive a tangible reward for voting, but reporter Tina Reed wrote in the Annapolis, Maryland newspaper, *The Capital*: "A ballot-full of businesses want to capitalize on election night by offering dirty martinis, Obama cookies and free bagels with your 'I voted' sticker."[1] Yes! Citizens could demonstrate patriotism by showing the ever-present "I voted" sticker and earning a dirty martini. Even the "Brat Man" wants to reward the voter with $1 off any menu item if the person voted in the primary.[2] We don't always get a reward like Wisconsin bratwurst when we do something of which others approve. But Americans do a lot to be accepted by others, especially those whose opinions they value—or maybe whoever will just give one a snack as a reward. Peer pressure appears to work for all kinds of social outcomes, good and bad.[3]

In fact, a group of political science scholars have a long-running research program trying to determine why people do and do not vote; the scholars find that social pressure to conform to norms of civic duty is an important part of the decision to vote. Political scientists Alan S. Gerber, Gregory A. Huber, David Doherty, and Conor M. Dowling (2015) show most recently that political participation such as voting does affect how others judge an individual (although about as much as they might judge someone who recycles or returns library books in a timely manner). Their research shows that people will also reward norm-consistent behavior and sanction those who do not take part in it.[4]

Why is it important to consider the importance of societal norms in the context of this book? In Chapter 1, I begin to develop the argument that the electoral system is an institution. However, in order to "be" an institution, the system must have a logic of appropriateness. This chapter will serve to show that there are a number of unwritten rules that underlie the stability of our institution of elections, specifically, and the government more broadly. Institutions comprise formal rules that are often (but not always) written down; however, institutions also comprise norms—expectations for behavior and beliefs shared when one is a part of the institution (Ostrom, 1990). Political scientist B. Guy Peters writes of the vital role these unwritten rules play that creates both conscious and unconscious choices on the part of Americans.

> Normative compliance, therefore, is central to the function of institutions from this theoretical perspective. The source of compliance then is derived from a normative commitment to the institution and its purposes. It may also, however, become habitualized and routinized so that conscious commitment and conscious decision-making are minimized. Individuals continue to respond in the ways expected, and needed, by the institution because they have become accustomed to doing so, and the various normative stances, as well as myths and stories associated, with the institution help to reinforce that routinization.
>
> (Peters, pages 41–42)

This chapter will show several key examples of the norms and values that undergird the institution of elections: voting is a privilege, voting is the duty of a citizen, our choices are our own—they are secret, elections are necessary because they are, and voting and elections have almost a religious symbolism today. Although these particular norms seem positive, some values and norms are not positive—our country has a history of voting discrimination. Further, although there is seemingly broad support for the right to vote, it is relatively easy for a person to abandon that perspective when presented with specific circumstances. Support for the right to vote depends on how one frames that right (see, for example, Chong and Druckman, 2007).

How Do Norms Operate?

Individuals may be accustomed to following norms, but rational-choice sociologist James Coleman in his 1990 book *Foundations of Social Theory* argued for the addition of another layer to this idea. He argues that norms are a system-level construct wherein the right to control an action is necessarily held, not by the individual taking the action, but is a socially defined right. Those people around an individual can and do control behavior through sanctions—that is, following a norm produces a positive sanction; failing to follow a norm could produce negative sanctions. That is, even if individuals do not internalize civic norms, they may nonetheless comply with them or believe in them if other individuals apply positive or negative sanctions for conforming with or violating norms. As such, enforcement of norms depends on repeated social interactions with others whose opinion one values. For example, one may have repeated social interactions with one's neighbors, or one may have repeated social interactions with one's church members. Certainly, one has repeated social interactions with one's parents and teachers. Thus, when individuals gather, there is opportunity to exchange information about expectations, but also to monitor others' behavior. However, individuals may vary in their level of social interaction and the extent to which they hold common norms and values.

It is important to emphasize that the norms—or expectations or "logic of appropriateness"—are shared—but like most public attitudes, they vary in intensity. Individuals within the collective have differing predispositions, which may derive from a variety of sources, not the least of which is that people from all over the world have settled in this country. (Political scientists Tom W. Rice and Jan L. Feldman have authored some particularly interesting scholarship on this point concerning what culture residents draw from their countries of origin.[5]) Crawford and Ostrom make the argument that rules are about shared understanding (1998). However, Ostrom (1998) argues that because norms are learned "in the social milieu," they will vary across cultures and individuals, within cultures and individuals, and within individuals across time. Thus, the extent to which those living here share the understandings is *a variable*, as are the expectations we hold for others' behavior and how much co-residents influence other residents' behavior.[6]

What will be revealed in the course of this book, however, is that in the United States, we do not have "one" election, but at least 51 (50 states plus the District of Columbia). Some would argue that this country has more than 10,000 different elections because elections are administered in local jurisdictions all over the country. The reader will see in Chapter 3 that the formal architecture of electoral laws spans at least three governmental levels: national, statewide, and local. What is fascinating is that there are a number of unwritten rules that span the country—they may vary in level and intensity in various parts of the country, but here I will argue that one can speak about the norms and values more generally because they touch so many areas of election administration. However, formal laws vary over space and time, but so do unwritten values and norms. An advantage of having the decentralized system is that scholars are able to compare jurisdictions, which do vary in both norms and values and laws. However, the disadvantage is more normative: that is, depending on the norms and values in the jurisdictions, discrimination may occur, as well as varying levels of participation in the system—and we see multiple examples of it over the years.

NORMS OF CIVIC COOPERATION: CIVIC DUTY

Among citizens and scholars who study voting behavior, there appears to be an accepted norm that voting is a civic duty for individuals (Riker and Ordeshook, 1968). When calculating the costs and benefits of voting, people do factor in whether they receive a civic duty benefit from voting. Indeed, public opinion polls show that Americans believe that individual voting is a civic obligation. The Pew Center for the People & the Press has been tracking American values in a survey since 1987. The survey queries a national sample of Americans about a variety of values-based issues, from the importance of prayer to the level of optimism that Americans have about Americans' abilities to solve problems. The survey also asks about political engagement. The 2012 survey found that 90 percent of Americans "completely" or "mostly" agreed with the statement "I feel it's my duty as a citizen to always vote."[7] Figure 2.1 charts the 15 times the Pew Center has asked that question; the levels of agreement

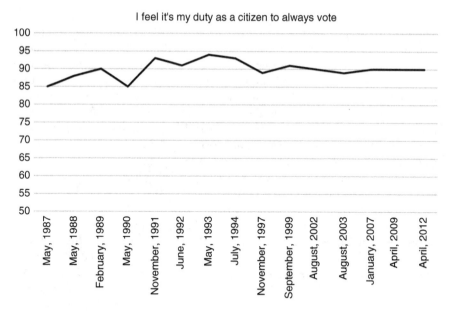

Figure 2.1   Civic duty over time
Source: Pew Research Center.

have stayed fairly constant for the past 25 years. Although the Pew Report notes that there is a pretty substantial age gap in belief in the duty to vote, the levels are still fairly high. In 2012, 98 percent of those over the age of 65 reported they agreed it was their duty to vote; 84 percent of those 18 to 29 agreed.

Other surveys find similar results. An Associated Press survey found that Americans believe it is their obligation to vote. When asked (in 2014) what "certain obligations that some people feel American citizens owe their country," three-quarters of Americans polled believe that "to vote in elections" is a "very important" obligation; 14 percent view voting as a "somewhat important" obligation.[8] Compared with the General Social Survey conducted in 1984, the numbers were 79 percent and 16 percent, respectively.[9]

Obviously, the belief in the "duty" or "obligation" to vote does not always translate into actual voting. It is important to note that civic duty is simply another "cost" or "benefit" of voting in the eyes of a rational-choice theorist. In fact, for many, "guilt" for not voting is part of the decision—the Pew Values Survey found that in 2012—as in 1987—67 percent of Americans "mostly" or "completely" agreed with the statement "I feel guilty when I don't get a chance to vote."

Stephen Knack is a World Bank economist who has analyzed how the feelings of civic duty may affect the probability that individuals will vote. His work was pathbreaking because it took the idea of civic duty one step further, considering not just a person's own sense of civic duty, but that of his or her friends, family, and social network. That is, social pressure or potential sanctions (or rewards such as praise) from others factors into the decision of whether or not to vote.

> Social sanctions thus permit a certain amount of 'substitutability' of feelings of duty, as someone with a low sense of civic obligation may nonetheless vote to avoid displeasing a friend or relative with a stronger sense of duty. For the individual, then, voter participation is a function of one's own sense of duty, of the strength of duty of one's family, friends, and other associates, and of the frequency and quality of interaction with these potential enforcers.
>
> (Knack, 1992: 138)

Knack's variety of evidence suggests that members of social networks can and do monitor those with whom they share connections.

As noted in the introduction, there has been a growing body of experimental political science literature showing that, indeed, social pressure plays an important role in voting. In a typical political science experiment, scholars will show a randomly assigned sample of individuals one message about voting, and another randomly assigned sample another. Gerber, Green, and Larimer (2010), in showing the results of a "feedback intervention" experiment, where people's past behavior was publicized, argue that "[t]he results reported here and in other social pressure experiments attest to the formidable effects of surveillance on compliance with social norms" (Gerber, Green, and Larimer, 2010: 416; see also Davenport, 2010). Gerber and Green (2000) note that face-to-face interactions with voters may increase voter turnout, as does the communication of social sanctions for failure to vote (Gerber, Green, and Larimer, 2008). Communicating the message that "everyone ELSE votes" also encourages people to vote (Gerber and Rogers, 2009). The research presented in the first part of this chapter uses multiple methods, not just experiments, to develop the causal mechanism behind this work: people really do reward and sanction others for their behavior.

THE SECRET BALLOT

The secret ballot is an instrumental part of our formally written rules, but consider our attitudes toward the secret ballot. As explained by Political Scientist Jerrold Rusk (1970), Americans have not always used secret ballots. Harvard University historian Jill Lepore noted that colonial Americans voted in the open; to do it any other way was not gentlemanly. "Colonial Pennsylvanians commonly voted by tossing beans into a hat. Paper voting wasn't meant to conceal anyone's vote; it was just easier than counting beans. Our forebears considered casting a 'secret ballot' cowardly, underhanded, and despicable; as one South Carolinian put it, voting secretly would 'destroy that noble generous openness that is characteristick [sic] of an Englishman."[10] At the same time, however, scholars point out that early-American voting laws were based on the idea that no one should be influenced by other individuals in casting their vote—a tenet of democracy was autonomy in decision making. (This justification worked variously in disenfranchising those in poverty, those who did not own land, those who had not lived in a community long, and, of course, women.) For a long time, however, political parties printed ballots of different colors so it was easy to discern for whom a voter placed his vote.

Today, in the United States, the secret ballot is paramount. In a *Washington Times* poll, 71 percent of Americans said that the "right to a secret ballot in elections" is protected by the US Constitution—interesting given that the Constitution does not guarantee the right to vote, much less the secret ballot.[11] Countless time is poured into how computer scientists can ensure that the vote conducted on an electronic voting machine is completely unknowable by others. Even the screens surrounding voting machines are a subject for passionate debate. One example: in Wilkes Barre, Pennsylvania, county commissioners rejected several privacy screen options because they were not cost effective and did not resemble the curtains used for older voting machines.

> The need for more voting privacy keeps coming up since the electronic machines were implemented three elections ago, but Luzerne County officials still don't have a solution. ... Election Board member Joe Cosgrove said he is surprised that someone hasn't been able to invent something, and he suggested looking into cardboard. 'I think the voters experienced an almost sanctuary-like setting for over 60 years and expected that this sacred quality of their vote would continue in the electronic age, and I don't think they feel that that's the case,' he said.[12]

And voters with disabilities called it a win when federal law mandated that local jurisdictions had to have voting equipment to allow them to vote privately.

In our country, a voter may identify himself or herself in order to vote, but his or her decisions on the ballot are supposed to be private. Interestingly, recent research examined perceptions of privacy (combined with strong descriptive norms about a desirable vote choice) by manipulating the "feel" of the polling place itself and then assessed the dependent variable (perceptions of privacy). Those in the political minority were much more likely to believe that pollworkers had seen their ballots (Karpowitz, et al., 2011: 669). These findings suggest that individuals might be willing to go against community norms, but they would be very uncomfortable in doing so, even in the "privacy" of the voting booth (see also Gerber, et al., forthcoming). These purported norms of cooperation extend further than simply whether or not someone should fulfill his or her civic duty and vote; they also extend to how someone should vote.

WE CAN'T HAVE GOVERNMENT WITHOUT ELECTIONS...

So strong is our feeling about the importance of elections that US citizens tend to hold elections for offices that many do not expect. Although the actual number of localities that elect a dogcatcher may be near zero, we do elect some offices for which expertise—not the ability to march in a parade—may be required.[13] Vermont elects a "lister" in localities—the person who appraises property for property tax reasons.[14] In many states, a coroner (not necessarily the person who performs autopsies) is a partisan elected official. Apparently, local contests for coroner include all the trappings of local politics, according to a story on National Public Radio featuring a partisan coroner race in upstate New York: "And in St. Lawrence County, this behind-the-scenes job comes with all the trappings of a small-town election: yard signs, party dinners and—for Warner—an entire summer marching in parades."[15] Ironically, we also elect approximately half of those individuals who are involved in the day-to-day work of running elections—approximately half of local election officials are elected, and about half of them are elected on a partisan basis, prompting many observers to call for changes to the way in which we select these individuals (Kimball and Kropf, 2006; White, et al., 2015).

THE APOTHEOSIS OF GEORGE WASHINGTON

As Americans, do we hold an almost religious belief about the goodness of our institutions of government, but most especially elections? In the light of day, elections are simply a process, and like all large, unwieldy processes, things can go wrong. Yet, the language we use and the political rhetoric surrounding elections imply that things do not and must not go wrong. An example: when a citizen walks into the United States Capitol rotunda, especially striking is what one sees when one looks to the top of the rotunda: a fresco painting: *The Apotheosis of George Washington*. The fresco was created by Constantino Brumidi in 1865, which perhaps reflected how Americans generally feel about their founders and arguably our country more generally: "In the central group of the fresco, Brumidi depicted George Washington rising to the heavens in glory, flanked by female figures representing Liberty and Victory/Fame. A rainbow arches at his feet, and thirteen maidens symbolizing the original states flank the three central figures."[16] Almost every school child learns about George Washington today. In February 2010, a CNN/Opinion Research Corporation Poll found that fully 22 percent of Americans thought George Washington never "lied to the public while he was president."[17] In 1994, fully 84 percent of Americans reported they viewed George Washington as a hero.[18]

In contemplating what George Washington symbolizes for our country, consider the arguments of political scientist Lorraine C. Minnite, who describes this American way of thinking as "myth." She writes that the myth includes "celebratory and cautionary narratives" (page 90). "U.S. exceptionalism extols the Constitution as a work of genius that ushered on to the historical stage a new age of freedom and equality. Indeed, in its telling and ritual retelling, the celebratory story takes on the luster of divine right. This is a purity myth like those that prop up the idea of a city on a hill or a chosen people or white supremacy" (page 91). She argues that the idea of limiting voting to those who can figure it out and eliminating voter fraud fits well into our mythic ideas. Even if voter fraud is not a common occurrence, it threatens the purity of the system by the perspective Minnite describes.

It may be too much to say that individuals believe in "legitimizing myths," but we certainly hold our country and the tenets of democracy as special. Pew Center scholars Andrew Kohut and Bruce Stokes wrote about this so-called "American exceptionalism" based on analyzing the results of several public opinion polls. They write: "Nothing is more vexing to foreigners than Americans' belief that America is a shining city on a hill—a place apart where a better way of life exists, one to which all other peoples should aspire. And, compared with Western Europeans, average Americans are more likely to express their pride and patriotism. In 1999, when Americans were asked to account for their country's success in the twentieth century, they credited the 'American system.' Many among the public may have been frustrated by how the system operated, but they liked the design."[19] Yet, after researching the issue of "American exceptionalism" Pew Center scholars Kohut and Stokes noted that their poll showed Americans were not necessarily evangelistic: "Americans are accused of believing 'Aren't we great? Do as we do!' In reality, they are far more likely to say, 'We think the American way is great; we assume you want to be like us, but, if you don't, that's really not our concern.'" So maybe we do not spread the word, but belief in our institution runs strongly. Indeed, a 2013 Gallup Poll reported that 85 percent of Americans felt "extremely" or "very proud" to be Americans.[20] Another public opinion survey reported that 69 percent of Americans were "very likely" to sing the national anthem.[21] The survey does not report the percentage of Americans who can actually reach the high notes in the anthem.

If it is fair to call the belief in our institution something like a religion, what characteristics do our institutional beliefs and values share with religion? The term "Christmas and Easter" Catholics may sound familiar to some. Similarly, there are "sometimes voters" who may choose to vote in a presidential election, but only rarely in a midterm election, and even more rarely in a local election or a primary.[22] There are debates over dogma in religion—why else are there so many religions? In our system of elections, there are debates over who should vote and whether voting is a right or a privilege. How much knowledge should a person have? How far do we go to preserve the "purity" of elections? There is even disagreement over the interpretation of the major texts of various religions and debate over how hierarchical an established church should be. Some churches give little control to individual parishes about who should be the leader of the church. Similarly, in the United States, scholars and policymakers debate over how much control the federal government and even the state governments should have over the organization of elections.

Very closely related to the ideal of election purity, is the idea that "every vote should count." Legal scholar Edward B. Foley wrote that citizens have not really internalized the idea that elections are *not* perfect and *cannot* be perfect. It is *not* just because nationally, the system is large and encompasses tens of thousands of moving parts (although the reader will see in the book that the electoral institution is big and unwieldy).

> But perfection is unattainable, and not just because of the technological limitations or the inevitability of human error, but because there are other important human values that necessarily compete with the ideal of "making every vote count." As a society we appropriately will not give up our commitments to those other human values, and yet we are not yet willing to admit the existence of this values conflict and the sacrifice it demands to the achievement of equal voting rights.
>
> (2006: 98)

For example, we institute voter registration so that those who are not eligible will not vote and so that voters will not vote more than once to protect the integrity of the election. In order to check the eligibility of voters, Foley argues, we must have a deadline for registration. This means that some people who move to the state after the deadline will be disenfranchised. On the other hand, if one moves the deadline closer to the election date, or eliminates it altogether, there is a distinct possibility that someone will vote who is not eligible to do so. If we wanted a perfect election, then election policymakers might have to require citizenship papers, but then also some sort of incontrovertible identification, such as DNA tests (which, of course, are never wrong). All in all, there are many trade-offs that policymakers and local election officials make in order to administer elections. In the 2000 election, Palm Beach County, Florida Supervisor of Elections Theresa LePore designed the infamous butterfly ballot, which featured two columns—and voters thought they had to vote in both. She says she designed the ballot that way because there were so many presidential candidates and she wanted to list them in a font large enough so that elderly voters could actually see them. It was a trade-off that helped put that election in the history books (Wand, et al., 2001; Kropf, 2014).

HISTORY OF VOTING DISCRIMINATION

Perhaps the reader believes that all the institutional norms and values mentioned thus far are positive. However, keep in mind that the terminology "logic of appropriateness" speaks more to what is acceptable during certain times, not necessarily what is positive. What has been appropriate at certain times is that the system may exclude some voters, particularly where there is a fairly widespread belief in the system that it is appropriate to do so. Furthermore, policymakers of all different partisan identifications have been continuously adept at using the attitudes about who should vote for political gain. Consider the struggle for the African American vote: in the wake of the Civil War and Reconstruction, the Southern Democratic elite worried about having former slaves with power—people who might actually vote with the Populists and the Republicans (the reader will note that even the way that Americans refer to race is a part of the institution formally in law and policy, and informally, in everyday conversation. For instance, consider how a book copy editor might regard variation in the use of terms regarding race within one book manuscript. In fact, in this particular book I use the terms "African American" and "Black" interchangeably, depending on the context and the use in source documents—the same is the case for "Latino" and "Hispanic" and "White" and "Caucasian"). Worry about retaining control over the reins of power made it logical to articulate racist views. Most would not see other types of discrimination in the same category as our country's history of racism and slavery (they are not), but these types are nonetheless discrimination in voting: many legal immigrants pay taxes and have children in school, but there are those citizens who strongly voice the opinion immigrants should *not* vote, even in school board elections or elections that might determine their level of property taxes.

That history of voting discrimination highlights a key point about the election institution's important values and norms: having that voice—the vote—is important enough for countless citizens to fight and die.

THE NORM (?) OF CONTRASTING POPULAR RHETORIC
WITH REAL BELIEFS

Conventional wisdom (another way of saying "informal rules"?) suggests that voting is a right, and an individual one at that; however, many Americans have a contrary view. Consider the story that began Chapter 1: the man who was not allowed to vote because he had a guardian. He had a guardian because of his cognitive impairment. Did you think he should or should not be able to vote? Did you consider his mental capacity? Or, did you get mad that he was not able to vote when he wanted to? Although popular rhetoric is consistent with a belief in the right to vote, both policy and public opinion make it appear more as a privilege for those who are able to pass some barrier to voting, including those barriers US voters take for granted such as voter registration. Think back to the 2000 election ultimately decided by the US Supreme Court: legal scholar Spencer Overton analyzes various election administration issues and analyzed the *Bush v. Gore* decision, which ended a recount in Florida, effectively giving the election to George W. Bush. He makes the argument that in *Bush v. Gore*, the "Court embraced merit-based assumptions that conditioned political recognition on an individual voter's capacity to produce a machine-readable ballot" (2001: 472). Thus, barriers are not just what potential voters do before an election, but as the growing literature on ballot design and usability indicates, are also produced because the method of communicating one's vote is not easy to use (Kropf and Kimball, 2012, especially chapter 5).

Overton (2001) illustrates that there are at least two conceptions about participation in democracy: an inclusion-based theory of democracy and a merit-based theory of democracy. In an inclusion-based theory, Overton notes, "[u]nder this vision, political participation is a right, and courts and democratic decision makers have a responsibility to create an environment that allows for, and even encourages, participation by all citizens" (page 474). Under a merit-based theory, Overton notes that individuals must meet a certain set of criteria in order to vote. "The merit-based vision of democracy also enhances societal well-being, the argument goes, because better political decisions arise from an electorate made up of citizens who are either competent enough or care enough to meet the criteria" (page 477). In other words, a "burden of proof" is on the voter. In his book *Why Americans Don't Vote*, political scientist Ruy A. Teixeira argues that voting is an individual enterprise for which the voter must bear the lion's share of the responsibility.

> The individual must surmount the bureaucratic obstacles necessary to vote. The individual must make sense out of a narrow range of political alternatives, within which his or her own individual viewpoint may very well not be represented. The individual must, by and large, mobilize himself or herself to go down to the polls and cast a ballot
>
> (1987: 8)

In the United States, taking these steps is taken for granted. There are certainly reasons why we have many administrative barriers in place—for example, registration for voting is said to decrease fraud. Not only that, but policymakers have reduced a number of barriers. For example, the Voting Rights Act of 1965 ended the practice of literacy tests before voting. Pollsters today may not have asked if individuals should be able to read and write in order to vote, but in 1963, when Gallup asked a national sample of Americans that question, 56 percent of Americans said "yes, they should."[23] Americans today might respond: if a person wants to vote, he or she will figure it out.

WHERE DOES "ACCESS V. INTEGRITY" FIT?

In the past 15 years, it has been common rhetoric that US election laws fit in the trade-off between access and integrity. Certainly, voting rights appear to be a matter of access if one considers stopping vote denial rather than stopping vote dilution. If one considers the idea of vote dilution, it could be that voting rights are really more about integrity in the sense that if a person is allowed to vote who is not "eligible" to do so, another person's vote is cancelled out.

Commonly, policymakers and scholars alike cite these values, with conventional wisdom dictating that Democrats generally want to increase access to the ballot—expand the electorate—and Republicans want to increase integrity—make it more difficult for people to commit fraud (for example, see Kropf and Kimball, 2012). These are indeed important values, reflected over time in our expansion of the electorate, but also the contraction of the electorate (as the reader will see later in this book). However, the rhetoric surrounding these values sometimes obscures the idea that elections are about the struggle for power, and in a democracy, the arena of action just happens to be in the electorate. The struggle for power also occurs in creating the arena—the institutions that define the rules of the game. Part of the struggle for power is the creation of political parties as part of the electoral institution from the very beginning.

Election reform research finds that attempts to win the game of politics often override values (or use them as rhetoric to convince), even if some partisans do so unconsciously. Provisional ballots became a nationwide program as a part of the Help America Vote Act of 2002. The program provides a failsafe ballot and access for those individuals who think they should be on a voter registration list but are not. The registration and ballots of these voters are verified (or not verified!) later after the hustle and bustle of Election Day. Kimball, Kropf, and Battles (2006) show that in the counting of provisional ballots, in Democratic-voting counties with Democrats in charge of administering elections, more provisional ballots count. In Republican-voting counties with Democrats in charge, fewer count. Similarly, in Republican-voting counties with a Republican in charge, more provisional votes count. In other words, winning matters, although this work did not establish the smoking gun of a partisan election official saying, "I want my party to win."

Even though laws affect turnout at the margins, with today's polarized politics, it may seem to citizens and policymakers (politicians) alike that elections are close and that laws will make a difference between winning and losing. Hopefully, at this point, readers who chose to read all of the chapters in this book have seen that the history of voting is not just ideological, but also about the battle for power: the battle to win elections. Institutional theory would suggest that politicians (not just Republicans, not just Democrats) have the incentive to stay in power once they are in office. Although ideological debates continue about access to the electoral institution of voting versus integrity of the electoral institution, a quick look at history gives the savvy reader insight into why politicians may want to effect change (or not) in electoral institutions.

Certainly, more than one scholar has suggested that voting changes and "reforms" often have political goals. Historian Alexander Keyssar argues that political advantage is a key reason for both expansion and contraction of the electorate in the United States. In discussing the design of ballots in North Carolina, public policy scholars James Hamilton and Helen Ladd (1996) argue "[s]ince institutions are designed by individuals who have preferences over political outcomes, the technologies of aggregation are likely to be chosen strategically" (page 260). They conclude their research, asserting, "[t]he bottom line for policymakers concerned with election law may simply be an acknowledgment that in a system where ballot formats may have an impact on voter choices, the ability to design ballot formats may simply be one of the electoral advantages of incumbency" (page 277).

Political scientists William D. Hicks, Seth C. McKee, Mitchell D. Sellers, and Daniel A. Smith (2015) examine voter identification legislation (from 2001 to 2012). They note that voter identification rules are part of a political game. They make a similar argument to that made throughout my book: "[p]erhaps the foremost objective of a political party is to win elective office (Aldrich, 1995). Principles become secondary as ideological platforms serve the purpose of assembling coalitions designed to capture the most votes (Downs, 1957)" (2015: 19). Hicks and his colleagues also show convincing evidence that voter identification legislation is introduced not just for integrity, but also for political reasons: to tip the political scale toward "maintaining Republican support while curtailing Democratic electoral gains" (page 18). They conclude by noting, "The right to vote has been treated with the esteem worthy of the most sacred democratic principle in American politics. Yet in the new millennium, the protection of voting rights palpably changed" (page 29).

I make the argument that the principle of voting rights has *not* "palpably changed" because the expansion and contraction of voting rights have operated under politics since their founding. In order to understand my argument, one needs to examine not just contraction of the electorate, but also expansion. Expansion is also political. Political scientist Corrine M. McConnaughy (2013) develops a theory concerning expansion of the electorate, and her scholarship dramatically shows the effects of politics, including information flow and institutional capacity in effecting change in suffrage. McConnaughy analyzes the history of woman suffrage in the United States; she is indeed not the first to do so. However, she makes a very compelling theoretical argument about the history of expansion of the franchise: she discusses "strategic and programmatic enfranchisement." She argues that strategic enfranchisement "is essentially the dominant framework of existing elite-centered accounts of suffrage expansion. This is where a single party acts to enfranchise a new group of voters expecting to reap electoral rewards from that group" (page 35).[24] This is difficult for a party because it needs to have accurate information about the group and its partisan intentions, it must have the incentive to make changes because of partisan competition, and it must have the capacity to make changes. In other words, a party must have the advantage in a legislature sufficient to make changes. She argues that this framework is not sufficient to explain suffrage changes, but in fact, politicians also make changes to satisfy their current supporters—that is programmatic expansion. The briefness of this discussion of her work belies the complex and intelligent theory building. My larger point is the contest for power has mattered and continues to matter.

CONCLUSION

The reader should not walk away from this chapter believing then that norms and values do not matter or that they are subsumed by politics. The opposite is true. For most folks, the values outlined herein define how many Americans think about elections. The degree to which we hold the norms and values does vary, however, which can give us insights about the operation of the institutions of elections in the United States and explain why the United States has one type of formal rule over another. There are trade-offs among values.

Furthermore, Ostrom (1990: 88–89) suggests that in collective action situations, extensive sets of norms develop so that people may govern themselves. As we see in this chapter, those norms define proper behavior.

> Many of these norms make it feasible for individuals to live in close interdependence on many fronts without excessive conflict. Further a reputation for keeping promises, honest dealings, and reliability in one arena is a valuable asset. Prudent, long-term self-interest reinforces the acceptance of the norms of proper behavior.

Ostrom's work is about not wasting a common resource, but I argue that the ideas certainly apply. Some will argue that voter turnout in this country negates the ideas that voting is a civic duty, yet enough people vote. Our democracy has not collapsed. Some can and will free-ride on the legitimacy created when others vote. The question is: Do we need government to make voting mandatory? Or is altering the laws we have—such as voter registration—enough? Or can any law change have effects without changes in informal rules? Or can we change the laws without changes in informal rules? We have to decide what it is we value the most at any one time because as legal scholar Edward B. Foley makes clear, when we value one part of the process, there is inevitably a trade-off in another.[25]

The norms of civic cooperation—the duty to vote—is not the only one mentioned herein. The country also holds widely shared beliefs about the secret ballot and having one's vote be private and not influenced by those more powerful. Citizens of the United States also hold beliefs about the exceptionalism of this country, which from its founding almost parallels the belief in religion. We will see in future chapters that many actors in the electoral institution hold these values, but others will use these values to frame policy choices so that they can benefit; from the Bill of Rights to the Civil War and from the civil rights era to today, we see policy choices made in order for some to gain power. And yet, we still have elections.

CHAPTER 3

THE MULTIPLE LABORATORIES OF DEMOCRACY

NOTICE THAT IN SOUTH CAROLINA, one cannot buy alcohol on Election Day. South Carolina's General Statutes make it clear:

South Carolina General Statutes: SECTION 61-6-4160. Sunday sales; election day.

> It is ***unlawful to sell alcoholic liquors*** on Sunday except as authorized by law, on state-wide ***election days***, or during periods proclaimed by the Governor in the interest of law and order or public morals and decorum. Full authority to proclaim these periods is conferred upon the Governor in addition to all his other powers. A person who violates this section is guilty of a misdemeanor and, upon conviction, must be punished as follows …[1] [emphasis added]

Maybe that should not seem too surprising, except for the fact that there are interesting contrasts in other states. In Colorado, where voters decided by an initiative on the ballot in 2012 that marijuana for recreational use was legal, there do not appear to be any particular regulations that govern marijuana use and sale on Election Day. Notably, Colorado voters had the opportunity to petition to place the marijuana question on the ballot for voter consideration in 2012, whereas, in South Carolina, voters cannot petition to bring such questions before the voters for consideration.[2] South Carolina does not have a law providing for the initiative petition, a process by which citizens can propose and pass a law or constitutional amendment, thereby bypassing the state legislature.

Furthermore, every voter in the United States is able to vote for a candidate for president (or, rather, everyone is able to vote for "electors" who together elect the president). However, not everyone faces the same ballot, even for the one national office. For example, in 2012, voters in Colorado had the opportunity to choose actress Roseanne Barr, a presidential candidate for the Peace and Freedom Party.

More than 50,000 voters chose her, for a grand total of 0 percent![3] In fact, there were 16 presidential choices on the Colorado ballot. In comparison, although South Carolina voters could have chosen Obama or Romney, they also could have chosen Jill Stein, the Green Party candidate, or Virgil H. Goode, Jr., the Constitution Party candidate. South Carolina only had five presidential candidates on the ballot. Every state is different because the responsibility for elections has always rested in the states legally and in localities legally and in practice. In other words, we have 51 different presidential elections every four years (if we include Washington, DC). The differences among states are legion; one state even caused controversy in 2006 because of a rule about enforcement of the rules concerning the weight of paper allowed for voter registration forms![4] All told, we have 51 separate presidential elections, but what is even more fascinating is that scholars have found that election administration is based in approximately 10,072 local jurisdictions (counties, townships, cities; sometimes combinations of both counties and cities—there are actually differing assessments of how many) that organize and operate the nuts and bolts of allowing a citizen to cast his or her vote.[5] Add to this the fact that most polls are staffed by individuals who are approximately once-or-twice-a-year election volunteers, and one could argue that elections are different in almost every polling place in the country (and citizens are also voting early and absentee by mail). Given the degree of local control, we actually have a lot more than 51 separate elections! The sheer size of the efforts to hold a countywide, citywide, or statewide election makes perfection interesting to contemplate, but probably impossible to achieve. But imagine achieving "perfect results" when a federal election is held around the date of the first Tuesday after the first Monday in November.[6]

All in all, however, simply describing the vast variation in laws (and implementation of those laws) can serve to demonstrate how confusing the legal architecture for elections can be. The major feature of our institution of elections is that it is not just one institution! Written laws may affect the behavior of the potential voter. Variation across states and even localities gives scholars leverage to see what effects on behavior may be. Yet, at the same time, variation across states and localities may result in similar voters being treated differently. However, different states and localities are, in fact, different—a rural county is different from Los Angeles—so it makes sense that citizens may vote with different rules. And, under the rules of the Electoral College, every state has its own contest for those Electoral College votes. As long as each voter within a state is treated with the same amount of "fairness," then maybe it does not matter that voters are treated differently in different states.

Whereas Chapter 2 served to engage the reader in some of the unwritten rules of elections, this chapter is designed to help the reader see what formal institutions affect voting. The chapter shows that voting is governed on multiple levels—all the way down to the polling place on Election Day. The chapter lays the groundwork for later discussion about the effects of rules on behavior.

This chapter starts with the middle of what I call an electoral institution hierarchy. Consider the idea that in terms of structure, the electoral institution resembles a pyramid of formal rules, although the power structure is not necessarily pyramidal.

In thinking about actors in the system, the federal government is relatively small in terms of formal rules it offers the system. States come next in the pyramid, with at least 51 different actors and political arenas, all with their own architectures of election rules. Local jurisdictions such as townships and counties are next, with differing degrees of accountability to voters and to state government. Finally, there is the arena of action wherein voters cast a ballot: a polling place (although not necessarily a precinct and not necessarily on Election Day; sometimes a voter casts his or her vote by walking to the mailbox, the kitchen table, and back to the mailbox again). Election Day "volunteers" staff the polling places, and potential voters vote.

In this chapter, I first explain why the discussion of formal rules begins with the states. The chapter cannot cover every single rule in every single state, however. There are simply too many different rules. The chapter will progress through the middle of the pyramid all the way down to pollworkers and the individual voters. The next chapter starts at the pinnacle of the pyramid—the very top—but perhaps the most important actor in the scheme is the nation's 130+ million voters who form the basis of the pyramid of institutions.

FEDERAL ELEMENTS OF THE ELECTORAL INSTITUTION

The federal government resides at the smallest point of the election pyramid; not because it is not important, but because there is only one national government, with a surprisingly small set of laws, mostly focused on voting access. In Chapter 4, I discuss various formal rules affecting access to the polls. Here, in Chapter 3, I will discuss the state institutions, local institutions, and the polling places first. Why? The answer is that the framers of the US Constitution did not make a decision as to who was allowed to vote. Historian Alexander Keyssar suggests the founders were hot and tired when writing the document that summer and the issues were complicated. Keyssar writes that "[t]he convention's debates about suffrage, held during the doldrums of late July and early August, were brief, and the final document made little mention of the breadth of the franchise" (page 4). Ultimately, the framers decided to leave the qualifications to vote up the states; the same qualifications that states set for the lower house of the state legislature would be the way in which the House of Representatives was selected. Keyssar suggests that the framers compromised to prevent a "potentially explosive policy problem," but that that the federal government did not receive "any clear power or mechanism, other than through constitutional amendment, to institute a national conception of voting rights, to express a national vision of democracy" (page 20). Most powerfully, Keyssar notes that "[t]he solution they devised, however, had a legacy—a long and sometimes problematic legacy" (page 20). He argues that the representatives from the states enabled a long history of civil rights violations.

STATE INSTITUTIONS AND ACTORS

States vary in the methods of administering elections. By federal law (beginning at least with the National Voter Registration Act passed in 1993—also known as the

Motor Voter Act), the federal government requires each state to have a chief election officer. Often that person is a secretary of state, but that also varies—some states, such as North Carolina, have a state board of elections appointed by the governor. Legal scholar Richard Hasen outlined the ways in which these state election leaders are selected:

> In thirty-three states, the secretary of state (or other statewide official charged with responsibilities as the Chief Elections Officer of the state (CELO) is elected through a partisan election process. No state currently elects the CELO through a nonpartisan election. The remaining states use an appointments process. Many states let the governor appoint the CELO, sometimes subject to confirmation of a house or both houses of the state legislature. Some states use various appointments measures for boards or commissions to run elections. Most of these commissions use a bipartisan model that either splits representation on the board evenly between the two major parties, or gives an advantage to the majority party in the state [footnotes removed from original].
>
> (2005: 974)

The source of power for both state-level actors and local actors (township, county, city jurisdictions who run elections) is specified by state constitutions, state laws, and administrative codes; state legislatures also have the power to provide funding to local jurisdictions in order for those jurisdictions to operate state elections. For example, according to legal scholar Joshua A. Douglas, 49 states "explicitly grant the right to vote through specific language in their state constitutions" (2014: 101).[7] Over time, state legislatures have passed laws designating who runs elections within the state and how those individuals are selected. Administrative code (promulgated by the agency that is operated by the chief election officer) designates a variety of day-to-day issues, such as that voting equipment in North Carolina should meet several standards, including "(7) It shall prevent the voter from voting for the same persons more than once for the same office;(8) It shall permit the voter to vote for or against only the question(s) the voter may have the right to vote" (08 NCAC 04 .0301).[8]

Many Americans likely would have been surprised to know that prior to the 2004 election, there was no central repository for turnout data from across the entire country, or that even such basic data as how "turnout" is defined varied throughout the country. For many years, turnout in Texas was defined with respect to the number of votes for the highest office on the ballot rather than the total number of voters who actually arrived at the polls. Furthermore, states still vary on whether they calculate turnout based on the number of people who checked in to vote and were marked in a voter registration paper record or whether one should count the number of votes cast on a voting machine or paper ballots actually processed. As a result of the 2000 election and the growth of scholarly research about election administration, the federal government began gathering data for midterm and general elections through the Election Assistance Commission (EAC) Election Administration and Voting Survey (EAVS). The survey is voluntary on the part of the states and as a result, the response rate from the states is not 100 percent, although the response has grown over time. One can especially see that there is variation in the states examining the evolution over time of the idea of election performance indicators across states.[9] As a part of its election initiatives, the Pew Center for the States began calculating an Election Performance Index in 2008, which allows for comparison among states on 17 key factors, including how complete the states' responses are to the EAC Election Administration and Voting Survey, as well as issues such as whether online voter registration is possible or whether the state has voter look-up tools where a potential voter can check his or her registration and where to vote (see Figure 3.1).[10]

Scholars and policymakers can compare voting among states because there is such a wide variation in the legal architecture and capacity to implement and enforce elections. One only need spend a few minutes examining the National Conference of State Legislatures website, an interest group that monitors state issues, to see that there is great variation in the types of election laws that state legislatures have passed. For example, as of this writing, three states—Oregon, Washington, and Colorado— use all-mail voting. Another 33 allow voting in advance of Election Day without an excuse—but locations where one can do so vary. Some states use grocery stores, shopping malls, or schools for early voting. Another seven allow voters to be on a permanent absentee voting list. And consider identification required for voting—some states require government-issued photo identification; still others simply require the potential voter to state his or her name.

And indeed, the 50 states of the United States and the District of Columba all vary with respect to the level of control that they exert over localities concerning election administration. For example, states such as Kansas leave many ballot design and other issues up to the 105 county clerks. For these reasons, the federal legislation the Help America Vote Act (HAVA) was largely state focused in that it required states to take action; the legislation ordered that states establish a chief election officer, mandated states to create state plans, and noted that states could receive funding for new equipment and other reforms. States would be responsible for funneling the federal funds to local jurisdictions. By not mandating uniformity in equipment, administration, and designs but asking the states to centralize election administration more, the federal legislation would strive to provide equal protection within states, rather than among states.

STATE RULEMAKING, ADMINISTRATIVE PROCEDURES, AND IMPLEMENTATION

After a political body passes a law, administrators are charged with implementing statutes, but most of the time, statutes require further specifications, and sometimes are rather vague (which often provides political cover for legislators). Often such rulemaking flies under the radar because voters tend to pay more attention to what the political branches of government do. What has received relatively little attention from scholars is the process for creating state administrative rules and for interpreting statutes (interpretive rules). Public administration scholar Neal Woods studies state-level administrative rulemaking and defines one category of rulemaking to be quite a bit like legislation. He defines it as "… the exercise of legal authority that

34

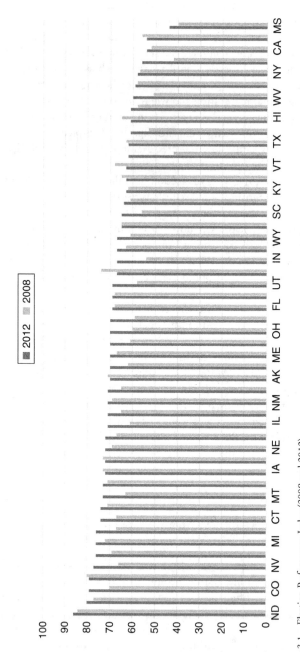

Figure 3.1   Election Performance Index (2008 and 2012)
Source: Data from The Pew Charitable Trusts.

has been delegated by the legislature to an agency. Administrative rules 'fill in the blanks' of legislative statutes and, like the statutes themselves, carry the force of law" (Woods, 2009: 518).[11] Public administration scholar Dr. Cornelius M. Kerwin, who has written one of the most important (perhaps only?) texts about rulemaking, notes that interpretive rules "… occur when agencies are compelled to explain to the public how they interpret existing law and policy. Although interpretive rules may stretch law or rules to fit new or unanticipated circumstances, they do not impose new legal obligations" (Kerwin, 2003: 22). Another category, according to Kerwin, is procedural rules, which define how the public may participate in rulemaking.

Rules may be as seemingly innocuous as this rule established in North Carolina in 2004:

> (a) The chairman of the county board of elections in a county where a voting system is used shall conduct an instructional meeting before any primary or election to instruct the precinct officials in the use of the voting system. The chairman may use any persons deemed knowledgeable or useful to the instruction of the precinct officials. The instructions on the use and operation of the voting system shall be according to manufacturer's instructions furnished with the voting system, whether the system is purchased or leased by the county board of elections. The precinct officials shall be qualified to instruct the voters on the use of the voting system.[12]

However, rules may also draw criticism from aggrieved parties, such as parties trying to register voters in the summer of 2008 in Ohio. *The New Times* reported,

> Mr. Blackwell's office has issued rules and materials that appear to require that paid registration workers, and perhaps even volunteers, personally take the forms they collect to an election office. Organizations that run registration drives generally have the people who register voters bring the forms back to supervisors, who can then review them for errors. Under Mr. Blackwell's edict, everyone involved could be committing a crime. Mr. Blackwell's rules also appear to prohibit people who register voters from sending the forms in by mail.[13]

Blackwell also received criticism because of his 2004 decision to enforce a statute already on the books concerning the weight of paper on which Ohio voter registrations were to be completed (Hasen, 2012).

STATE COURTS AND VOTING RIGHTS

Voting rights have had a complex legal path, with legal parties pursuing multiple arenas of action simultaneously. Across the country, state laws and state court decisions concerning election administration are structured in different ways. Yet, as noted before, all but one state constitution contains "the right to vote." Thus, it would seem appropriate that state laws might be challenged in state courts as potential violations of state-granted rights. Indeed, a number of state courts have considered claims concerning voter photo identification. Using photo identification cases as an example, legal scholar Joshua Douglas explains that parties in state courts and judges deciding cases have used the legal reasoning that either (1) "locksteps," or follows along with the federal constitution and federal precedent in voting cases, even though state constitutions grant a higher amount of protection for the right to vote; or (2) first examines the federal constitution for its level of protection, but then considers the state constitution if its protections are more robust; or, (3) considers the state constitution an "independent source" of voting rights, and may only consider the federal constitution if the state constitution does not provide adequate coverage.[14] Douglas finds that voter photo identification is not necessarily always found unconstitutional under state constitutions, but legal reasoning for those decisions does vary and may depend in part on how much the state judges defer to the US Constitution. This reliance on state constitutions for protection of rights is known as "new judicial federalism" and is used intermittently and sometimes only when attorneys believe that state judges might be sympathetic to the argument (Tarr, 1994: 74). However, as the reader will see, state courts may affect election administration, not only because of voting rights, but also because of a variety of state laws, even those that govern the language of ballot measures related to voting.

There are several examples where judges invoke state constitutional reasoning in state voting cases. An example is North Carolina, whose challenges to voter identification have proceeded in separate ways. For example there is one case with a federal Voting Rights Act claim and one challenging that the case under the state constitution under the idea that every "qualified" person has the right to vote under the North Carolina constitution. *The Charlotte Observer* interviewed the lead attorney for the case, Mr. Press Millen:

> The qualifications set out there are minimal, said Millen, who represents the challengers. They require only a residency period, registration and that a person not be a felon, unless the rights of citizenship have been restored. The North Carolina Constitution, Millen said, "explicitly allows the General Assembly to enact general laws governing the registration of voters," and over the past 147 years pages and pages of laws related to that topic have been added to the General Statutes. In contrast, voter qualifications, he said, are strictly off-limits.[15]

As of this writing, both the state and the federal North Carolina cases were still under consideration. Another example is Missouri where the state legislature passed a photo identification law in 2006—one of the first in the nation. The Missouri Supreme Court ruled:

> The trial court properly held that SB 1014's photo ID requirement violates the equal protection clause of article I, section 2 of the state constitution. It also properly held that the photo ID requirement violates the right to vote as guaranteed by article I, section 25 of the state constitution, which provides more expansive and concrete protection to the right to vote than the federal constitution. In reaching these conclusions, this Court applies strict scrutiny analysis, in which any limitation on a fundamental right must serve compelling state interests and must be narrowly tailored

to meet those interests. SB 1014's photo ID requirement fails to pass constitutional scrutiny because it creates a heavy burden on the fundamental right to vote and is not narrowly tailored to meet a compelling state interest.[16]

In other words, an amendment to the Missouri constitution would be necessary in order to allow for a photo identification requirement. The state legislature would have to place a referendum on the ballot for Missouri voters to consider, which they did in 2011. However, the referendum did not appear on the ballot because of a court case about the language that would appear on the ballot for voters to consider. Among other findings, the court ruled that the ballot "title states that passing the amendment would enact the 'Voter Protection Act,' which is insufficient and unfair because the proposed amendment does not contain the language 'voter protection act,' or even the word 'protection'" (Harwin, 2013: 217).

LOCAL JURISDICTIONS AND THE LOCAL ELECTION DIRECTOR/BOARD/COUNTY CLERK

Local election jurisdictions range in size from about 123 voters to 4.7 million (Loving County, Texas, to Los Angeles), but most are relatively small, according to director of Election Data Services and longtime election expert Kimball Brace. Brace reports that only about 400 out of 10,000 jurisdictions have more than 100,000 registered voters. Although larger jurisdictions often have large staff and on-staff technology experts, many smaller jurisdictions are relying on the voting equipment vendors for technical assistance and troubleshooting.

The task of organizing elections may be defined in state law, but somebody at the local level must be responsible for organizing the prosaic job of simply making sure an election happens: finding polling locations, ensuring that pollworkers staff the polling places, making sure that each polling place has the proper signage and balloting materials/equipment, and making sure that a primarily voluntary workforce of pollworkers knows about changes in election law from the last time they worked— never mind about getting the proper number of ballots and/or pieces of voting equipment in each polling place. And, such factors do not even count the work the people who run elections do between elections to ensure that the voter lists are up-to-date (among many other administrative duties) in order to ensure that those who are eligible are able to vote. The individuals at the local level face a number of challenges in running elections. The General Accounting Office outlined the reasons for the challenges in a 2001 report; despite changes stemming from the problematic 2000 election, many of these challenges remain today:

First, the GAO notes there are tremendous differences in how standardized state election rules are. As an example, Oklahoma has standardized rules governing elections, leaving little to administrative discretion at the local level. In contrast, in Pennsylvania there is almost no standardization among the 67 counties. Second, voting technology is a major determinant of how election officials implement elections. ... Third, the size of the jurisdiction presents different challenges: Los Angeles County, California, (with over 4 million registered voters) faces more difficulty maintaining up-to-date voter lists than Petroleum, Montana (with 367 registered voters).

(Kimball and Kropf, 2006: 1258)

These officials typically operate elections at the county level, although there is a tremendous amount of variation in the unit of local government that runs an election. For example, in states in the Northeast, townships and cities run the elections. In Michigan and Wisconsin, county officials, as well as city and town officials, run elections. (Local election authority is shared by an elected partisan county clerk, a three-person county election commission—that is, the county clerk, judge of probate court, and county treasurer—and a township or city election commission.) The local election authority is defined under state law in the separate states of the United States. Although some states select the person who runs elections in the same way in every county, many states vary among jurisdictions within the state based on characteristics such as population.

Although there are limited public opinion surveys analyzing the topic of public preferences on election administration, 2005 research conducted by political scientists R. Michael Alvarez, Thad Hall, and Morgan Llewellyn indicated that approximately three-quarters of Americans believe that local election administration should be in the hands of an elected official. Three-quarters also indicated the person should not have a party affiliation. The most preferred governing option in that survey was a nonpartisan, elected board of elections in every county. Yet, political scientists David Kimball and the present author, Martha Kropf (2006), found that in analyzing local jurisdictions—counties and townships—a vast majority of local election officials (LEOs) are elected. About half are selected with explicit consideration of partisanship—some of these partisans are elected, as is the case for county clerks throughout much of Kansas; others are appointed by the governor, some with a board with a partisan distribution (e.g., North Carolina counties are governed by an election board, with two members from the governor's party and one member of the other major party; North Carolina election boards hire a civil servant to run the day-to-day process of elections—an election director). Mississippi has elected election boards, but with about half elected on a partisan basis and the other half appointed.

Many policymakers and scholars believe that local election administration must be nonpartisan (or with bipartisan control, such as election boards, who hire an election director, do in North Carolina). There is some evidence of differing partisan attitudes and behavior, depending on partisanship. Along with my colleagues Timothy Vercellotti and David C. Kimball, I found that local election official partisanship does affect attitudes toward provisional voting—when officials are more supportive, more provisional votes are cast and counted in the local jurisdictions the officials serve (Kropf et al., 2013). However, in other research, Kimball and I along with Donald Moynihan, Carol L. Silva and Brady Baybeck found that in fact, partisanship affects attitudes toward election administration only in the largest precincts (Kimball, et al., 2013).

Although some public administration scholars speak about "representative bureaucracies," it is interesting to note that in terms of demographics—or descriptive representation—there may not be a lot of representation going on among local election officials. For example, the Congressional Research Service reports that three-quarters of the local officials are women, and only about 5 percent are minorities (Fischer and Coleman, 2008). My research with Moynihan, Silva, and Kimball found that in the jurisdictions flagged by the Voting Rights Act as the Section 5 jurisdictions (pre-Shelby, 2013),[17] only about 5 percent had a history of devices or tests that discriminated against minority voters. Further, the study notes that African American local election officials were significantly less likely to support a photo identification policy and were significantly less likely to believe fraud was a problem. Finally, the most recent study about LEO service examines responses to requests for information from Latino individuals. Harvard University political scientists Ariel R. White, Noah L. Nathan, and Julie K. Faller conducted an experiment wherein they emailed local election directors to ask about photo ID requirements:

> Analyzing over 5,300 replies, we find clear, causally identified evidence of bias against Latinos in the responsiveness of local election officials. Emails from Latino names are roughly five percentage points less likely to receive a reply to a question about voter ID requirements than those from non-Latino whites. Replies that Latino emailers do receive are less likely to convey accurate information about ID requirements. There is some evidence that this bias is greater in responses to questions about voter ID compared to a baseline question, but this is not statistically significant across model specifications.
>
> (White et al., 2015: 2)

However, more research in the area of the partisanship of local election officials needs to be conducted. Perhaps a motivation to serve the "public" keeps partisan attitudes in check and ensures that officials represent their constituents. In other words, informal norms governing election administration may actually govern how these local officials run elections. There are democratic and civic norms of cooperation that may very well affect local election officials—who often have considerable discretion to implement policy because they are so distant from state officials—which make them want to implement the election simply according to the law and/or most fairly.

THE POLLING PLACE AND THE POLLWORKER

There is no way an election could happen (short of more advanced Internet voting and all-mail voting, as is the case at the time of this writing in Oregon, Colorado, and Washington) without a largely volunteer force of citizens to work as pollworkers. Typically, pollworkers are paid very little[18] (compared with the full day they typically work); they work in the polling place, opening and closing it, checking people in, asking for identification, setting up voting machinery, adjudicating issues with people who are convinced they are registered to vote, etc. According to the EAC EAVS, close to 900,000 pollworkers worked on Election Day in 2012 in 50 states (about 7 pollworkers for every polling place). According to the 30 states that reported age data for pollworkers, almost one-quarter of them were over the age of 71, despite federal grant programs to recruit college-aged pollworkers (grants administered through the Election Assistance Commission). State law addresses the types of pollworkers who staff the polls and even governs the differing titles by which they are known: for example, election judges (and chief judges), booth workers, commissioners, etc. Although some states may designate that a polling place must have a member of both major parties as judges, these individuals are not the same as party poll observers or those who may challenge voters as members of the political parties.

The EAVS found that 44 percent of jurisdictions reported a "somewhat difficult" or "very difficult" time with pollworker recruitment for the 2012 election.[19] Scholars Barry C. Burden and Jeffrey Milyo analyzed these data as a part of a report for the Presidential Commission on Election Administration (a group charged by President Barack Obama in his 2013 State of the Union address to study problems in election administration):

> Many states report little difficulty across all jurisdictions (DC, Michigan, and New York) while others report difficulty in every local jurisdiction (Alaska, Connecticut, Delaware, Hawaii, Kentucky, and Louisiana). At least one state reported that it was "very difficult" to find poll workers in every county. Examining the states where difficulty was common does not reveal obvious relationships between this measure and other outcomes such as levels of voter turnout, political competitiveness, or waiting times.[20]
>
> (pages 5–6)

Burden and Milyo suggest that because the question on the survey is not related to turnout or other outcomes such as how long potential voters waited in line, there may be a problem with the way in which the difficulty of recruiting is assessed. Clearly, however, pollworker recruitment is cited as an issue, leading some to suggest that Election Day should be a holiday—not necessarily to increase turnout of voters, but to allow full-time employees to be pollworkers![21] Still others note that the only qualification that one must have to be a pollworker is a pulse!

No election director can be in every voting precinct at the same time, so in elections, there is very little supervision of pollworkers. Political scientists R. Michael Alvarez and Thad Hall (2006) call this a principal-agent problem in that the election directors in counties must delegate responsibility to pollworkers on Election Day. In other words, a "principal" cannot be in every place she or he must be to complete task(s) such as provision of government services (such as holding an election), so she or he hires "agents" to complete the task(s) for him or her; that agent may or may not share the same attitudes as the principal. The pollworker must make a variety of decisions, which the county/town official in charge of elections must hope are consistent with the pollworker's training (if, in fact, a pollworker is trained—that is not necessarily the case). The regular county election staff is typically not in the precinct polling place when a voter is checking in at a front table; a pollworker has to make decisions about what direction to take. Consider asking for voter identification. Even if the state law does not specify that one needs identification to vote, the pollworker might believe so strongly that it should be the law that he or she asks for it anyway! If the voter is lacking the proper ID, then a voter may be turned away simply because of the principal-agent problem and not the written law of the state. Furthermore, in a state that does require photo identification, the pollworker can decide if the identification is acceptable or not; for example, who decides whether the picture on the ID matches the voter? In each case, the attitude of the pollworker becomes the law.[22] In that sense, the pollworker is a street-level bureaucrat, acting as a government worker directly providing a service (the ability to vote) to the people (see Lipsky, 1980). And it is not clear that pollworkers intentionally discriminate—pollworkers are paid next to nothing to work a very long and stressful day—and they only work, at most, one or two days every year. It should not be surprising that even with good training, they take action that may be unconscious or that seems perfectly logical to them.

Indeed, research provides evidence that in the case of voter identification, pollworkers may mistakenly ask certain people to identify themselves. A group of political scientists led by Lonna Atkeson studied pollworkers in New Mexico; at the time of the study, the state had not required photo ID, so pollworkers could not require it for voters at the polls on Election Day. Yet, Atkeson and her colleagues (2010: 70) found that pollworkers often did ask for ID. They found that the potential voters whom pollworkers asked were most likely to be Hispanic men, compared with White voters.[23] Political scientist Rachel Cobb and her colleagues conducted an exit poll of voters in Boston, where only two types of potential voters are required to show an "acceptable ID": first-time voters who registered by mail and failed to provide a copy of their photo ID and voters who are inactive.[24] Cobb and her colleagues found that pollworkers were more likely to ask for ID from non-English speakers (rather than English speakers) and from those who are Black or Hispanic, compared with similar voters who are White. Pollworkers were less likely to ask for ID from those who reported having "more than college" education than from similar voters with "less than college" education. In the national Congressional Cooperative Election Survey, political scientist Stephen Ansolabehere (2009) found similar results regarding requests for identification among states that require such ID and those that do not. The three studies cited here are careful to consider other variables that may cause pollworkers to ask for identification. The study by Cobb and colleagues is particularly interesting in that the scholars even considered how crowded the polling place was at the time the survey was taken and whether or not minorities were more likely to be first-time voters or inactive voters.

Yet, pollworkers are involved in more than just checking citizens in at voting time—they assist voters, offer the voters curbside voting or not (as in North Carolina), and answer questions about eligibility and location if the voter is registered in a different precinct. Although these decisions are governed by election law, it is difficult to remember the various subtleties of law, especially if the polling place is busy.

Clearly, pollworkers are key. Thad E. Hall, J. Quin Monson, and Kelly D. Patterson (2009) studied how voters viewed the service provided by the pollworkers on Election Day in Ohio and Utah. The voter perception of pollworker job performance affects how confident voters are in "fair election outcomes" and how confident the voters are that their ballots were "counted accurately." Taking into account a variety of other voter variables, the scholars found that the rating of job performance did matter to how confident voters felt.

FUNDING MECHANISMS FOR ELECTIONS

Because budgeting is such an important part of the political landscape, the reader should wonder why those studying institutional theory do not mention the structures of funding more prominently. One can reasonably hypothesize that the method by which elections are funded will affect the amount *and* certainty of funding, and thus the activities in which localities are able to promote voting and educate voters. If that is the case, then the value elections hold vis-á-vis other funding priorities must certainly play a role in voting behavior and election outcomes (for example: Do people know how to use voting equipment? Will they turn out to vote, and will they have the correct identification?). If a locality cannot afford to have the proper voting equipment or as many pieces of equipment as necessary given its population, that could affect the ability of the jurisdiction to process all the voters. Interestingly, both budget practice and accounting practice vary among states and, most likely, localities. In fact, scholars who conduct accounting research hypothesize that institutional theory (laws, values, and norms) affects what accounting standards are adopted by states (Carpenter, 2001)! When scholars and policymakers study the amount spent on elections, it seems that these varying practices across the country make it as difficult to calculate the accurate amount spent as it was to calculate voter turnout across the country more than a decade ago and to a certain extent today. Those examining budgets often use case studies with a small number of jurisdictions or rely on reports from election administrators. For example, the Pew Center has a series of reports about state-level funding for elections.

However, limited evidence indicates that local officials are embedded in a local government and funding for elections largely comes from local tax dollars, although state budgets may contribute some funds to cover the costs. In 2001, Ernest Hawkins, at the time, Sacramento County, California, Registrar of Voters and president of the National Association of County Recorders, Election Officials and Clerks, explained that in some states such as California, localities "charge" the state, school district, or special district (for example, a rural water district) for costs of running an election for an office in that jurisdiction.[25] Yet the federal government does not pay for elections for federal offices; if they did 15 years ago, Hawkins suggests that it might have cost more than $59 million. To cover those costs, local election officials must compete with other governmental bodies. Hawkins put it this way:

Funds that are allocated for conducting elections come from the same pool of funds that are needed to operate the libraries, maintain parks, fix the roads, provide health and welfare services, enforce law, protect adults and children and the whole host of local services.[26]

Boone County, Missouri, county clerk Wendy Noren told me in an interview in 2003 that elections are often considered a low priority by county commissioners who have other, more visible priorities, such as roads that potential voters drive on every day (Kropf, 2005). Presidential Commission on Election Administration commissioner and former Maricopa County Election Department's federal compliance officer Tammy Patrick noted that there are several expenses that many do not consider, such as processing of write-in candidates on ballots, a county deputy on call for potential election security calls, and troubleshooting hotlines and other communications in case of troubles on Election Day.[27]

Political science scholars Heather M. Creek and Kimberly A. Karnes (2010) note that different funding practices leave some jurisdictions with a lower capacity to run an election:

Rural districts quite often work not only with limited resources due to their small populations and limited tax bases, but must also serve expansive areas. The process of becoming HAVA-compliant requires resources such as staff, funding, technical expertise, and buildings accessible to the disabled that can be used for polling places. These are all costs that we expect would be greater burdens on rural than urban districts.

(page 276)

Creek and Karnes provide a detailed case study of three states with very different funding mechanisms where voting equipment was concerned in the wake of HAVA. More than ten years beyond HAVA, local election administrators are now worried about purchasing new equipment, as much of the current equipment is reaching the end of its life.

CONCLUSION

From a historical perspective and practically speaking, it makes sense that US elections are administered in such a decentralized manner. At our country's founding, distances among voters within a state were greater, both figuratively and literally. The growth of transportation and communications technology in our country has significantly shortened distances and made more centralized elections possible, yet more centralized elections are not really politically possible at this point. We have a highly path-dependent system of election administration in the United States. That is to say, we have a system now that is built upon institutions created at the founding of our country, and before, in the period of colonization. Political scientist Alec Ewald argues that the US system of voting has gradually become more centralized, but the development of centralization has been "gradual and uneven" (page 18). He writes that

> Americans arrived in the early national period via a particular set of experiences, and ideas born of those experiences shaped and defined their policy choices. At the same time, part of the messiness of democratic lawmaking is that it can build on prior policies and institutional arrangements without clearing them away.
>
> (page 25)

Yet, he also develops the idea that US elections are governed more at the local level than many Americans believe or understand. Practically speaking, very little of the formal legal system governing elections is created at the national level.

CHAPTER 4

THE FEDERAL PART
OF THE INSTITUTION

WHEN A TYPICAL US CITIZEN CONSIDERS "ELECTION MONITORS," he or she might consider a team of US observers traveling to other countries, such as Kenya when it held its 2013 national election. In Kenya, according to the Carter Center, "[t]he country has a longstanding history of ethnic-fueled electoral violence, which culminated in postelection violence in 2007–2008 that left more than 1,000 people dead and over 600,000 internally displaced."[1] International election monitoring is provided by organizations worldwide in order "to support efforts to strengthen democratic processes and institutions and to support the conduct of elections that meet international standards, are peaceful, and have credible results."[2]

One might never consider monitors observing a local election in Alabama—at least not in today's world. But, in Evergreen, Alabama, federal monitors did oversee the election held on June 18, 2013, in the central-Alabama town of almost 4,000 people. *New York Times* reporter Adam Liptak illustrated the reasoning for the observers with a story of a man who greatly valued his right to vote:

> Jerome Gray, a 74-year-old black man, has voted in every election since 1974 in this verdant little outpost of some 4,000 people halfway between Mobile and Montgomery. Casting a ballot, he said, is a way to honor the legacy of the Voting Rights Act of 1965, a civil rights landmark born from a bloody confrontation 70 miles north of here, in Selma.
> The franchise remains fragile in Evergreen, Mr. Gray said. Last summer, he was kicked off the voting rolls by a clerk who had improperly culled the list based on utility records.[3]

Yet others claimed there was no basis for the observers. According to Alabama Media Group reporter Brendan Kirby recorded a statement that showed the emotions raised by the federal intervention.

> [Incumbent Council Member] Skinner, who got 51.6 percent of the vote in a field that included two white candidates and two black candidates, said the results refute the caricature of Evergreen painted by naysayers during the federal litigation over the racial makeup of the voting districts. "It shows there's no racial divide here. There's not," he said. "That's made up."[4]

However, on January 14, 2014, a federal judge ordered the federal supervision under Section 3 of the Voting Rights Act to continue until 2020. This meant that federal monitors could observe the election and that changes to voter registration and city council districts had to be cleared with the Department of Justice before they went into effect.[5] Although city officials first tried to fight the extension,[6] they ultimately came to an agreement with the plaintiffs. In addition to the federal monitors, even though the part of the Voting Rights Act that required voting jurisdictions to ask permission to make changes in voting law had been overturned by the Supreme Court in June 2013 in the case *Shelby v. Holder*, Evergreen would need to have voting changes concerning districting and eligibility cleared by the federal government.[7]

The plaintiffs filed the lawsuit partially because voters such as Jerome Gray, mentioned in the opening story, were placed on a "problem voter" list. In establishing who was eligible to vote in the city election, the city began not with the county voter registration list, "but worked from the list of persons billed by the municipal utility system, and placed those persons who paid municipal utility bills on the list of eligible voters."[8] According to the lawsuit, 30 percent of the eligible voters in the city were on the county registration list but not the utility bill list, so were considered "problems" and omitted from the registry. Furthermore, the city council districts based on the 2010 Census apparently packed the vast majority of the African American population into two districts. Two-thirds of the population is African American, but the council only had one Black member. The litigation had delayed the local city council and mayor's election until June 2013, but ultimately, 15 federal election monitors observed the five polling places across the small city. According to a court-appointed special master, no incidents occurred. However, with three majority Black districts created, only one Black candidate won a seat, even with the new court-ordered plan. Voter turnout was low.

Election monitors are fairly common. In every presidential and midterm election, the attorney general announces lists of jurisdictions where monitors will oversee 28 jurisdictions in person, where the Justice Department most likely received a complaint or request for the monitoring.[9] The monitored jurisdictions include those that have been "certified" as requiring monitors for federal elections under the Voting Rights Act. According to the Department of Justice, 153 counties or parishes[10] in 11 states have been certified for federal monitors in the past. As of early 2015, fewer than ten are certified under Section 3a of the Voting Rights Act.[11] Monitors are in place not just for racial discrimination, but also for purposes of ensuring that election officials provide ballots and other election materials in languages other than English (for example, in Orange County, New York, a number of individuals are from Puerto Rico, an American territory, and their first language is Spanish).[12] The Justice Department also notes that ensuring those with disabilities can vote has been a priority.

The previous chapter made the institution of elections sound very decentralized, and for good reason—the institution *is* decentralized, even hyperdecentralized. One should not take for granted today that Congress now can do nothing in the face of overwhelming and unwieldy state and local power over elections, as the example of federal monitoring shows. The Elections Clause of the US Constitution states: "The Times, Place and Manner of holding Elections for Senators and Representatives, shall be prescribed in each State by the Legislature thereof; but the Congress may at any time by law make or alter such Regulations, except as to the Places of chusing Senators" (US Constitution, Article I, Section 4). How much power this clause imparts is a subject of debate.

Three overriding themes emerge in this chapter: first, when the political context allows, the federal government makes some changes to the institution of elections, despite the hyperdecentralization, but it can be an uphill battle. The second theme is that the federal part of the formal "rules" has largely focused on access to voting rather than administration. However, as the reader will see in later chapters, making sure individuals have the right to vote is really known as a series of "first-generation" battles. The second generation of battles focused more on making sure that minorities could elect candidates of their choice. The final theme? The federal courts—especially the Supreme Court—often have the final say as to what the laws mean and in their "enforcement," even though opinions often invoke "legislative intent." An administrative agency in the federal government—the Department of Justice (DOJ)—has "enforcement" powers over much of the federal laws (although a relatively new Election Assistance Commission (EAC) has had charge of distributing funds for voting equipment incentives[13]), but more often than not, the Justice Department files a lawsuit in court, although certainly, as indicated by the introduction, the DOJ has sent monitors to protect voting rights.

A SURPRISINGLY LIMITED ROLE FOR FEDERAL LAWMAKERS

An interesting balance has developed in terms of election administration. Public administration scholars and Auburn University professors Kathleen Hale and Mitchell Brown have helped educate (and certify) election officials for many years as a part of the National Association of Election Officials. They characterize attitudes toward election administration in the federal system as divided:

> In terms of the broad normative themes that support American federalism, the mechanics of elections—how, when, where, who—are typically seen as the province of states and localities; the equity of elections—access to and fairness of the process—are typically seen as responsibilities of the federal level.[14]

This is ironic given that the "right to vote" is not explicitly in the US Constitution, but time brought changes that informed state governments that they could not deny the right to vote based on race (Fifteenth Amendment), sex (Nineteenth Amendment), or age (Twenty-Sixth Amendment). Furthermore, the Constitution now reads that "[t]he right of citizens of the United States to vote in any primary or other election for President or Vice President, for electors for President or Vice President, or for Senator or Representative in Congress, shall not be denied or abridged by the United States or any State by reason of failure to pay poll tax or other tax" (Twenty-Fourth Amendment). All of these amendments state that "Congress shall have power to enforce this article by appropriate legislation."

One way to analyze the role the federal government has had in elections is to consider the various pieces of legislation the US Congress has passed where it concerns both election administration and voting rights. The timing of the passage of legislation has signaled the political importance of voting rights and emblemizes the waxing and waning of voting rights, which have been affected by the political environment (external triggering events and partisan control of institutions of government) at the time. And the level of enforcement of those laws (mostly by the Department of Justice's Civil Rights Division, with a Voting section and a Disability Rights section), most likely reflects the political environment at the time of the DOJ action (or inaction).[15] And, even when the Department of Justice does not sue states or localities in an attempt to enforce the law, private citizens and interest groups have filled that void. Thus, if an election authority allegedly violates a federal law, the DOJ or an individual (often represented by an interest group such as the American Civil Liberties Union or the NAACP) will bring suit in federal court. Throughout history, a number of legal decisions have emanated from the federal courts concerning issues such as gerrymandering, violations of the Voting Rights Act, and many others.

Numerous pieces of legislation have been passed at the federal level throughout history with the intent of regulating elections in some manner. The constitutional changes allowed voting to various groups, but the twentieth-century statutory changes tend to focus on access to the voting process, with the exception of the Help America Vote Act of 2002, which was more administrative in nature. Many of the pre- or early-twentieth-century changes dealt with arguably minor administrative issues. For example, in 1872, Congress established that representatives be chosen at the same time—on the Tuesday after the first Monday in November. When the Constitution was amended to allow for direct elections of senators, Congress also passed a law for the election on the same day as the House of Representatives (1914).[16] However, it is notable that the Help America Vote Act of 2002 was the first piece of federal legislation passed that provided federal funding for localities' election administration. Political scientist Alec C. Ewald argues that nineteenth-century national changes "were relatively scattered, and many were reversed or abandoned after partisan or doctrinal shifts" (page 72). However, he argues that each of the changes in the twentieth century have served as scaffolding for succeeding changes. Most Americans are probably surprised at how few national laws there are regarding elections, especially since the ones that exist are high profile (the Voting Rights Act) or tend to touch almost every citizen (the National Voter Registration Act [NVRA], also known as the Motor Voter Act).

VOTING RIGHTS ACT OF 1965
(AMENDED 1970, 1975, 1982, 2006)

Variously called "the most effective civil rights statute ever enacted in the United States,"[17] "the crown jewel of the Civil Rights movement,"[18] "a revolutionary measure,"[19] and "a sacred symbol of American democracy,"[20] but with parts that are "fraught with controversy,"[21] the Voting Rights Act (VRA) was passed in 1965 with a bipartisan majority. The VRA was intended to enforce the Fourteenth and Fifteenth Amendments to the Constitution, which had been circumvented continually, particularly in the South.[22] The VRA represented a dramatic shift in power toward the federal government, especially because of Section 5.

SECTION 5/SECTION 4B

Section 5 specified that election laws were essentially frozen, but only in certain jurisdictions. Local and state governments could make no changes—not even small ones—to election law without asking permission from the Department of Justice or the DC federal district court. The US Commission on Civil Rights (USCCR) is a government agency created by the Civil Rights Act of 1957 whose mission is to collect information and evidence about civil rights enforcement, including voting rights. The USCCR gathered a variety of evidence concerning VRA enforcement for hearings held about the reauthorization of the VRA. They noted in that report the various types of laws that needed preclearance:

1. redistricting plans, annexations, and de-annexations;
2. methods of elections (for example, from at-large to single-member districts, the use of a majority vote requirement, or from elective to appointive and vice versa) or the number of elected officials;
3. precinct lines, polling place locations, and absentee or early voting locations;
4. ballot format, balloting rules, polling place procedures, early voting and absentee voting procedures, ballot initiatives, referenda, and recall procedures;
5. special election dates;
6. voter registration;
7. the procedures and standards for becoming a candidate for elective office and campaign finance requirements;
8. the public electoral functions adopted by political parties; and
9. the languages in which jurisdictions provide voting materials and information to the public.[23]

The Voting Rights Act defined those jurisdictions that would be subject to the freeze in those laws in Section 4b. The DOJ or the district court would not allow the law to go forward if it had either the purpose or result of discrimination against minority voters. This part of the law was supposed to be temporary, but lawmakers kept extending it (Tokaji, 2014).

What distinguished the Section 4b jurisdictions that had to obtain the "preclearance?" Those jurisdictions had a history of the use of "tests or devices" (such as a literacy test to determine whether someone was "able" to vote), which prevented people from voting, as well as voter registration or turnout in the jurisdiction under 50 percent of the population. The federal government had never before told a state or local government it had to ask permission before changing its own law. However, litigating each case of voting discrimination had proven a formidable burden before passage of the VRA. According to legal scholar Richard L. Hasen, Southern states challenged the new law in court; in the first such case, *South Carolina v. Katzenbach* (1966), the Supreme Court ruled that Congress acted appropriately in passing the law—it enforced the Fifteenth Amendment.[24] In fact, the majority opinion read,

> Two points emerge vividly from the voluminous legislative history of the Act contained in the committee hearings and floor debates. First: Congress felt itself confronted by an insidious and pervasive evil which had been perpetuated in certain parts of our country through unremitting and ingenious defiance of the Constitution. Second: Congress concluded that the unsuccessful remedies which it had prescribed in the past would have to be replaced by sterner and more elaborate measures in order to satisfy the clear commands of the Fifteenth Amendment.[25]

The US Congress most recently renewed the section requiring that the state and local governments obtain permission in 2006.

However, on June 25, 2013, the Supreme Court struck down the coverage formula in Section 4b in *Shelby v. Holder* on a vote of 5-4. Chief Justice John Roberts wrote the majority opinion:

> Coverage today is based on decades-old data and eradicated practices. The formula captures States by reference to literacy tests and low voter registration and turnout in the 1960s and early 1970s. But such tests have been banned for over 40 years. And voter registration and turnout numbers in covered States have risen dramatically.

Legal scholars such as Samuel Issacharoff argue that one way of looking at the decision is to consider that racial discrimination or electoral manipulation that affects minorities is just as likely to occur in states such as Ohio as it is in states such as Mississippi (2013: 117). Essentially, the opinion indicated that if the US Congress wanted to pass a more updated coverage formula, it should. Although members of Congress have proposed legislation altering the coverage formula, members of Congress had not seriously considered such formulas, at least as of early 2015.

The election of the nation's first Black president (for two terms) triggered a discussion about the continuing relevance of Section 5. Political scientists and legal scholars Stephen Ansolabehere, Nathaniel Persily, and Charles Stewart III (2013) note that advocates of Section 5 believe it proved its worth:

> In the run up to the 2012 election, section 5 proved it had bite, as photo ID and other laws were prevented from going into effect by the Department of Justice (DOJ) or the district court in Texas, South Carolina, and Florida, and Texas's congressional redistricting plan was found to be intentionally discriminatory.[26]

(page 206)

Ansolabehere and his colleagues analyzed different sources of data to show that there is racially polarized voting within the former Section 5 jurisdictions. This degree of correlation between vote choice and voter race (taking into account other factors known to affect vote choice) is an indicator of a variety of problems, say the scholars. They argued that racially polarized voting indicates that minorities may have less of an opportunity of electing candidates of their choice. Not only that, but if race is a large determinant of voting, then it is also possible that politicians will follow the will of the majority, which in effect discriminates against the minority because the politicians will be more responsive to those that vote for them—the disadvantage is specific to African Americans in this case. Finally, the polarization is not due to state law itself being intentionally discriminatory, but "private choices occur in a state-structured environment" (page 209). This polarization in the Section 5 jurisdictions compared to non-Section 5 jurisdictions "demonstrate[s] the coverage formula's continuing relevance" (page 220).

Critics of the Supreme Court ruling are also quick to point out that states—particularly those with Republican majorities in their state legislatures—were quick to pass restrictive voting legislation. An example is North Carolina, where the Republican governor signed into law a controversial voter reform bill on August 12, 2013, just about six weeks after the *Shelby v. Holder* decision (dated June 25, 2013), and over strong Democratic opposition. Note that the General Assembly presented the bill to the governor on July 29, 2013.[27] The North Carolina bill contained photo identification for voters, ended same-day voter registration during early voting, cut a week off of early voting (although early voting was to be open in more places), stopped pre-registration of 16- to 17-year-olds, and ended the ability for voters to cast provisional votes in precincts other than their officially assigned precincts. These issues quickly became the subject of lawsuits under Section 2 of the Voting Rights Act (see the following section). As of this writing, these lawsuits are wending their way through the courts.

SECTION 2 VERSUS SECTION 5

It is important to note that the *Shelby* finding does not mean the VRA is no longer in force. In particular, Section 2 of the act basically forbids discrimination in voting. It states that

> [n]o voting qualification or prerequisite to voting, or standard, practice, or procedure shall be imposed or applied by any State or political subdivision to deny or abridge the right of any citizen of the United States to vote on account of race or color.[28]

The issue is that Section 2 requires a case-by-case approach, rather than the "stop it before it starts" approach to discrimination in Section 5. In other words, the burden of proof is on those filing the lawsuit (the plaintiffs) rather than the jurisdiction having the burden to show the law change does not disadvantage minority voters.[29]

What makes Section 2 interesting, however, is that Congress amended the Section in 1982. The Voting Rights Act changed the face of African American registration and voting, increasing both dramatically. Yet, some observers began to realize that an increase in registration and voting did not necessarily mean an increase in descriptive or substantive representation. In other words, voting discrimination moved from outright "vote denial" to more subtle "vote dilution." The US Congress addressed that with changes to the act in 1982. University of Michigan legal scholar Ellen Katz and a team of students examined cases decided on the basis of Section 2 and in the context of the research discussed the background of amendments to the Voting Rights Act passed in 1982:

> By the summer of 1975, black citizens in Mobile were registering and voting without hindrance, a feat that would have seemed impossible a decade earlier. And yet, ten years after passage of the Voting Rights Act, black residents in Mobile noticed that their participation seemed to be making little difference to the substance and structure of local governance. At the time, African Americans comprised approximately one third of the city's population, white and black voters consistently supported different candidates, and no African-American candidate had ever won a seat on the three-person city commission. Housing remained segregated, black city employees were concentrated in the lowest city salary classification, and "a significant difference and sluggishness" characterized the City's provision of city services to black residents when compared to that provided to whites.[30]

Katz and her colleagues stated that, at the time, the lower courts found that the at-large electoral system diluted African American voting strength.[31] When local legislatures are structured so as to select representation on an at-large basis, it makes it much more difficult for a minority to gain any sort of representation. However, in *Bolden v. City of Mobile*, the Supreme Court overturned that decision, saying that neither Section 2 of the VRA nor the Constitution proscribed electoral laws, just "produced racially discriminatory results." (Katz et al., 2006: 647). Thus, in 1982, Congress amended the Voting Rights Act to bar electoral structures that had a discriminatory *result*. For the most part, a plaintiff does not need to have a smoking gun to establish voting discrimination, but one must show that there are discriminatory effects.

Furthermore, as noted in the introduction, parts of the VRA establish a similar system of preclearance, based on a lawsuit. A federal court found that the city mentioned in the introductory story, Evergreen, Alabama, violated the Voting Rights Act in terms of both voting access (determining eligibility) and vote dilution (in terms of the drawing of the city council districts). Thus, with the ruling, the city came under DOJ supervision, but with electoral changes only related to those two points subject to preclearance.

The critical difference between Section 2 and Section 5 is that Section 2 cannot stop legislation before it is even enacted. Section 2 requires that some sort of alleged violation must occur and then someone must file a lawsuit under Section 2. However, Section 2 took on increased importance after the *Shelby County v. Holder* decision. In fact, the Justice Department sued a number of Southern states who passed voter identification legislation in the wake of *Shelby* using the Section 2 law.

LANGUAGE MINORITIES

In the 1975 amendments to the VRA, Congress added consideration of "language minorities." That is, for certain election jurisdictions, the Voting Rights Act requires that bilingual (or multilingual) voting information be available: a number of individuals have not had adequate education in English in order to read the ballot and other election material. In fact, some places, such as Los Angeles, have up to seven languages (with an eighth Asian language "unspecified").[32] Still others, such as Orange County, New York, have a number of American citizens educated in a school flying an American flag, as Puerto Rico does, but not providing instruction in English. According to the Department of Justice,

> [a]mong other factors, the denial of the right to vote of such minority group citizens is ordinarily directly related to the unequal educational opportunities afforded them resulting in high illiteracy and low voting participation. The Congress declares that, in order to enforce the guarantees of the fourteenth and fifteenth amendments to the United States Constitution, it is necessary to eliminate such discrimination by prohibiting these practices, and by prescribing other remedial devices.

Interestingly, CNN conducted a poll in 2006, wherein they found that a majority (about 53 percent) of Americans believe that a person should *not* "be permitted to vote if they cannot read or write English."[33] And certainly, in examining the effectiveness of protections, organizations such as the Asian American Legal Defense and Education Fund documented cases in a recent report that those with limited language skills receive little to no help from pollworkers and sometimes even harassment.

> In Philadelphia, PA, at the Jefferson Alumni Hall poll site, an elderly Chinese American voter unsuccessfully attempted to vote. The Judge of Elections and another poll worker held the curtains to his voting machine wide open as the voter cast his vote, violating his right to privacy. Then the Judge of Elections instructed the voter to push certain buttons and vote for certain candidates. The poll worker then instructed him to vote for additional candidates. The voter had intended only to vote for the presidential candidate. No Chinese interpreter was present at this poll site. Had an interpreter been present, the LEP [low English proficiency] voter would have been able to vote for whomever he wished.[34]

Such harassment is the reason for the election law—so that knowing English does not become the "literacy test" for citizens wishing to vote.

ACCESSIBILITY FOR INDIVIDUALS WITH DISABILITIES

Consistent with the idea that the federal government's role in election administration has mostly been in the realm of protecting access to voting, the Americans with Disabilities Act (ADA) specifically mentions voting as an area wherein those with disabilities have experienced discrimination. However, the first federal concern was with those who are 65 and older accessing the polls (Voting Accessibility for the Elderly and Handicapped Act of 1984). Then, more generally, the ADA provided that state and local governments should make public services—such as voting—available. The General Accounting Office (GAO) has conducted a variety of studies concerning the level of accessibility for those with disabilities. GAO's Barbara Bovbjerg testified before the National Council on Disabilities, explaining that the law is not just about physical modifications to polling places:

> State and local governments may generally comply with ADA accessibility requirements in a variety of ways, such as reassigning services to accessible buildings or alternative accessible sites. ... Public accommodations must make reasonable modifications in policies, practices, or procedures to facilitate access for people with disabilities. These facilities are also required to remove physical barriers in existing buildings when it is "readily achievable" to do so; that is, when the removal can be done without much difficulty or expense, given the entity's resources.[35]

(page 4)

Even commercial (nongovernmental buildings) must be accessible if they are used for voting. However, Bovbjerg noted that the GAO study found that only about one-quarter of polling places "had no potential impediments in the path from the parking [lot] to the voting area" (page 1), but 45 percent of polling places at least had curb-side voting. According to the report, about one-third of localities the GAO surveyed said they used long-term care homes as polling places (presumably effectively ensuring accessibility). Interestingly, the federal government began administering a grant program through the Department of Health and Human Services for accessibility when it passed the Help America Vote Act of 2002.

NATIONAL VOTER REGISTRATION ACT OF 1993

Most Americans know this law by the most common place in which it is implemented: local offices of state Departments of Motor Vehicles (DMV). The so-called "Motor Voter" law mandated that citizens be able to register in offices wherein they received social services such as food stamps, as well as the DMV. It also instituted uniform requirements governing the removal of voters from the register; instituted a uniform, federally provided voter registration form;[36] and allowed all voters to be able to register to vote by mail. Supporters argued that the law was needed because of low voter registration and turnout. Scholars and voting rights activists Frances Fox Piven and Richard A. Cloward noted the difficulties with various registration laws across the country in 1988, about seven years before the implementation of the Motor Voter law:

> Thus in many places people must travel to a county seat to register, often without benefit of public transportation, and then only during working hours. Even the twenty-four states that allow people to register by mail have no system to make the mail-in forms widely available, so that one must still go to a board of elections. For poorer and less

educated people, voter registration forms are frequently difficult to understand. And elections officials can be intimidating. Such arrangements are typically justified with the argument that voting shouldn't be easy, that people ought to earn the privilege by surmounting the obstacles embedded in the registration process. But the voter registration system is supposed to be a method of listing eligible voters, not of weeding out those whom politicians consider undeserving.[37]

(page 869)

Thus, the NVRA sought to provide more uniform and open voter registration. However, when the act first went into effect, seven states went to court to challenge it, but lost. And in 2008, two voting-access interest groups, Project Vote and Demos, reported that there was a decline in the number of registrations at public agencies; in addition, the report notes that there remained a large number of unregistered voting-age citizens whose incomes were under $25,000 year.[38] However, groups such as the Heritage Foundation responded by saying that welfare reform (passed in 1996) reduced the caseload, and therefore the voter registrations.

VOTING ACCESS FOR OVERSEAS VOTERS

There have been several efforts over the years to centralize voting for military members and their spouses, starting in 1955 with the Federal Voting Assistance Program (FVAP). A 1964 FVAP report lamented, "[a]s late as 1955, and despite the experience of World Wars I, II, and Korea, the United States had no completely satisfactory system to permit members of the Armed Forces and overseas civilian employees to take part in local, state and national elections through the use of absentee ballots."[39] The US Secretary of Defense is the individual charged with implementing federal laws ensuring that soldiers and other government employees working overseas can register and vote.[40] In 1986, the Uniformed and Overseas Citizens Absentee Voting Act (UOCAVA) was passed to centralize all previous federal laws concerning absentee voting for the military.[41] The FVAP administers the nuts and bolts of overseas voting, ranging from answering "frequently asked questions" such as "What is a postmark and how do I get one?" to providing an electronic transmission service for overseas voters to request, receive, and submit ballots. In response to claims that several soldiers were not receiving ballots on time in order to vote and submit them by the deadline, Congress passed an amendment to UOCAVA—the Military and Overseas Voter Empowerment Act (MOVE) in 2009. Most importantly, MOVE required states and localities to provide absentee ballots to overseas voter at least 45 days before an election.[42]

HIGHER EDUCATION ACT OF 1965 (1998 AND 2008 AMENDMENTS)

Federal government involvement in voting participation does come in some other strange places as well. For example, in order for a college/university to be eligible to participate in federal student aid programs (Stafford Loans, Pell Grants, etc.), the institution must participate in a "good faith" effort to distribute voter registration forms to "each student enrolled in a degree or certificate program and physically in attendance at the institution, and to make such forms widely available to students at the institution."[43] Amendments added in 2008 said that universities could distribute forms electronically, although any email distribution must be about voter registration alone.[44]

HELP AMERICA VOTE ACT OF 2002

The Help America Vote Act of 2002 (HAVA) represented a significant level of involvement in the nuts and bolts of election administration, but scholars and policy-makers both argue it was carefully crafted in order to respect the idea of federalism on which the electoral system was based. Congress passed the act in response to the 2000 election and various administration and counting problems identified in the voting process.[45] The largest proportion of the act's budget was focused on incentives for election jurisdictions (states, counties, cities, townships) to replace outdated voting equipment,[46] although some funds were allocated to grants for accessibility, as briefly mentioned earlier.[47] At the time, many jurisdictions used punchcard ballots, which had been in use since the early 1960s. Punchcard ballots were the "poster child" of the 2000 election because problems with using these ballots became the focus of headlines. Thus, the act called for voting equipment that met certain standards:

> Title III of the Act specified that voting systems used in federal elections should meet several standards. First, the voter should be able to verify independently and privately that his vote was cast as intended. Furthermore, the voter should be able to change the ballot if he desires. If the person casts too many votes for a contest, the system should provide notification and allow the opportunity to correct any mistake.
>
> (Kropf and Kimball, 2012: 25)

Not only that, but each precinct in the country was required to have at least one piece of voting equipment that allowed those who are disabled to vote in private and independently. In total, Congress budgeted $3.86 billion dollars in HAVA, most of which was granted to the states in order to purchase newer equipment.[48] According to the Congressional Research Service, as of December 2014, only $3.54 billion of the monies had been appropriated.[49]

Second, although many states had provisions in state law that provided for fail-safe balloting (approximately 27), HAVA required these provisional ballot rules to be instituted in every state.[50]

> To avoid turning people away from the polls on Election Day, Section 302 of the HAVA required states to allow people to vote a provisional ballot when they believe they are registered but their names do not appear on the voter list at their polling place. The justification for provisional voting was that sometimes people are wrongly removed from the voting registry because of database errors or because the would-be voter recently moved. Data entry errors and general administrative mistakes are also possible.
>
> (Kropf and Kimball, 2012: 26, note removed)

Once cast, these provisional ballots would be separated from other ballots, and the decision of whether or not the ballots would be counted into the total would be decided by local election officials after the election. However, HAVA left it up to state discretion whether or not provisional votes, which were otherwise valid but cast in the wrong precinct, would count toward the contests for which the voter was eligible. In the 2004 election, 17 had provisions in place to count provisional ballots cast outside the correct precinct (or at least the portion of the ballot that applied to the individual—if a person, for example, votes in the incorrect district for city council, his or her vote for city council would not count, but his or her state or federal election votes would count). In 2004, 27 did not count those cast at the wrong precinct. By 2014, only 22 state governments chose not to count any of the ballots cast in the incorrect precinct.[51]

VOTER REGISTRATION DATABASES

Another key part of HAVA called for each state to create a "single, uniform, official, centralized, interactive computerized statewide voter registration list defined, maintained, and administered at the State level that contains the name and registration information of every legally registered voter in the State and assigns a unique identifier to each legally registered voter in the State."[52] The EAC issued voluntary guidelines that suggested that the databases either could be coordinated from the top (at the state level) or local jurisdictions could all be connected, with data combined (Hall, 2013).

These statewide electronic voter registration lists enable state partnerships in order to check for duplicate registrations—where a citizen is registered to vote in more than one location. People may be registered in multiple locations, not necessarily because they wish to commit fraud; they may simply move, especially if they live in an area where multiple states are linked—such as the Washington, DC area, where people tend to live in northern Virginia, DC, or Maryland.[53] Thus, several states have created efforts to cross-check voter registration lists from other states.[54] However, matching is not a straightforward exercise, according to the experts working with the National Research Council; in fact there is a fairly large amount of research examining how to perform matches in large databases, with scholars having different points of view:

> Errors in record-level matching may be false positives (a match is indicated when in fact the two records refer to different individuals) or false negatives (a nonmatch is indicated when the two records refer to the same individual). What is an acceptable upper limit on a given type of error depends on the application in question. For example, if the voter registration database is being checked against a database of felons or dead people, a low rate of false positives is needed to reduce the likelihood that eligible voters are removed from the VRD. Just how low a rate is acceptable is a policy choice.[55]
>
> (page B2)

There are at least two different interstate cooperatives comparing voter registration databases. One of the first states to pioneer an effort to compare voter rolls was

Kansas, in which cooperating states sign a memorandum of understanding. More than 20 states participated in the cross-checking program in the beginning of 2013.[56] The cross-checking has caught people double-voting,[57] but many fewer than were simply matched by the database comparisons, as identified by Kansas Secretary of State Kris Kobach in a presentation before the National Association of State Election Directors. Another effort involved more than just comparing voter registration databases; seven states participate in the Electronic Registration Information Center (ERIC), supported by the Pew Charitable Trusts. ERIC is designed to

> connect information in state voter files with data from state motor vehicle offices, death records, and change of address information to identify eligible but unregistered individuals and identify outdated entries and duplicate entries within and across states to help clean up voter rolls.[58]
>
> (page 1)

HAVA AND THE CREATION OF THE ELECTION ASSISTANCE COMMISSION

HAVA created a new federal agency: the Election Assistance Commission (EAC). The EAC could not write rules to implement federal policy; rather, it would serve as a clearinghouse of election research in addition to providing best practices for issues such as ballot design and design of election signage and other information (Montjoy, 2005).[59] The EAC now hosts the Election Administration and Voting Survey, with data about voter turnout, absentee ballots, and voting equipment from 2004 to 2012. However, there was some question about midway through the agency's tenure when the commission's handling of a voter identification and election fraud research report was questioned, when the agency failed to release the report.[60] In 2007, Congress investigated the EAC and asked the inspector general to review the obligations of the agency.

However, in terms of ballot and equipment standards, research indicates that only a few jurisdictions have adopted the suggestions for the graphic design of ballots (Kropf, 2014). The EAC has also issued voluntary voting system guidelines (VVSGs) in cooperation with the National Institute of Standards and Technology. Public administration scholars Hale and Brown show that the vast majority of states have opted out of the VVSGs and that election officials and voting equipment venders both find the national standards unhelpful.

> They also report that their ability to acquire new equipment is stymied by a time-consuming, expensive, and ineffective federal certification process that, although voluntary, has become the de facto standard for voting equipment manufacturers. Not in the least, election officials are not confident that states can fill the void in the absence of any federal certification process, even though the current process is expensive and slow at its best.
>
> (page 429)

Hale and Brown find that just 12 states fully adopted the guidelines, whereas another 23 have adopted the federal standards in some way. As current voting equipment ages out, Hale and Brown report that local jurisdictions are worried that they will not be able to purchase new equipment that meets federal standards.

The EAC has been consistently handicapped because of a lack of commissioners, which occurred because of political pressure to close the agency.[61] In the beginning, although the law specified that the commission would be in place by February 2003, it took until about February 2004 for the body to operate because of delays in the nomination and confirmation of commissioners.[62] Because the body was charged with distributing the grant-funding portion of the HAVA appropriation (states had to meet various requirements such as publishing state plans for reform in order to obtain the funds), no grant funds could be distributed until the commission was in place.[63] Then, according to one newspaper report (*USA Today*), the EAC "languished without commissioners" from 2010 to December 2014, the equivalent, the paper reported, of "two election cycles, to put it in Washington terms."[64] According to the Center for Public Integrity,

> [i]t's endowed with almost no regulatory powers. All four commissioner positions [sic] have been vacant since 2011, and it hasn't conducted a public meeting since then. It hasn't had a quorum of three commissioners—what's needed for the EAC to conduct votes, write policy and issue advisory opinions—since 2010. The commission has no permanent executive director or general counsel. It used to distribute grants to states so they may better administer elections. But today, lacking leaders, the EAC no longer make[s] grants.[65]

In December 2014, the Senate confirmed three commissioners, allowing the commission to have a quorum.

THE DEPARTMENT OF JUSTICE

Ultimately, enforcement of many of the federal laws has been up to the Department of Justice's Voting Section, part of the Civil Rights Division of the Department of Justice (organized under the Civil Rights Act of 1957). According to the DOJ Office of the Inspector General (OIG):

> The Voting Section is responsible for enforcing federal voting laws, including investigating and litigating civil matters throughout the United States and its territories, conducting administrative review of changes in voting practices and procedures in certain jurisdictions, and monitoring elections in various parts of the country. The Voting Section is staffed with approximately 100 employees, comprising attorneys, social scientists, civil rights analysts, and support personnel. Since 1995, the Voting Section has generally employed 35–40 attorneys at any given time, although the number of Section attorneys in that period has fluctuated between 31 (1998) and 45 attorneys (2010). The structure of the Section's management team has varied over time, but Section leadership has generally included a Section Chief and several Deputy Section Chiefs and Special Litigation Counsels. The Section's staff, including its management team, is comprised entirely of career employees.[66]

(page 9)

The OIG provided this information as part of an extension of investigation of charges of political influence over the actions of the Department of Justice—under both Republican and Democratic administrations. Yet ultimately, the OIG did not find evidence for partisanship affecting the enforcement of voting laws. However, the OIG concluded that "[t]he conduct that we discovered and document in this report reflects a disappointing lack of professionalism by some Department employees over an extended period of time, during two administrations, and across various facets of the Voting Section's operations" (page 258). Other offices administering politically charged legislation did not indicate that liberals and conservatives behaved so badly toward each other. Legal scholar Richard L. Hasen put it thusly, "... if the people charged with maintaining a level playing field can't keep the peace, what hope is there for anyone else"?[67]

All in all, the DOJ helped the United States make very real strides in voting rights for minorities. The DOJ is probably struggling with many of the same issues the rest of the country is—how much progress has really been made for minorities in our country? The reaction when *Shelby v. Holder* was announced certainly is illustrative of the discomfort many Americans have regarding issues of race. Some like to say they do not see race, but a quick look at current events concerning controversial police shootings remind us that race is very relevant. And, moreover, it is probably difficult for most Americans to imagine people born in the United States who may not be literate in English, as some in Alaska are.

FEDERAL COURTS

The purpose of this book is not to cover the intricacies of the federal court system: certainly there are three levels of federal courts—district courts where federal voting lawsuits begin (94 districts), courts of appeals (there are 12), and, of course, the Supreme Court. This chapter has made it clear that a number of federal agencies implement various types of federal voting legislation, including the Justice Department. Legal scholar Jennifer Nou (2013) argues that "... the emerging portrait of federal election administration is one in which some of the most important election-related statutes are being implemented, if at all, by courts" (page 151). Her scholarship argued that the courts themselves, have few tools of their own for enforcement of law and must rely on other policymakers to do so—even Alexander Hamilton made the argument that the courts are "the weakest branch" (Franklin and Kosacki, 1989). The public's view of the courts as legitimate is arguably more important than that of the other branches. Although there were several court decisions concerning elections before the 1960s, in general, federal courts did not become involved in "political questions" such as election administration. The 1960 case *Baker v. Carr* about redistricting in Tennessee signaled a sea change in court willingness to become involved in the nuts and bolts of elections, and sometimes very involved, particularly in redistricting cases.[68]

Right after the Supreme Court agreed to hear the *Crawford v. Marion County* case (Indiana voter identification case), legal scholar Daniel P. Tokaji (2007) made the argument that election administration cases should stay with the lower courts. He argued that the lower federal courts have done a "respectable if imperfect job" of handling election administration cases, especially given their "factual complexity."

> Even more serious is the potential damage to the Court's credibility that might flow from further intervention in a hot-button issue that tends to divide legislators along party lines. When lower courts make mistakes, their opinions do much less damage than erroneous decisions from the Supreme Court. That is true not only because their precedential impact is narrower, but because lower court decisions receive far less attention.[69]
>
> (page 1093)

The Supreme Court did indeed uphold the Indiana government–issued photo identification requirement. According to Justice John Paul Stevens, who wrote the majority opinion in the case, one of the three appeals court judges did say the law seemed political.

> The dissenting judge, viewing the justification for the law as "hollow"—more precisely as "a not-too-thinly-veiled attempt to discourage election-day turnout by certain folks believed to skew Democratic"—would have applied a stricter standard, something he described as "close to 'strict scrutiny light.' *Id.*, at 954, 956 (opinion of Evans, J.)."[70]

The majority opinion, however, stated that the burden was on only a limited number of individuals, for example, "elderly persons born out-of-state, who may have difficulty obtaining a birth certificate" but the state's interest in "integrity and reliability of the electoral process" was greater.

EXAMPLE OF FEDERAL INVOLVEMENT

All in all, the federal government becomes involved in more ways than sending observers; the Department of Justice and federal courts have suggested alternative methods of electing representatives as a way to address racial imbalance in representation. Yet such solutions sometimes contrast with long-held beliefs about election administration and voting. Take for example the case of Port Chester, New York.

In December 2006, the Department of Justice filed a lawsuit against a Westchester County, New York village, Port Chester (otherwise known as "the 'poor stepchild' in a county of wealthy enclaves"[71]). Before 2010, no Hispanic[72] person had ever been elected to the Port Chester board of trustees, even though about one-quarter of its citizen voting age population was Latino[73] and almost half of its total population is Latino. Cesar Ruiz, a Peruvian immigrant who was raised in Port Chester, filed a DOJ complaint after having failed in an attempt at running for the board.[74] Thus, the Department of Justice contended that the village's method of electing trustees— the village elected them at-large, that is, elected by and representing the entire village—violated Section 2 of the Voting Rights Act. In other words, the method of electing representatives diluted the votes of Hispanics and they could not elect a representative of their choice, even when Hispanics voted as a bloc. The majority of voters simply overwhelmed their choices. This is an example of "vote dilution" rather than "vote denial."[75] The structure of the institution affects the right to vote—not in terms of an individual (or group of individuals) being allowed to cast a vote, but rather, in terms of a group not being able to elect a representative (see Chapter 9).

In keeping with requirements of Section 2 lawsuits, the DOJ charged there was a history of discrimination against Hispanics in the state and county. Ultimately, the court sided with the DOJ, and the village had to change its method of electing trustees, among other actions. Thus, in 2010, the village began to use a method called "cumulative voting."[76] Every voter had six votes to cast (that is, the voters had as many votes as there were seats on the board)—a voter could cast all six for one candidate if he or she felt strongly enough about the candidate.[77] The village mounted an educational campaign about the method, which appeared to work. In an exit poll, most people reported they understood the system, and many used multiple votes.[78] The system worked in terms of enabling representation: the village elected its first-ever Hispanic representative.

The village used an alternative election mechanism—a different, but definitely not new way of electing representatives. Yet even though empirical evidence indicated that people understood the system, it seemed counter to "normal" principals of voting. An Associated Press reporter found an example:

> Arthur Furano voted early—five days before Election Day. And he voted often, flipping the lever six times for his favorite candidate. Furano cast multiple votes on the instructions of a federal judge and the US Department of Justice as part of a new election system crafted to help boost Hispanic representation. ... "That was very strange," Arthur Furano, 80, said after voting. "I'm not sure I liked it. All my life, I've heard, 'one man, one vote.'"[79]

The village of Port Chester is also not the first to experience this sort of lawsuit. The courts have considered part of our right to vote the ability to be able to choose a representative and actually have a fighting chance at electing that representative. Often, such cases are addressed by ordering the entity to create smaller districts rather than electing representatives at-large. Here, some individuals believe that alternative methods are more difficult to implement because people like Furano, who was introduced earlier, are used to voting in a certain way. This idea of "one man one vote" is powerful rhetoric against the method of voting because it has been an accepted maxim about voting since the 1960s.

CONCLUSION

The character of the relationship between the federal and state governments has changed over time, depending on political context. Political scientist Alex Ewald suggests that for a time in the late 1800s, among judges and members of Congress, it became almost "common sense" that Congress should have power over elections. Ewald writes, however, that "just as national institutions together built a doctrine and a practice of expanded national power to supervise voting practices, so together did they eventually abandon it" (page 64). He suggests that partisanship was part of the reason for the change in focus toward states; but changes in state law concerning Australian Ballots (secret ballot reforms, see Chapter 1) also trumped the nascent federal efforts. Although states passed such laws, they often passed the burden of paying for ballots onto localities (Ewald, 2009: 69) and local officials were thought of as "agents of the state." The federal government, in contrast, exercised such delegation in a very limited and restrained way.

CHAPTER 5

ACQUIRING VOTING RIGHTS

IN THE SUMMER OF 2013, the US Supreme Court changed the course of electoral history by striking down Section 4b of the Voting Rights Act (VRA). This part of the federal VRA defined jurisdictions that had a history of voting discrimination against minority populations. In effect, before the summer of 2013, election law was frozen in nine whole states and parts of six other states (56 counties and two townships), which were defined as "covered" jurisdictions and subject to Section 5 of the act.[1] Every time one of those jurisdictions wanted to make even the smallest voting change, they had to apply to the Department of Justice (DOJ) or the DC Federal District Court. Together, the DOJ and the court halted a number of election changes deemed to be discriminatory to both African Americans and Native Americans.

Yet, as noted previously, this national-level legislation has not been the norm in the United States. Some observers suggest that we have reached a point in our country wherein we no longer need the legal structure created by the Voting Rights Act; after all, we have universal suffrage at this point in our country and we elected an African American president. Actually, that we have universal suffrage in our country is not exactly the case; our progress toward universal suffrage has not been a linear progression or easily developed. In point of fact, this chapter markedly shows how the institution of voting is not only about the laws created, but also the attitudes toward those who might cast a vote. It is in considering the development of the right to vote that one sees the most obvious causal effects of institutional theory—this country's legal apparatus and its implementation has had a direct effect on the utilization of the franchise in the United States. This chapter highlights some of the storied history of the articulation of the right, in both formal and informal ways.

This chapter articulates three key themes: first, in considering the development of suffrage, its development was not a steady movement forward. Keyssar notes that it was explicitly nonlinear:

> The evolution of democracy rarely followed a straight path, and it always has been accompanied by profound antidemocratic countercurrents. The history of suffrage in the United States is a history of both expansion and contraction, of inclusion and

exclusion, of shifts in direction and momentum at different places and at different times.

(page XXIII)

The quote from the *Shelby* dissent is indicative of that nonlinear, parametric development; African Americans in the United States briefly had the legal ability to register and vote following the passage of the Thirteenth, Fourteenth, and Fifteenth Amendments to the Constitution, only to have the vote severely curtailed. Some individuals argue that today, we have been seeing the beginning of yet another era of curtailment, especially for those who are primarily Democratic voters (see Chapter 10). The nonlinear movement has occurred for women, immigrants, and even for college students (or maybe more accurately, those aged 18 to 20).

The second theme has to do with the idea that political scientist Richard Valelly labels "institutional complementarity." He explains that "[t]he operation of each part of the emerging regime was all the stronger because it worked in a larger context of other measures" (page 127). In other words, no single law worked by itself to allow or disallow the right to vote. Moreover, when new parts of the electoral institution are created, the new factors interact with structural inequalities, currently existing laws, and institutional norms already in existence. Those who seek to maintain power know this. Keyssar wrote that suffrage was allowed or not based on identity (immutable characteristics of the potential voter such as race, sex, or age) or behavior (did the potential voter establish residence, have enough knowledge, or commit a felony). For those wanting power, restrictions based on behavior complemented characteristics (even those not temporary) long correlated with immutable factors such as race or age. In other words, if the potential voter is a former slave, then he might not have adequate education to meet literacy requirements. Additionally, election laws are necessarily implemented at the local level, and those administering the laws have discretion to implement them—especially in ways expected by those in power.

The third theme is simply that the United States does not yet have universal suffrage: for example, states vary in terms of laws governing voting for individuals who are over 18 but who have a guardian and for individuals with mental or cognitive incapacities, such as traumatic brain injuries. States also vary with respect to those who have committed certain types of felonies. In terms of suffrage, even college students may fall into a grey area. The United States has progressed very far, but it is not correct to say we have universal suffrage.

All in all, then, what this chapter illustrates is a history of institutions—both formal and informal—that has changed over time, but not in a perfectly linear manner. This chapter proceeds by detailing what might be thought of as the chronological order of the development of suffrage. What we see is an unfolding of the history of suffrage, which is driven by a variety of factors. Keyssar details a variety of reasons for changes in who could vote: what is especially notable is how partisan politics and winning elections seemed to be a key driver for such changes throughout time, although not the only one. War, economic change and development, and even changes in attitudes (toward race and sex, for example) effected change in the formal institutions.

Yet, what the reader will see by the end of the chapter is that the United States is not perfectly democratic; there do remain questions about which specific groups should vote (e.g., felons, but also those with mental disabilities and even college students).

THE FOUNDERS AND THE CONSTITUTION

In keeping with the hierarchy of electoral institutions, it is important to begin with the Constitution of the United States, which set in motion the idea that states would shape the development of the right to vote in the United States (or lack thereof). As noted in Chapter 2, scholars today are quick to note that the US Constitution *lacks* an articulated "right to vote."[2] The framers left the definition of who could vote to the states to decide. It was only much later in the context of amendments that the Constitution had more to say concerning race and suffrage, sex and suffrage, and age and suffrage—not to mention poll taxes. Yet even such amendments did not say that every citizen of our country had the right to vote.

Furthermore, the framers seemed to have a manifest distrust of the masses in creating the national government. Historian Sean Wilentz (2005) writes that "[p]hilosophically, the assumption prevailed that democracy, although an essential feature of any well-ordered government, was also dangerous and ought to be kept strictly within bounds" (page 7). Even though the revolution was built on the ideas of "sovereignty and representation," Wilentz finds that even the most patriotic thought that government belonged in the hands of those most wise. Given the colonial British roots, he suggests, the founders worried that those who had no property would be manipulated by those for whom they worked (they were incapable of independent judgment) or would figure out a way to use politics to gain access to land.[3] Wilentz puts it bluntly

> The Revolution, by destroying the old forms of monarchical government and virtual representation, opened up lines of argument and ways of thinking that severely undermined hierarchical assumptions. The most hard-headed of the revolutionary leaders understood this and, for the most part, found it frightening.
>
> (page 9)

This distrust is reflected in the structure of the national government as articulated in the Constitution. For example, the president of the United States was not directly elected. Rather, he (or she) was elected by a group of "electors" appointed

> in such Manner as the Legislature thereof may direct, a Number of Electors, equal to the whole Number of Senators and Representatives to which the State may be entitled in the Congress: but no Senator or Representative, or Person holding an Office of Trust or Profit under the United States, shall be appointed an Elector.[4]

Indeed, that we should have a more "democratic" system and directly elect the president has been the subject of legions of scholars and activists to this day. The

Constitution also set the parameters for the types of participation. Furthermore, the framers also provided for indirect election of senators. Certainly, there was a House of Representatives, explicitly created to represent "the people," especially in issues of taxes because revenue bills originated there. Yet the House was moderated by the Senate (all laws had to pass both chambers with the same language), which was elected in such a way as to represent the states, and was often elected by the legislature of the state from where they came. So although the legislative branch was supposed to represent the people, the branch was considerably limited, and the system, with its built-in checks, exhibited a significant bias toward the status quo—that is, slow and incremental change in public policy over time. That was by design so that the masses could not quickly and easily change policy. However, even with this distrust, the framers left voter eligibility in the hands of the states—there was disagreement, and the framers built support for the new Constitution on the rhetoric of democracy.

LIMITS BEFORE THE CONSTITUTION

States established that White men with property (of course, each state had different laws) were allowed to vote. Yet, new research about early voter eligibility and turnout indicates that the proportion of individuals who could vote was actually higher than many historians have noted in the colonies, and later the American states. Oxford historian Daniel Ratcliffe suggests that the availability of land made the difference in terms of allowing more White males to vote:

> By contrast, the abundance and availability of land in North America meant that large numbers of colonists satisfied similarly defined requirements. This was especially true where the requirement was expressed in terms of acreage rather than value, as was customarily the case in the southern colonies: It was much easier to acquire (and to measure) 50 acres than land worth £50 either at sale or in annual rents. Six colonies also allowed alternative qualifications to freehold ownership in the form of personal property or payment of taxes, opening the suffrage to owners of urban property, and even to those prosperous farmers who rented their land or held it on some form of leasehold. Consequently, as early as the 1720s the suffrage was uniquely wide in the colonies.
>
> (2013: 221)

Moreover, Radcliffe notes that the states did not adopt additional restrictions on suffrage in the aftermath of the adoption of the Constitution, and some states rolled back property requirements. By 1792, only 7 out of 15 states required property to vote (Robertson, 2013). Two opposing forces affected the franchise: inflation made property restrictions less important by increasing the value of smaller parcels, but urbanization reduced the amount of property that any one person owned (Robertson, 2013).

BLACK/AFRICAN AMERICANS

Ironically, as the franchise and attitudes in favor of democracy (for White males) increased during the early 1800s, support for explicit limitations on the franchise for women and Blacks increased. In the early 1800s, several Northern states began to limit African American voting, including New York, according to City University of New York history professor Paul J. Polgar. New York's 1821 Constitutional Convention created a property requirement for Black voters, but not for White voters. He provides evidence that the opposition to African American voting in New York in the early 1800s was based not just in racism and prejudice, but also in partisan competition between the Federalists and the Republicans (Polgar, 2011).[5] Free Black voters were a firm Federalist bloc, even though the Republicans had made attempts to appeal to them (Federalists tended to oppose slavery). Polgar argues that the Republican Party of that time also used racism and prejudice to suppress non-supportive votes. Along with analyzing data[6] attesting to the level of partisan competition, Polgar relates intriguing details that almost sound contemporary:

> After controlling the State Assembly for eight straight years, the Republicans finally lost their majority in 1809. The economic depression New York was undergoing as a result of the Jefferson administration's embargo had resurrected the Federalist Party. When the Republicans retook the State Assembly a year later, they passed a bill that required free black voters to obtain certificates of freedom in order to vote in elections. The Republicans framed their actions as returning legitimacy to state elections by accusing Federalists of illegally enlisting the votes of bondspersons.[7]
>
> (pages 8–9)

Historians suggest the history of Black suffrage was rather akin to two sets of Reconstruction: one immediately after the Civil War wherein African American participation skyrocketed; yet what institutions give, they can also take away. The other took place 100 years later with the passage of the Voting Rights Act (Valelly, 2008).

By the start of the Civil War, 25 states out of 31 excluded African Americans from voting, and New York, as noted earlier, had separate requirements for Black and White males. The five states allowing African Americans to vote were in New England (Keyssar, 2000: 69).[8] By the end of the Civil War, three amendments were part of the Constitution: the Thirteenth (freeing the slaves), the Fourteenth (equal protection and citizenship), and the Fifteenth (1869; the right to vote should not be denied based on race). Yet, following Reconstruction, the federal government did not enforce the Fifteenth Amendment (very well), and Southern state governments worked to circumvent the ability of Black Americans to vote via changes to state constitutions. Not only that, but Blacks were subject to vigilante violence on the part of those who worried about political domination.

Why didn't the federal government enforce the Fifteenth Amendment? Indeed, Congress did pass two Enforcement Acts in 1870 and 1871 making interfering with voting a federal crime and made a number of fraud-related election crimes illegal. Additionally, in June 1870, Congress created a Justice Department that would provide the enforcement. However, these two acts lasted only about two decades. Valelly (2008) makes a compelling argument that the federal government did not have a "monopoly on coercion," making it impossible for Blacks to exercise political rights. Those trying to build the Republican Party in the South had reduced capacity because the federal government lacked that control (even in Reconstruction). Political scientist Alec Ewald develops a variety of arguments about the acts, but ultimately attributes the acts' failure to the idea that only the Republican Party supported them.

Another set of scholars provided evidence that enforcement in the South made sense politically speaking for the Republicans, given scarce resources. Political scientists Scott C. James and Brian L. Lawson (1999) develop a theory suggesting that the Republicans in power did not need the African American votes to win the presidency. In particular, they argue that design of the Electoral College incentivized the same sort of activity it does today: the same way that candidates spend most of their time in the battleground states, the Republicans of the time spent most of their federal voting rights enforcement resources in swing states.

> As the data suggest, this shift in the sectional incidence of prosecutions reflected a systemic alteration in the political economy of nineteenth-century voting rights enforcement, with the decline of southern prosecutions and the growth of swing state activity closely tracking partisan turnover in the White House. The watershed was the presidential election of 1884. Near defeat in 1876 and the emergence of the Solid South drove home to Republicans their tenuous hold on the executive branch, precipitating a reallocation of scarce federal enforcement resources away from the former Confederacy and toward the northern states we have designated as swing.[9]
>
> (page 124)

Given that resources to enforce voting rights were constrained (sending marshals and examiners to various jurisdictions was resource intensive), the Republicans in power had to be strategic in their use. "Strategic" meant they worked to protect their political position, especially in the presidency. James and Lawson analyze the use of prosecutions, deputies, and election supervisors to provide evidence for their Electoral College competition theory. They note that several scholars have come to similar conclusions about the end of the voting rights enforcement, but with a slightly different cause:

> We are not the first to connect Gilded Age electoral competition theoretically to the collapse of African American voting rights. Reaching conclusions different from our own, Valelly (1995) maintains that it was the decline of national party competition in 1896—itself the product of party system change—that precipitated the Republican abandonment of the South. Because the GOP could now secure national majorities without southern votes, the impulse to intervene on behalf of African Americans shrank correspondingly.
>
> (page 128)

The bottom line, of course, is that the Enforcement Acts did not last long, and no real enforcement of voting rights happened again until the Voting Rights Act was passed in 1965.

The case of Wilmington, North Carolina's 1898 race riot and coup d'état illustrates well both the relative amount of power that African Americans had achieved after the Civil War and how they lost power in the wake of Reconstruction. A little context: in Wilmington, Blacks outnumbered Whites and Blacks held a number of local offices such as justice of the peace, deputy clerk of court, and coroner; there were Black mail carriers and firefighters. The so-called "Black Second" was a congressional district packed with Black Republican voters; four different Black members of Congress were elected during the last 30 years of the 1800s (Christensen, 2008). Yet, it was not only racism that created the powder keg that led to rioting on the part of Democrats/conservatives in Wilmington, according to historian Jerome A. McDuffie (1979: 63–64); it was the loss of political power, especially to those deemed inferior.

> It was not just racism that led the Conservatives to take their final stand on the platform of white-supremacy. The ultimate provocation was the consolidation of the black vote in support of a political party that supported Reconstruction at the very moment when the radical impetus of Reconstruction had sharpened the class character of North Carolina politics. The Conservatives view the Republicans as a dangerous alliance of inferior blacks, incompetent whites, and traitorous Unionists.[10]

In 2000, the North Carolina state legislature created a race riot commission to study the events to give an official imprimatur to them. According to the report, members of the Democratic Party (White elites) overthrew a "legitimately elected municipal government" and banished more than 2,000 African American citizens from the city; the report also confirmed that around 60 people were killed.[11] In other research, the introduction to one collection of essays noted, "[n]o one, black or white, could deny that the racial massacre signaled a sea change in how white Americans would regard civil rights for African Americans. White people in Wilmington had violently seized their government, and no one had acted to stop them (page 5)."[12] In other words, it seemed that by the beginning of the twentieth century, despite the Fifteenth Amendment, Black citizens had lost the franchise.

In the years following Reconstruction until the passage of the Voting Rights Act, it was not just formal institutions that prevented African Americans from voting, but also informal institutions. Today's voters probably cannot imagine the murder, lynching, arson, and other terrorist activity that prevented African Americans from voting. And the account here does not mean to downplay the terror generated by lynching or other violent actions; they are more effectively articulated in other sources.[13] They key takeaway here is that these actions were enforcement of the norms of the time; wealthy elites used racist attitudes about former slaves in order to regain power following Reconstruction and to protect or preserve their power. Historians note that such tactics, along with legal-institutional changes, managed to preserve the power structure of the White elite Democrats. And although the violent activities were politically effective at suppressing political participation, historians argue they were, by nature, inefficient. Thus, those who wished to regain and then preserve the Southern power structure also used several quasi-Constitutional/legal methods to suppress the vote.

Valelly suggests that the Republicans knew that the Fifteenth Amendment might be open to circumvention when it passed.

> During the drafting of the Fifteenth Amendment, several Republicans—southern Republicans in particular—warned their party colleagues that they ought to textually

inhibit any future efforts at apparently color-blind property and educational restrictions on suffrage. They urged their colleagues to draft language that could prevent such
tactics. But eventually, Republicans agreed that the important thing was to write an
amendment that could be ratified as quickly as possible, and the version of the Fifteenth
Amendment that is now in the Constitution appeared to fill that bill.

(Valelly: 123)

States capitalized on the idea that they set the requirements for voting—changing
both their state constitutions and state statutes. Democrats from the Southern states
had a variety of methods that seemed color blind such as poll taxes, cumulative poll
taxes, literacy tests, state residence requirements, county residence requirements, pre-
cinct/ward residence requirements, and White primaries. Valelly notes that the states
learned from each other, something akin to the "policy diffusion" literature that
political scientists study now. Historian Keyssar observes that the literacy tests were
particularly potent at barring Black participation, given the level of illiteracy; local
administrators had discretion to implement these requirements.

Many of the disfranchising laws were designed expressly to be administered in a discriminatory fashion, permitting whites to vote while barring blacks. Small errors in registration procedures or marking ballots might or might not be ignored at the whim of
election officials; taxes might be paid easily or only with difficulty; tax receipts might or
might not be issued.

(page 89)

At the same time, several states—both Northern and Southern—were passing
Australian ballot laws. As briefly mentioned in the first chapter of this book, many
believed that Australian ballots would limit the influence of political parties/bosses;
however, such ballots also served as an implicit literacy test because the ballot required
one to read. Valelly notes that elites expected the ballot to disfranchise (page 127).
By 1900, Black voting was down to practically zero. Many of the legal mechanisms
utilized to reduce the Black vote did appear color blind simply because our founders
had been debating several of them for some time.

In considering the ways the Voting Rights Act, but not the Enforcement Acts
(previous federal attempt to enforce voting rights) succeeded in increasing Black suffrage, Valelly argues that the central government had more of an institutional capacity in the 1960s and after to enforce the voting rights centrally, including a stronger
military, than it had in the wake of the Civil War.

In 1957, Congress created a fact-finding body, the United States Commission on Civil
Rights, it reorganized the Justice Department, adding a Civil Rights Division, and
it authorized the attorney general to institute civil actions in federal courts to enjoin
actions that would deprive a citizen of voting rights. In 1960, Congress addressed such
problems as obstruction of court orders and the destruction of federal election records,
also authorizing court appointment of voting referees.

(2008: 39–40)

When the Voting Rights Act passed in 1965, one of the most controversial sections was the preclearance section. Those jurisdictions that have a history of discrimination had to ask permission to make any changes. In other words, instead of the Justice Department pursuing lawsuits and fighting voting discrimination in a case-by-case manner, they could prevent the discrimination. A case-by-case method could simply result in the guilty parties slightly changing a law after the lawsuit, as pointed out in the *South Carolina v. Katzenbach* opinion—the first case to challenge Section 5—articulated by Chief Justice Earl Warren:

> The previous legislation has proved ineffective for a number of reasons. Voting suits are unusually onerous to prepare, sometimes requiring as many as 6,000 man-hours spent combing through registration records in preparation for trial. Litigation has been exceedingly slow, in part because of the ample opportunities for delay afforded voting officials and others involved in the proceedings. Even when favorable decisions have finally been obtained, some of the States affected have merely switched to discriminatory devices not covered by the federal decrees, or have enacted difficult new tests designed to prolong the existing disparity between white and Negro registration.[14]

Indeed, Section 5 of the Voting Rights Act was a new approach to the racial discrimination in voting that would, as articulated by Justice Ruth Bader Ginsberg in her dissent to the *Shelby v. Holder* finding, resemble "battling the Hydra." However, as noted in Chapter 4, the Supreme Court struck down the formula that defined which jurisdictions were subject to Section 5 in June 2013.

In early 2015, citizens remembered the 1965 Selma march, which was a triggering event for the passage of the Voting Rights Act. CBS Television anchor Bob Schieffer interviewed Congressman John Lewis (D-GA), who helped plan the march from Selma to Montgomery.

> When the marchers crossed the Edmund Pettus Bridge, they were confronted by state troopers and sheriffs who came toward them, beating them with night sticks, using tear gas and trampling them with horses. Lewis, who was in the front, was the first person to be hit.[15]

In news coverage of a reenactment of the march, a CBS News Poll asked Americans if the Voting Rights Act is necessary today. Interestingly, a majority of Americans say yes, but there is a deep racial divide, with 86 percent of African Americans saying it is necessary and only 55 percent of Caucasians.[16] The poll showed that nearly two-thirds of Americans say they do not have enough information to evaluate whether or not the Supreme Court should have overturned Section 5.[17] Finally, of the people who answered the poll, 12 percent of African Americans reported they had trouble voting; only 7 percent of White Americans had trouble.[18]

IMMIGRANT VOTING

As noted in the first chapter of this book, most Americans today believe that voting is a basic duty of a citizen. Given the current political climate, this also means that noncitizens are explicitly barred from voting. In an article entitled "The Threat of Non-Citizen Voting," Heritage Foundation scholar Hans A. von Spakovsky writes, "Americans may disagree on many areas of immigration policy, but not on the basic principle that only citizens—and not non-citizens, whether legally present or not—should be able to vote in elections."[19] He is right. The German Marshall Fund did ask in 2010 whether noncitizens should vote—but only in local elections, and not national ones (wherein it is explicitly illegal by statute). Their research found that almost two-thirds of Americans believe "[v]oting in municipal elections is a right that should be reserved for only American citizens."[20] These attitudes are not necessarily consistent with the history of this country (illustrating the nonlinearity of the development of voting rights), and the reader will soon see that there are a number of local elections wherein noncitizens do vote, especially since they pay local taxes.

At the founding of this country (and even before), the most important qualifier for voting was the ownership of property,[21] although, obviously, there was a question about whether women could "own" property or be a head of a household. According to one of the early scholars studying noncitizen voting, Gerald M. Rosberg (1977), the states (and colonies before that) varied in whether "citizens" could vote or "inhabitants" could vote, and what "citizenship" even meant was not completely clear.

> Generalizations are difficult not only because of the problem of determining how the formal rules of suffrage were translated into practice, but also because the concept of citizenship did not have the same meaning as it has today. Until the Constitution centralized the power to naturalize aliens in the national government, no single definition of citizenship was applicable throughout the American states.
>
> (page 1094)

Keyssar notes that the federal government changed the formula for citizenship every year until about 1802, when foreign-born White males became eligible to naturalize after five years (2000: 27). Keyssar then notes that until 1830, states revised their constitutions to ensure that the word "inhabitant" was replaced with "citizen" for voting; all new states until 1840 followed that language. Rosberg suggests it was the War of 1812 that actually had an effect on the tightening of citizenship and voting—it created a rise of "national consciousness."

Keyssar writes that residency requirements and rollbacks in noncitizen voting went hand in hand because policymakers began to express grave concerns about nonresidents voting, particularly those from other countries. Keyssar details the partisan struggle in New York in the 1830s.

> Early [proposals] for a registry were unmistakably designed to hinder the voting of Irish Catholic immigrants and thereby reduce Democratic electoral strength. In 1840, Whigs succeeded in passing a registry law that applied only to New York City, which contained the largest concentration of Irish voters.
>
> (2000: 52–53)

The restrictions on noncitizen voting also occurred about the same time as many states decreased or eliminated the property requirement for voting (Raskin, 1993).

However, Keyssar and Rosberg both note that between 1840 and 1900, a number of states began allowing noncitizens to vote again. Rosberg writes:

> At a convention in February 1856, the Know-Nothing Party denounced Wisconsin and other states that had allowed aliens to vote. But their real concern was not so much with aliens as with "foreigners," and their goal was to restrict the political power of all persons of foreign birth. The party's platform included a demand for a 21-year residence requirement for naturalization. But the practice of alien voting survived the attacks, and after the Civil War it spread to at least thirteen more states, all of them in the South or West and all of them evidently anxious to lure new settlers.
>
> (pages 1098–1099)

In 1874, the Supreme Court ruled on a Missouri case wherein a woman, Virginia Minor, a women's suffrage leader in Missouri, tried to register to vote, and made the claim that the Fourteenth Amendment protected her "privileges" as a citizen, among those being suffrage. However, the court opinion stated that, indeed, Minor was a citizen, but voting was not a right of citizenship—Chief Justice Morrison Waite cited the idea that noncitizens could vote in some states, but that voting was not necessarily an inherent part of citizenship.[22]

> Besides this, citizenship has not in all cases been made a condition precedent to the enjoyment of the right of suffrage. Thus, in Missouri, persons of foreign birth, who have declared their intention to become citizens of the United States, may under certain circumstances vote. The same provision is to be found in the constitutions of Alabama, Arkansas, Florida, Georgia, Indiana, Kansas, Minnesota, and Texas.
>
> Certainly, if the courts can consider any question settled, this is one. For nearly ninety years the people have acted upon the idea that the Constitution, when it conferred citizenship, did not necessarily confer the right of suffrage.[23]

However, despite these statements, a movement against noncitizen voting began again in the late nineteenth century and into the early twentieth century. political scientist Leon E. Aylsworth noted in 1931 that "[f]or the first time in over a hundred years, a national election was held in 1928 in which no alien in any state had the right to cast a vote for a candidate for any office—national, state or local" (page 114).[24] Thus, from 1776 until 1926, up to 40 states had some sort of experience with immigrants voting, reports political scientist and immigrant voting advocate Ron Hayduk (2006).[25]

According to the US Government Office of Citizenship and Immigration Services, from 1900 to 1920, the United States allowed more than 14.5 million immigrants to enter the country, but new laws requiring literacy and then World War I reduced the number immensely.[26] Further, the US attitude toward open immigration also changed—one legal scholar writing in 1993 advocating for noncitizen suffrage called the attitudes "xenophobic nationalism attending WWI" (Raskin, 1993: 1395). The United States Citizenship and Immigration Services (USCIS) noted that policymakers viewed immigration as a national security issue more than it had before. Even when immigration began to rise again from 1950 to 1965, voting was a low-profile issue. In 1968, New York City began allowing noncitizens "whose children were in public schools to vote in community school board elections" (Keyssar, 2000: 252). The arguments in favor of immigrants voting included that they often own homes, have jobs, and pay taxes. Moreover, according to the Air Force News Service, 35,000 immigrants currently serve on active duty, and 8,000 more join every year.[27] The argument against immigrant voting is that they are not fully invested in the United States, nor are they fully assimilated.

When thinking about immigrants and voting, probably the first thing people are considering is that perhaps "illegal aliens" (undocumented immigrants) are trying to vote and affect election results. Yet, according to 2012 estimates, there are approximately 13.3 million so-called "legal permanent residents" (LPRs) in the United States who are green-card holders and can hold a job and pay taxes (Rytina, 2013).[28] Another 10.3 million are undocumented, according to 2005 estimates (Passel, 2005).[29] US statutes state that it is "unlawful for any alien to vote" in *federal* elections, unless there are other things on the ballot the state or locality might allow. However, the other offices/purposes must be separate from the federal contest.[30]

Depending on the independence of the municipality from the state (e.g., does a city have home rule), some local jurisdictions have allowed noncitizens to vote, and several others have considered it. For example, Takoma Park, Maryland, near Washington, DC allows noncitizens to vote in local elections. According to the Maryland Municipal League,

> [w]hile the Maryland Constitution requires citizenship as a prerequisite for voting in state elections, the law is otherwise silent on the issue. Therefore, individual municipalities are free to choose whether or not to allow non-citizen residents to vote. Currently, five municipalities in Maryland permit non-citizen residents to vote: Barnesville, Garrett Park, Glen Echo, Martin's Additions, Somerset and Takoma Park.[31]

According to Hayduk, noncitizens currently vote in school council elections in Chicago. In Massachusetts, at least two towns—Amherst[32] and Cambridge[33]—passed ordinances allowing citizens to vote, but because state law says that noncitizens cannot vote, the state legislature would have to give them an exemption, but has not done it.[34] The move by Cambridge prompted one editorial writer to state that the proposal would basically make them citizens:

> It would do this via a shortcut, waiving all the requirements customarily expected of those wishing to be naturalized, including any knowledge of the United States and its history, any requirement for even the most derisory knowledge of English, or the necessity of any intent to become a citizen.[35]

By 2010, Brookline, Newton, Chelsea, Boston, and Summerville all considered similar ordinances.[36] San Francisco considered a similar ballot measure in 2010, but it was defeated (Table 5.1).

Table 5.1 The wording and vote of San Francisco ballot measure

Measure D – Non-Citizen Voting in School Board Elections[a]

Shall the City allow non-citizen residents of San Francisco who are 18 years of age or older and have children living in the San Francisco Unified School District to vote for members of the Board of Education?

	Votes	Percent
Yes	118,608	45.09%
No	144,418	54.91%

This measure requires 50%+1 affirmative votes to pass.

Note: [a] http://www.sfelections.org/results/20101102/, accessed February 16, 2015.

It is with noncitizen voting that some of the most interesting arguments are made concerning the "logic of appropriateness" where it concerns our institution of elections. For example, advocates dismiss arguments, such as those made by a Maryland delegate in 2012, that noncitizens have dark reasons for wanting the franchise. According to the *Washington Post*, "Del. Patrick L. McDonough (R-Baltimore County) warned "that even Osama bin Laden would have been allowed to vote in Takoma Park."[37] In the *Michigan Law Review* Rosburg argued that

> [a]n alien who has managed to gain entry into the United States is subject, to the same extent as any citizen, to the laws relating to espionage, sabotage, public disorder, and the rest. And the resident alien can even be prosecuted for treason—the crime against allegiance—since he owes at least a temporary allegiance while present in the United States and is no freer than a citizen to give aid and comfort to the country's enemies. Moreover, a resident alien who is an anarchist, a communist, an advocate of sabotage or destruction of private property, or any one of a great many other things, can be removed from the country altogether by deportation.
>
> (pages 1125–1126; notes eliminated)

However, the issue of immigrant voting remains a controversial one, and some empirical research indicates that noncitizens do, in fact, vote when it is not allowed. Based on the results of the Congressional Cooperative Election Survey (CCES; conducted online) political scientists Jesse T. Richman, Gulshan A. Chattha, and David C. Earnest note that the CCES did validate a small number of noncitizens voting, but several others reported voting in both the 2008 and 2010 elections. Although the sample sizes of noncitizens are very small (about 800 in both years out of 90,000 respondents), making estimation very difficult because of the large potential size of subsample errors, these scholars argue that noncitizen voting could have changed the result of the North Carolina election in 2008 giving Obama the win instead of McCain.

COLLEGE STUDENTS

The minimum age for voting of 21 was rarely questioned (except during periods of major war; see Keyssar, 2000: 225), making the issue of traditionally aged college students voting moot for much of US history.[38] In May 1939, a Gallup Poll asked Americans, "Do you favor reducing the age at which American citizens can vote from 21 to 18?" Eighty-three percent of Americans said no.[39] In the midst of World War II, Gallup asked the question slightly differently, "At the present time American citizens cannot vote until they become 21 years of age. Would you favor changing the law to allow men and women 18, 19, and 20 years old to vote?" Fifty-two percent said no.[40] Keyssar explains that during World War II, two US senators proposed a constitutional amendment, but "it died a quiet death," and only one state—Georgia—made the voting age 18.

The lack of support for the Vietnam War changed the shape of opinion (Keyssar, 2000: 226). Opinions about 18-, 19-, and 20-year-olds voting changed by another 15 percentage points Of course, again, Gallup changed the question, too: "Do you think persons 18, 19 and 20 years of age should be permitted to vote or not?" Thirty-seven percent said no in September 1970.[41] In June 1970, Congress amended the Voting Rights Act to allow all individuals aged 18 to 21 to vote in federal and state elections and limited the residency requirement to 30 days. Not surprisingly, some states challenged this; in *Mitchell v. Oregon* (1970), the US Supreme Court decided that the federal government could only require that those 18 to 21 could vote in federal elections, but not state elections.[42] Faced with the prospect of seriously complicated elections with two different age groups for different offices, the US Congress passed an amendment in March, and by June, enough states had ratified it to create the Twenty-Sixth Amendment. It took another Supreme Court case (*Dunn v. Blumstein*, 405 U.S. 330 [1972]) to change lengthy residency requirements for eligibility to vote in state and local elections; In Tennessee, where the case was filed, the state had required a prospective voter to live in the state for a year, and the county where registered for at least three months. Such residency requirements had made it much more challenging for college students to register and vote and did not, according to the *Dunn* ruling "serve a compelling state interest."

What the constitutional amendment and court cases did not make clear was "what is a resident"—the court does allow states to define residency, or "bona fide residency."[43] Political scientists Richard G. Niemi, Michael J. Hanmer, and Thomas H. Jackson (2009) note that among and within different states, there are different practices where college student voter registration is concerned. Niemi and his colleagues note that Missouri and Iowa are two states wherein students are informed they "may register either in their home town or in their college town" (page 337). The scholars also analyze Idaho law as an example of a "potentially restrictive" law, which gives factors to consider when determining one's residence:

> Consider also factor 10, which asks where one spends most of the year. Perhaps recognizing that college students usually live on their college campuses more than in their parents' homes, the question goes on to ask why one spends time elsewhere. Answers to such a query are subject to interpretation and call to mind how, in the pre-Civil-Rights-era South, responses to literacy questions were taken to mean whatever the registrar wanted.

The screen ends by warning students that violations of registration laws "can subject you to criminal penalties".

(page 338)

As for Virginia and South Carolina, the scholars found variation across the state in terms of local practice where registering students is involved. Michael O'Loughlin and Corey Unangst prepared a report about college student voting for the Institute of Public Affairs and Civic Engagement at Salisbury University (2006: 8):

> Federal law however excludes any "community commitment" or even a "good conduct" criteria for voting rights for non-student adults who also may be transient. Movement of people in and out of communities is quite common in American society, yet few suggest that voting rights for those citizens ought to be dependent on their actual or intended longevity within a community, except when it comes to college students.

In their analysis, as of 2006, O'Loughlin and Unangst classified 38 states as having a choice for students (not including North Dakota, which does not have voter registration). The remaining are restrictive states.

All of this is seemingly at odds with the national law, which states that colleges must make voter registration forms available to college students or risk losing federal aid (see Chapter 4). But residents of local communities often worry about having their votes overwhelmed by college students who might only live in the town part-time. Phillip Ardoin, Charles S. Bell, and Michael Raggozzino conducted research where they found that college students are more likely to vote Democratic, but tend to roll-off for local contests (that is, not cast a vote).[44]

Various state legislatures have proposed statutes that would affect college student voting. For example, in 2013, senators in North Carolina introduced a bill titled the "Equalize Voter Rights Bill," which would have eliminated a "personal exemption" on the parent's North Carolina taxes if the child registered to vote anywhere other than in their hometown. That particular bill died in committee, but the General Assembly did pass another bill aimed more broadly than simply at college students, enacting such things as cutting the number of days on which early voting is allowed,[45] eliminating same-day voter registration during early voting, requiring a government-issued voter photo identification with a current address (starting with the primary in 2016), and specifying that provisional votes that are cast outside the voter's correct precinct would no longer count. Several students (along with the NAACP, the ACLU, and later, the Justice Department) filed suit charging that the Voter Information Verification Act violated the Twenty-Sixth Amendment to the Constitution, a type of lawsuit that has never been filed before.[46]

Sponsors of such bills (at the time of this writing, Republicans) argue that they are trying to prevent college students from voting in more than one location. However, opponents argue that such legislation is intended to prevent college students from voting because the popular perception is that they vote Democratic.[47] Although the franchise issues of college students are nowhere as problematic as the history of racial discrimination, policy surrounding college student voting is fraught with inconsistencies and confusion.

UNIVERSAL SUFFRAGE?

The previous three examples are case studies that indicate that voting rights have ebbed and flowed in the United States. Now, many argue that the United States has universal suffrage—but that is not the case. There are limitations and threats of limitations on voting: the "threats" are ones that are generally acceptable to most citizens, but they are still limitations.

REGISTRATION

Voter registration establishes who is eligible to vote and where and for whom or what (offices, contests) individuals can vote. Registration is the first step of voting in all states, except for North Dakota, which has no voter registration.[48] There is no national registry of voters; rather, as the rest of the electoral system, it is decentralized; when HAVA passed, it was the first requirement that states have a centralized voter registration list. Differing states have differing systems. The majority require that voters be registered beforehand (the time before ranges from 8 days to 30 days, according to the National Conference of State Legislatures). As of this writing, only ten states allow Election Day registration (or same-day registration in the case of early voting). Some, such as North Carolina between 2007 and 2013, allowed "same-day registration" but only during early voting. Scholars have consistently shown that Election Day registration increases turnout (see for example, Leighley and Nagler, 2014).

However, it is not just the act of having to register that may limit voting; it is also the chaotic state of the voter registration lists. One of the most important recent frontiers in policy scholarship has been the work analyzing problems with voter registration lists. According to political scientists Stephen Ansolabehere and Eitan Hersch (2010),[49] validation of voting lists is only recently possible due to private companies compiling state lists and advances in computer power. At the time of their analysis, the scholars found that more than 185 million individuals were registered to vote. About 1 in 1,000 had an address error in the database. Ansolabehere and Hersch note that election offices

> may neglect to note a voter's ZIP code, for example. Other times, due to illegible handwriting on the part of voters or faulty data entry on the part of officials, street numbers, street names, cities and ZIP codes may be entered incorrectly or contain typos. (2010)

Further, up to 1 in 25 addresses may not be deliverable. This is a problem when the local election office needs to send voting information or a ballot request to addresses, but it may also pose a problem if voters are required to show government-issued photo identification with a current address. The research estimates that 1 in 365 may not have correct birthdays. There are also deadwood and potential duplicates.[50]

There are ways to minimize errors and potential issues with voter registration. One example is cutting out the data entry person and allowing online voter registration (see Chapter 8). Also, same-day registration allows a voter to register if he or she is not on the list on Election Day. Finally, the Pew Charitable Trusts is supporting the Electronic Registration Information Center (ERIC). The system allows states to collaborate to use "matching [tools] to improve the accuracy and efficiency of state voter registration systems."[51]

FELONS

Whether or not those who committed felonies should be allowed to have voting rights has also been a long-debated subject. Some states do not allow those who have committed felonies to vote, even after prison and probation (12, according to The Sentencing Project, an organization that advocates on this issue, but with variation in the type of felonies and whether it is the first or second felony). Still others, such as Vermont and Maine, have never had such restrictions, and even allow those in prison to vote. As of 2014, The Sentencing Project notes that close to 6 million individuals are not allowed to vote.[52] As stated in the introduction to this chapter, Keyssar noted that immutable characteristics and behavior characteristics have been used to justify curtailing voting rights. Having committed a crime is one of the most obvious behavioral limitations. And, there are certainly a number of normative arguments both for and against felons having voting rights, but the fact remains that there are many who cannot vote. The Sentencing Project also states that "Black Americans of voting age are four times more likely to lose their voting rights than the rest of the adult population" (2014: 2).

INDIVIDUALS WITH COGNITIVE IMPAIRMENTS

An additional group who still faces formal rule barriers, as well as informal views about their ability to vote, is those with cognitive impairments. There is great variation in the types of cognitive impairments, including issues such as autism spectrum disorders, traumatic brain injuries, those with Alzheimer's (and other usually age-related cognitive decline), and those who were born with an intellectual disability. Mental illness may also affect one's right to vote. Not only is there variation in the types of cognitive disorders, there is also a great deal of variation in the physical manifestations of the injuries and impairments. For traumatic brain injuries (TBI) in particular, the issue became even more relevant because of the National Football League (5,000 former players sued the NFL for hiding the danger of concussions[53]) and because of the high survivability of the recent conflicts in Afghanistan and Iraq—soldiers were less likely to die and more likely to return home with TBI (Tanielian et al., 2008; Corrigan and Cole, 2008). According to the Brain Injury Association of America, "TBI is defined as an alteration in brain function, or other evidence of brain pathology, caused by an external force."

The real legal question is what qualifications must a person with such impairments meet to be able to vote? Who decides whether they are able to vote? Scholars have been studying the issue of cognitive impairments and voting for at least two decades. There are state laws that could bar those with cognitive impairments from voting, explicit in constitutional language, statute, or precedence from court decisions (Hurme and Appelbaum, 2007). In New Jersey, prior to a 2007 constitutional change, the constitutional language was, "No idiot or insane person shall enjoy the right of suffrage." Apparently, as of 2008, nine states still use similar language in their state laws and constitutions.

According to the Bazelon Center for Mental Health Law & National Disability Rights Network, in 2008, 15 states and the District of Columbia do not allow voting if the voter is "under guardianship" or a court determines the person is "mentally incompetent" or "mentally incapacitated."[54] The two groups note, however, that such hearings rarely involve issues having to do with voting or making a choice. Rather, the hearings tend to revolve around issues other than voting. Another 20 states do not allow voting if a court determines a person cannot vote. Finally, three states disallow voting by individuals who are determined to be "non compos mentis," but according to the Bazelon Center, the three states implement the requirements differently. Only 11 states have no competency requirements for voting. As of this writing, in California, there is an active federal lawsuit concerning whether or not those under guardianship can vote or not. As of now, if a person is under guardianship, the person cannot vote, no matter if the person could make a voting choice or not.

There are informal barriers to voting as well. For example, it may be more difficult for someone who is cognitively impaired to obtain photo identification. Further, some of the impairments have more physical manifestations than others. According to political scientist Jessica Link and her colleagues, there is very little research about how pollworkers and caregivers react to the outward manifestations of issues such as TBI. In addition, states vary as to their laws on voter challenges.[55]

> ... we speculate that the outward signs such as apraxia and language deficits might draw a challenge to their ability to vote (some individuals with TBI may appear drunk), though scholars do not have empirical evidence as yet. There is, however, evidence that people with cognitive impairments are subject to stereotyping, stigma, and discrimination in the job market and other areas of life.[56]
>
> (page 54)

Scholars are learning more about cognitive impairments and voting, but advocates say the bottom line is that those who have impairments should not be "routinely required to meet higher burdens than others in order to vote."[57]

Scholars are learning more about how to assess someone's capacity to vote reliably, but that does not necessarily mean that such tests should be applied in the first place. Rather, if tests are applied, then such standards should be the same across voters. Studying those with Alzheimer's and related diseases, Appelbaum, Bonnie, and Karlawish (2005) use an assessment tool called the "Competency Assessment Tool for Voting" or CAT-V. They developed the test from criteria laid out in a 2001 federal district court decision, *Doe v. Rowe*. The test measures the individual's understanding of the voting process and the effects of voting. The individual gets to make a choice between Candidate A and Candidate B. (The questions together are known as the Doe Standard used in court). Appelbaum and his colleagues use these questions and two additional questions to assess "appreciation and reason" for the Competency Assessment Tool for Voting (CAT-V). However, Raad, Karlawish, and Appelbaum (2009: 627) argue that adding the reasoning and appreciation portion of the test may "disenfranchise some would be voters who met the Doe criteria—an unfortunate outcome." Raad and his colleagues argue that the Doe Standard works well for legally evaluating those with potential incapacity.

CONCLUSION

Many of the stories about the loss of the right to vote are ones we have heard before, but bear retelling. Others seem relatively new because they are based in what Americans are reading in the newspaper now and even seeing on ESPN. The important themes to learn, however, are that in these stories, old and new, we learn that the United States does not have universal suffrage, the process of gaining suffrage has been far from linear, and politics steeped in the rhetoric of this country's logic of appropriateness play a key role in determining who votes and who does not. The barriers to voting today are both direct and indirect. One would be hard pressed to find a legal statute or administrative rule that said "college students are not allowed to vote." On the other hand, the idea that noncitizens cannot vote is both direct and supported by informal rules that our country has recognized for about a century. The barriers to vote are not objectively obvious, however. Good people disagree about felons voting or whether a college student should vote in his or her home town or in his or her college town. Because there are arguments on both sides and because of the decentralization of elections, it is easy for politics to be involved with the decision making. That is part of the electoral institution.

CHAPTER 6

EXERCISING THE RIGHT TO VOTE

ONE OF THE NEWEST METHODS OF MOBILIZING CITIZENS to the polls appears to be "vote shaming." An example is from the former editor of an online newsletter for election scholars and election administrators across the country. "In his mailbox was an official-looking document detailing his voting history and comparing his voting history to his neighbors'." The election guru was rather indignant about this piece of campaign mail because his voting "grade" was not as high as his neighbors' grades because he had recently moved. He was quoted as saying:

> I got one out of four bars, when, honestly, I'm [a] super voter. I vote in regional, local, national, any election you hold, I'll vote in it. Because I moved in 2011, my federal election records indicate that, in [my new home], I voted in the November 2012 election and that's it. But that's completely wrong. I voted in every federal election since 1990.[1]

Why do voters receive such reports? Recent research indicates that voting is a function of your own sense of civic duty—but also that of your neighbors. For many citizens, such tactics are effective. Yet, the decision to vote is more than understanding the social expectations for political behavior. The legal environment in which those norms of civic cooperation are embedded is also vital to understanding the institutional structure underlying the decision of any one citizen to vote.

Voting is by necessity both a community and an individual activity, but one that political science evidence has long shown is affected by laws governing voting in the country. How important laws are is always questioned, especially given that how much citizens know about voting laws is affected by education and political interest. Yet, along with political interest and education, the written rules surrounding voting and informal practices administering the nuts and bolts of voting also have an effect on the likelihood of a person turning out to vote. But both individual attitudes and community expectations play a role in how the legal architecture will affect an individual. As articulated in Chapter 2, there is a vast architecture of laws governing voting, but it all comes down to the idea that given eligibility, an individual decides whether or not to vote.

The key theme of this chapter is that viewing the turnout decision from an institutional angle requires more than just considering the formal written laws. It also requires an understanding of the logic of appropriateness (norms) and an individual's perception of belonging to the community. In other words, institutionalism requires the scholar to think in an interdisciplinary way considering sociology and psychology, much like the idea suggested by political sociologist David Knoke (1990):

> The advancement of knowledge in voting research does not boil down to a zero-sum choice between the Michigan social psychological approach and the Columbia sociological approach. Rather, it lies in a judicious blending of relational with attitudinal elements into a comprehensive account of how voters' preferences are shaped through the interpersonal flow of political influences.[2]
>
> (page 36)

Yet scholars of new institutionalism have often places choices in a rational choice framework. Knoke rejects rational choice theory, arguing, "[c]omplex microsocial and macrosocial networks constrain and facilitate people's perceptions, attitudes, and actions in ways inexplicable by a rational utility-maximizing calculus" (page 39). I argue the theory is appropriate, and forms the basis for institutionalism. But sociological and psychological theories demonstrate the mechanism for why a group of individuals form something bigger than just them all together. Consider that a person must weigh the costs and benefits of voting before deciding to vote (rational choice). But, the way in which the person perceives the costs and benefits is driven by the sociological theory of groups and psychological theory concerning whether an individual perceives he or she is a part of the community.[3] In this chapter, I consider the traditional theories surrounding voting: rational choice/economic, group/sociological, and individual/psychological. Ultimately, I would argue that "new institutionalism" requires scholars to consider group dynamics and how an individual views himself or herself in relation to others.

When thinking about "institutions" as a concept, innumerable scholars have considered the effects of laws and requirements for voting on the likelihood that someone will vote. Although "norms," habit, and civic duty are also very common themes in considering turnout, typically scholars do not consider such concepts as a part of our institution, and only sometimes consider how such attitudes interact with written laws and practice. That is to say, very few scholars have considered "institutionalism" in a more holistic way, illustrating costs and benefits created by formal *and* informal rules, and how the formal rules are shaped and considered in light of informal rules. This chapter will conclude with a discussion about how institutions—both laws and the norms and expectations surrounding voting—affect the probability of voting.

RATIONAL CHOICE

Those who have studied the legal structures typically situate the research within an overused and abused, but important, rational-choice framework: an individual will vote if the costs are less than the benefit from a preferred candidate winning; later scholars added a benefit: the positive feeling an individual may derive from fulfilling his or her civic duty (in mathematical form: $C < PB + D$). Using that calculation, one might think that most, if not all, voters will abstain. Voting is not rational under traditional definitions of rationality. Bluntly put, the costs of voting will almost always outweigh the benefits—a person's vote makes very little difference to the final result of a political contest, so one person could hardly draw a benefit from changing the result. Yet people do vote. Thus, considering voting in the context of a larger theoretical framework, factoring in the constraints and opportunities created by formal laws, as well as the informal rules surrounding voting, can help to put this behavior into perspective.

Anthony Downs (1957) is one of the most commonly invoked scholars in discussing rationality in voting, yet he also wrote about why people vote despite higher cost than benefit:

> Participation in elections is one of the rules of the game in a democracy, because without it democracy cannot work. Since the consequences of universal failure to vote are both obvious and disastrous, and since the cost of voting is small, at least some men can rationally be motivated to vote even when their personal gains in the short run are outweighed by their personal costs.
>
> (page 269)

Riker and Ordeshook, also early proponents of rational-choice theory in political science, created the theoretical model that would take that democratic rule into account: they write that the so-called "D" or "duty" term may be conceptualized as "the satisfaction from compliance with the ethic of voting, which if the citizen is at all socialized into the democratic tradition is positive when he votes and negative (from guilt) when he does not" (1968: 28). Another possibility, they continue, is "the satisfaction from affirming allegiance to the political system: For many people, this is probably the main rationale for voting. It is also a highly political motive and to leave it out of the calculus would be absurd." Still another possibility is that voting is not a costly activity, nor is it a particularly beneficial one, so any perceived decrease in cost or increase in benefit may increase voting (Aldrich, 1993).

What these scholars are talking about is that those who vote play an important role in maintaining the system, not just by making a choice of one candidate or another, but simply by casting a vote. They are ensuring the survival of democracy. If we held an election and only a very select few voted, it would be very difficult to say that the candidate was legitimately elected by "the people."

People vote, but what appears to occur is that the costs are more burdensome for those who have the least resources—that is, time, money, education, or civic skills (for example, Verba, Schlozman, and Brady, 1995). Critics of rational-choice theory note that it "seems best suited to explaining voting on the margin only, by examining how changes in costs (the C term) affects turnout" (Hasen, 1996: 2146). Considering legal structure as a cost that can be increased and decreased, scholars often argue "voting is a form of political participation whose costs the government can most easily alter through institutional change" (Haspel and Knotts, 2005: 560). Brady and McNulty (2011) note "[b]ecause costs may differ across groups, Downs' insight suggests that partisan politicians might be able to manipulate election dates, places, modes, and times to encourage voting by their supporters and to hinder voting by their opponents" (page 115). Consider early voting—how long the state makes early voting available, where it is available, and even whether it is available on a Sunday makes a difference to the level of turnout, because it makes a difference to who has the time to vote. Costs are not equally distributed.

From the standpoint of democratic theory and full participation, one might hope that election reforms make it less costly for the less wealthy and those with less education to vote. In a study of 40 years of data, political scientists Jan E. Leighley and Jonathan Nagler (2014) show that

> both election day registration and absentee voting have positive effects on turnout. It appears that early voting's potentially positive effects are dependent on the length of the early voting period. ... Taken together, this evidence shows that electoral reforms over the past several decades have modestly increased voter turnout in presidential elections.
>
> (page 186)

However, Leighley and Nagler indicate that the bottom quintile of citizens by income have the lowest likelihood of taking advantage of reforms. Moreover, they acknowledge that scholars have consistently found a substantial income bias in voting, and their work does too.[4]

INDIVIDUAL/PSYCHOLOGICAL

What might be called "social psychological theory" is inherently about how the individual thinks or processes information. Political science research in the individual/psychological tradition—"the (University of) Michigan model"—focused early on partisanship as a "psychological orientation ... without going into great detail about the psychology behind that orientation" (Borgida, Federico, and Sullivan, 2009: 1). Since then, scholars have learned a great deal about factors such as socialization and its effects on partisanship (e.g., Jennings and Niemi, 1981), as well as how individuals reason about partisanship. And, as the field of political psychology has progressed, so have the individual-level explanations for attitudes such as partisanship and for political choices. Political psychologists have shown, for example, the subtleties of media effects on attitudes, given the ways in which individuals process information (e.g., Iyengar and Kinder, 1987; Barabas and Jerit, 2009; Prior, 2013). Some of the most exciting work has focused on political choices—a core part of the field has centered on questions about whether citizens could fulfil their democratic duty and vote (correctly) (Lau and Redlawsk, 2006; Goren, 2013). The political psychology field is dominated by vote-choice models because at its heart, psychology examines how people think and reason when they make decisions.

Making the decision to vote (not just for whom to vote) is also important—it has not been ignored by any stretch. A key line of long-running research in the psychological tradition emphasizes resources in terms of time, money, and civic skills, making participation possible (see for example, Verba, Schlozman, and Brady, 1995). Other research shows that political mobilization—asking someone to participate—affects the probability of political participation (Rosenstone and Hansen, 1993). Political psychology research also explains voter turnout in terms of a variety of attitudes, such as political interest, political knowledge, trust in government, and efficacy—a feeling that one's vote makes a difference (internal and external). Importantly, political science scholars Lawrence Bobo and Franklin D. Gilliam, Jr. (1990) connect group consciousness with the development of such attitudes. Bobo and Gilliam note that the consistent finding is that, controlling for socioeconomic status (income and education), African Americans are more likely to participate in politics (see for example, Tate, 1984).[5] Further, Bobo and Gilliam note the marked increase in the number of African American local elected officials as of the late 1980s. In analyzing whether or not Black officials in office increased the level of Black empowerment, and thus participation, they found an important connection.

> Our results show, first, that where blacks hold positions of political power, they are more active and participate at higher rates than whites of comparable socioeconomic status. Second, black empowerment is a contextual cue of likely policy responsiveness that encourages blacks to feel that participation has intrinsic value. This conclusion is based on the finding that empowerment leads to higher levels of political knowledge and that it leads to a more engaged (i.e., trusting and efficacious) orientation to politics.[6]
>
> (page 387)

The reader will note that Bobo and Gilliam explicitly state that they believe people participate in politics when the benefits outweigh the costs, which is important. However, the reader should also note that the reason the benefits outweigh the costs is psychological—having more African Americans in office changes attitudes among African American citizens that are known to predict participation.

This idea of "group consciousness" is part of a theory that is at once psychological and sociological. Scholars have invoked "social identity theory" as a theoretical explanation for voter turnout and other political behaviors.[7] Political scientists Leonie Huddy and Nadia Khatib (2007) define social identity as: "an awareness of one's objective membership in the group and a psychological sense of group attachment" (page 65). The idea of social identity posits there is an in-group with which a person identifies, and "others" are the out-group; the in-group, which is dominant, is mostly likely to define itself as a group vis-à-vis another group.[8] It is not simply that the individual is a member of some group, but that he or she identifies with the group as a whole. For example, scholars such as Leighley and Vedlitz (1999) examine "group closeness" (identity) and "out-group distance (affect toward other racial/ethnic groups)" as explanations for political participation among minority groups (page 1096). Scholars argue that racial identity is especially important to African Americans, given the shared history of slavery once the group arrived in the United States (Dawson, 1994; Bowler and Segura, 2012). A sense of belonging to a group and sharing a fate may be a piece of the puzzle explaining African American cognition, perceptions, and ultimately voting behavior, but other ethnic and racial groups do not share the same history within the group. Huddy and Virtanen (1995) found evidence of subgroup bias among Latinos:

> The tendency among Latinos to distinguish members of their own subgroup from other subgroups and to demonstrate a positive bias for fellow subgroup members was especially pronounced among Cubans, the Latino subgroup with the highest socioeconomic status. A drive toward positive distinctiveness may motivate Latinos to distinguish their own from other subgroups (especially from subgroups with lower status) so as to boost their subgroup's standing.[9]
>
> (page 104)

Bowler and Segura suggest one reason is that some racial and ethnic groups had ethnic identities that, before coming to the United States, were in conflict with each other.[10]

Some of the more recent social identity research supports many of the ideas presented in this book regarding norms and values. Social identity theory is particularly important because it encourages scholars to consider how attached any particular individual is to certain groups (demographic or otherwise), as well as the nation. Huddy and Khatib discussed how individuals may feel "a subjective or internalized sense of belonging to a nation" (page 65) and also sought to separate the concept of patriotism from the concept of "national identity."

> Social identity theory also predicts greater adherence to group norms among strong group identifiers, translating into greater civic involvement among strong national identifiers in the case of American identity. This prediction received impressive support in our data. Americans with a strong national identity paid more attention to politics, knew more about current events, and were more likely to vote. Moreover the connection between national attachment and civic engagement is not predicted by any other approach to patriotism.[11]
>
> (page 74)

In other words, the national identity is nonideological, as opposed to patriotism, which scholars have often suggested is strongly related to issue opinions that are strongly ideological such flag burning.

Finally, relatively new political science research related to how one thinks (or does not think, in this case) is the idea that voting becomes habit—something like eating popcorn at the movies[12] or putting on one's seatbelt upon getting in the car.[13] A team comprising both political science and psychology scholars John H. Aldrich, Jacob M. Montgomery, and Wendy Wood (2011), suggests that repetition of an action is necessary, but not sufficient to develop a habit.

> Habit involves repetition of a response under similar conditions so that the response becomes automatically activated when those conditions occur. Everyone necessarily starts off with no strength of habit for turnout at all. Turnout, like any other response, becomes automated through behavioral repetition.[14]
>
> (page 536)

Not only do contextual clues matter (a stable context helps retain voters—that is, it is harder to keep voting after one moves from one city to another), but the strength of habit matters. In other words, those without a "habit" of voting make "motivated" decisions based on norms of civic duty or strength of partisan intensity. Those with a habit were less likely to make such decisions, but still vote. Aldrich and his colleagues find the habitual voters and the "motivated decisions" voters are different groups.[15]

SOCIOLOGICAL OR GROUP THEORY

Sociological theory explains political behavior via social interdependencies among citizens. Early conceptions of the sociological approach to political participation (as conceived by scholars in the "Columbia University tradition") found that interpersonal contacts and group memberships (for example, social class, religion, political party) affected political behavior (for example, Lazarsfeld, Berelson, and Gaudet, 1944; Berelson, Lazarsfeld, and McPhee, 1954). According to political sociologists Jeff Manza, Clem Brooks, and Michael Sauder (2005), as political sociology moved forward, much of the scholarship on individual-level political behavior was left to rational-choice theorists and those studying psychology (see also Knoke, 1990). From the rational-choice perspective, sociologist James Coleman argued that a broad explanation for social action is in a sociological approach, which "sees the actor as socialized and action as governed by social norms, rules and obligations .... [this approach] sees social action as shaped, constrained, and redirected by the social context (page S95)"[16] This "social capital" approach gained a great amount of traction in the 1990s among political scientists, due to the publication of works by Robert Putnam such as *Making Democracy Work: Civic Traditions in Modern Italy* (1993) and *Bowling Alone: The Collapse and Revival of American Community* (2000). As conceptualized by Putnam, "social capital" in the form of group memberships—both formal and informal— played a key role in encouraging political participation such as voting. The key idea from this is that gatherings for social reasons encourage people to follow civic norms of cooperation, such as voting and other community political participation.

Although the idea of social capital has been relatively recently measured and analyzed by political scientists, the ideas behind social capital have had long roots in sociology (Portes, 1998). Sociologist (and apparently Putnam critic) Alejandro Portes writes with Erik Vickstrom (2011):

> a theoretical analysis of the organizational basis of modern society demonstrates that it does not depend on interpersonal networks or mutual expressions of trust. A simple excursion into the sociological classics suffices to remind us that the glue that keeps modern society together is not the mechanical solidarity associated with such networks, but a higher form of cohesion associated with a complex division of labor and the strength of institutions. Trust in these societies does not depend on mutual knowledge, but on universalistic rules and the capacity of institutions to compel their observance.
>
> (page 476)

Part of the debate about the worth of social networks is whether the United States' immigration and degree of ethnic heterogeneity create civic cooperation or attenuate it. Portes (2014) emphasizes that there is research that pre-WWII Germany had dense networks of associational memberships, yet ended up with a totalitarian government headed by Hitler and the Nazis.[17]

Most relevant to the present book on the election institution, sociologist James S. Coleman writes in his book *Foundations of Social Theory* (1990) that social capital is not necessarily organizational memberships per se. He writes, "[S]ocial organization constitutes social capital, facilitating the achievement of goals that could not be achieved in its absence or could be achieved only at a higher cost" (page 304). The resources inherent in social capital lie in the relationship between and among individuals and the ability of individuals to monitor each other's behavior. Social capital is made up of three components: obligations and expectations (norms), information potential (ability to obtain information from others about current events and/ or community expectations), and social organizations (including, but not limited to, group membership). Coleman notes that an especially important form of social capital is the prescriptive norms, which dictate that individuals should forego their self-interest to act in the interests of society. If social relations do not include expectations about collective action, social capital may do little to encourage activities such as voting. Public policy scholars have followed his intellectual lead, including economist Stephen Knack, who provides empirical evidence that interpersonal pressures enforcing norms of civic duty play a role in the decision of whether or not to vote.

Indeed, in the past two decades or so, political scientists have followed the idea of "norms" and produced some interesting findings using field experiments. The literature examines whether an individual's decision whether to vote is partially driven by social norms (e.g., Gerber and Green, 2000). That is to say, "... the desire to adhere to social norms fosters electoral participation by activating voters' intrinsic motivation to engage in prosocial behavior" (Panagopoulos, 2010: 369). The variety of large-scale field experiments has shown, for example, that individuals may be driven more by descriptive norms that indicate that many others take part in behavior such as voting (Gerber and Rogers, 2009). The research also indicates that knowing that others may monitor one's behavior and apply positive sanctions for norm compliance is more effective than the ability to apply negative sanctions for norm shirking (Panagopoulos, 2010).

Understanding norms and social interaction is a key part of what sociologists have offered political scientists concerning voter turnout, but other sociological scholarship also plays an important role. Although scholars have long examined aggregated election returns combined with census data to explain political phenomena (for example, Key, 1949), scholars had not combined the analysis of individual and collective information about the neighborhood, county, or other "social unit" in which the individuals lived (Knoke, 1990). Knoke argues that a 1950 article about how these geographic-level findings do not necessarily apply to individuals changed the focus of scholars more to individual-level data, until scholars realized they could combine the individual and the contextual or geographic data. Thus, those who study context argue that both community and individual-level factors influence a person's behavior (see for example, Putnam, 1966; Huckfeldt, 1979; Giles and Dantico, 1982).

This body of work considers community-level factors such as partisanship, level of education, and social class as correlates of participation. One study considers a person's social cooperation context by examining county-level factors, such as how many people respond to the Census Bureau when it sends out an initial mailing with a Census form (Knack and Kropf, 1996). Contextual analysis has also been conceptualized in terms of to whom each individual in the analysis talks. In their book, *Citizens, Politics, and Social Communication*, political scientists John Huckfeldt and John Sprague (1995) analyze not just information culled from individuals about political perceptions, but also asked individuals for the names of three persons with whom they discussed politics. The underlying idea is that people misperceive what their friends really believe, with a bias toward what they themselves believe. They were able to interview a sample of those so-called "discussants" in order to analyze the sociopolitical context of the original respondent. Their research showed that

> individual opinion and behavior is a product of social interaction, social communication, and the individual response to information obtained in this manner. Three sets of factors contribute to the responses: citizens' idiosyncratic social and political orientations, the information and viewpoints to which they are (socially) exposed, and the interplay between the two.
>
> (page 283)

An individual's context does in fact affect both attitudes and probability of voting.

Political scientists have had a long interest in political discussion, which arises naturally from the early sociological studies finding that interpersonal communication affects political participation (mostly decisions about for whom to vote). However, studies in context and social capital reignited a strong interest in political discussion as a means of transferring information, as well as having independent effects in terms of encouraging participation (for example, McClurg, 2006). Scholars have also been considering how disagreement within a network affects political participation. For example, political scientists Casey A. Klofstad, Anand Edward Sokhey, and Scott D. McClurg (2013) note that in the many studies about political disagreement, there is "serious disagreements about disagreement" (page 132). They expect that the differences in studies come from both how "disagreement" is measured and the types of statistical analyses utilized to show the effects of the disagreement. They argue those methods need to take into account that discussions are reciprocal, but also, to whom an individual talks is not randomly sampled. Expanding on other work, they find that there are differing types of political disagreement: both general disagreement and partisan disagreement.

> And, in pointing out these differences, we find that networks with disagreement salient enough to register as "general disagreement" seem to cut at the foundations of many important behaviors. Conversely, disagreement based on the absence of agreement (i.e., partisan disagreement) rather than the overt presence of conflict has no such impacts, despite the fact that other research demonstrates it to be an important covariate for a wide array of behaviors (e.g., Huckfeldt and Sprague 1995; Huckfeldt, Johnson, and Sprague 2004).[18]
>
> (page 132)

Taking into account the different ways of examining disagreement and the different statistical methods, they find that either type of disagreement had a statistically significant relationship with voter turnout.

Underlying all of the theory is the structure of relationships among both individuals and networks. One can analyze the structure in terms of where individuals are located within a structure of relationships (this person is friends with his coworker or his neighbor), but also within a network of many other structures of relationships (coworkers, neighbors). Some of the connections between these networks are very loose. (By loosely, scholars simply mean that the individuals in different networks who know each other do not know each other very well.[19]) One of the most-cited pieces of network theory scholarship is that of Mark S. Granovetter (1973) who posited that weak relationships (weak ties) among individuals are key to the diffusion of information among networks and individuals. Granovetter argues that linking individual and community levels (in the form of networks) is key to understanding outcomes. Weak ties make the linkages possible. He notes: "Such linkage generates paradoxes: weak ties, often denounced as generative of alienation (Wirth 1938) are here seen as indispensable to individuals' opportunities and to their integration into communities; strong ties, breeding local cohesion, lead to overall fragmentation" (page 1378).[20]

THE INSTITUTIONAL PERSPECTIVE

Political scientists have made institutional arguments for years, yet consider the "institution" mostly as a set of laws. In the well-known 1980 book *Who Votes?*, Rosenstone and Wolfinger find that how long before an election someone is allowed to register to vote has a strong effect on likelihood of voting. Still other scholars have incorporated the understanding of groups into rational-choice theory. For example, political scientist Jan Leighley shows that racial context affects how minorities— African Americans in particular—calculate the costs and benefits of participation.

> This contextual influence may indirectly reduce the costs of participating by affecting the likelihood of elite mobilization and the provision of relational goods, but more important, it increases the benefits of participating more directly. For minority individuals, the potential benefits of participating are greater as the racial/ethnic group increases in size because the group consequently enjoys a higher probability of being successful in its political efforts. For Anglos, an increase in minority group size acts as an informational cue of group threat—which again should increase the potential policy benefits of engaging in political activity.[21]

Another political scientist, Carole J. Uhlaner (1989), advances the idea of participation being a "political investment," but the decision to vote is made "within a social structure" (page 391).[23] The general point behind her argument is that when individuals are members of groups, group leaders can use this group identity to gain policy concessions on the part of politicians. As a member of a group, it is more rational to vote than as an individual because the group vote together has more pull than any one single vote.

Weighing these three major schools of thought (and the various combinations thereof) about voting and other political participation, and attempts at the scholarship considering the integration of these approaches, one can see why there is a common finding that the legal architecture surrounding voting has a relatively marginal impact. For an individual, the decision to vote is affected by costs of voting in terms of institutional barriers, but also may be affected by the individual's feelings about the importance of voting in maintaining democracy and feelings of civic duty. In part, the individual derives such attitudes from community interactions, especially if the individual does not personally feel like voting is important, but the individual's associates do (Coleman, 1990; Knack, 1992; Knack and Kropf, 1998). The "electoral institution" is something bigger than individuals aggregated together in a group.

The empirical analyses integrating both formal and informal rules are relatively rare, and many of them do measure "community context" via some sort of aggregation of individuals. Nevertheless, such work is path breaking as scholars attempt to handle some of these subtleties statistically. For example, political scientists Gimpel, Dyck, and Shaw (2006) and Dyck and Gimpel (2005) studied the interaction effects on those voters who might feel the cost of voting more than others because of a long commute to their job, but also feel the responsibility to vote because of a sense of civic duty (Dyck and Gimpel, 2005; Gimpel, Dyck, and Shaw, 2006). Gimpel, Dyck, and Shaw theorize that the largest increase in turnout will be among the voters with the highest education, and by extension, the highest levels of civic duty. The interaction between higher education and commuting distance is significantly related to a larger amount of absentee voting in this study. They found that "voters living in neighborhoods with the highest levels of combined education and commuting will vote absentee at a rate of 43%, compared with just 4% among those with the lowest values" (Gimpel, Dyck, and Shaw, 2006: 47). Voters with this interaction of long commutes and higher education are also more likely to vote early than those who did not have high levels of these variables (Gimpel, Dyck, and Shaw, 2006). Although higher education predicted a higher likelihood of voting, Dyck and Gimpel (2005) also found that distance is an important factor in voting. The closer a person is to his or her precinct, the more likely he or she is to vote. They found that absentee voting increases as distance to precinct increases (Dyck and Gimpel, 2005). Laws, attitudes and groups all affect voting.

CONCLUSION

Approximately 126 million Americans cast votes in the 2012 presidential election. In other chapters of this book, I described the electoral institution as a pyramid, with federal rules and laws representing the very top. State laws and conventions are next, followed by localities. Of course, there are tens of thousands of precincts (and, of course, the post office) enabling the 126 million Americans to cast votes. This chapter has served to outline the motivations for why individuals vote and how those motivations are captured within the context of new institutionalism. Those who live in the United States either vote or they do not vote based on motivations that have been theoretically developed by economists, psychologists, and sociologists.

If one examines the formative work in new institutionalism, one sees the critical importance of the "logic of appropriateness" (March and Olsen, 1983). Political scientist and the Nobel Memorial Prize in Economics Sciences winner Elinor Ostrom grew the theory of new institutionalism in a variety of ways while conducting field observations on the use of natural resources. Her book *Governing the Commons* (1990) shows that extensive sets of norms often develop to allow people to govern themselves. The "norms" define proper behavior. She writes:

> Many of these norms make it feasible for individuals to live in close interdependence on many fronts without excessive conflict. Further, a reputation for keeping promises, honest dealings, and reliability in one arena is a valuable asset. Prudent, long-term self-interest reinforces the acceptance of the norms of proper behavior.
>
> (pages 88–89)

Norms have allowed for the continuance and very stability of the long-term institution in the United States: our electoral system. Ostrom talked about governing without institutions. The argument here is that the US democratic government is not possible, save for the persistence of the electoral institution.

CHAPTER 7

FINDING THE TIME AND PLACE TO VOTE

EARLY VOTING—OR ALLOWING VOTERS TO vote in person before Election Day—has been allowed formally at least since 1988.[1] The idea behind early voting was that if voting times were more convenient, it would reduce the opportunity costs of voting. In other words, potential voters would not have to take off work (or give up other activities) in order to vote. If one examines newspapers covering the policy discussions, one can see that the goal of early voting was to increase voter turnout, not necessarily to relieve the pressure of long lines on Election Day, but it did not hurt that early voting might relieve long lines. For example, in North Carolina in January 1996 (about four years before North Carolina began to implement its one-stop voting—North Carolina's name for early voting), one can see that no-excuse early voting was one of many proposals being considered to "cure voter apathy" and "boost turnout at the polls."[2] There was bipartisan excitement by the year 2000. Political reporter Jim Morrill quoted the Mecklenburg County Republican Party Chair Frank Whitney as saying: "Voter turnout always determines an election, not the polls ... I have a feeling (early voting) will increase overall voter turnout."[3]

Times do change, and so does the character of voting as a part of the electoral institution. "The days of white-picket fences and going with your neighbors to the polls are gone," said Meredith B. Imwalle from the National Association of Secretaries of State way back in 2004. She continued, "States are trying to make it as easy as possible in this society of two-parent working households for people to vote on their own schedule."[4] Over the next decade after Imwalle made this statement, the United States has witnessed an astounding growth in state laws allowing voting before Election Day. As of the 2014 midterm election, political scientist Charles Stewart reported that 41 percent of voters cast their votes before Election Day, according to the survey he has been directing, The Survey of Performance of American Elections (SPAE). Stewart also noted that "in 15 states, the majority of votes were cast before Election Day. This was the case in 14 states in 2012 and 11 states in 2008."[5] This increase in voting before Election Day is in spite of the fact that state legislatures have scaled back the number of days for early voting in a number of states.

As formal institutions change, voting has seemingly become easier and easier for most voters. Most Americans have multiple times they could vote and have multiple locations where they could choose to vote. This chapter will discuss the locations and timing of voting today, as well as some of the direct implications—what do these policy changes mean for voter turnout and for managing ever-increasing costs of voting equipment? However, our informal rules also interact with the formal rules, creating the possibility of long-term effects of differing voting possibilities. As suggested by institutional theory outlined throughout this book, formal rules and informal rules interact. How do these changes to the electoral institution affect the right to vote?

The overriding themes of this chapter get to the heart of the interaction of formal and informal rules where it concerns the electoral institution. First, note that formal rule changes allowing the expansion of pre–Election Day voting expanded the right to vote and expanded voter turnout. In some sense, voting has returned to the community celebration it was in early American history—at least there are some good examples of it.[6] At the same time, the ability to vote at the precinct on Election Day has contracted due to budgetary constraints. We are seeing fewer neighborhood polling places because of the rise of more centralized voting locations. The second theme is that the change in the electoral institution also changes citizens' ability to enforce the norm of civic duty. In other words, voters are less likely to see (or not see) neighbors voting, and thus be able to monitor and sanction their behavior. Third, the expansion of voting opportunities has created opportunities for political parties to expand on mobilization. The unintended consequence of the success in mobilization has created a political backlash wherein state legislatures are limiting the days on which early voting is offered. Valelly's idea of institutional complementarity also matters here; laws enacted at the same time tend to work synergistically.

FINDING THE TIME AND PLACE TO VOTE

In colonial America, voting provided a chance for people from all over a jurisdiction to come together. According to historian Kate Kelly, "[s]ince colonial settlements were usually some distance apart, it was a time for friends and neighbors to meet, catch up on news and generally have a good time" (1991: 2). Different local jurisdictions did elections differently, but many times, the election was held using a voice vote and sometimes over a period of days. Things have changed. For example, federal law set Election Day as the first Tuesday after the first Monday in November, and states have established various other days for local elections. For the most part (unless one votes by mail) voters complete a ballot in privacy. And, states have a variety of laws concerning absentee voting (by mail; with or without an excuse); early voting (in person before Election Day); voting by mail alone; and even Internet, fax, and email voting (for overseas voters). Scholars often refer to such reforms as "convenience voting"—"understood to mean any model of balloting other than precinct-place voting" (Gronke, Galanes-Rosenbaum, Miller, and Toffey, 2008: 438).

These methods of voting are convenient because voters can choose when to cast a ballot or bypass potential barriers—for overseas voters, one large barrier has been the mail service. This chapter will also consider the precinct place on Election Day.

ABSENTEE VOTING

Today, all states have absentee voting, although there is variation in how it operates. Absentee voting has been in existence since at least the Civil War—but even then, explains policy scholar John C. Fortier, it was political. In the Union states, some of the impetus behind these battles was partisan, with Republicans pushing for soldier voting and Democrats opposing these efforts because the soldier vote was for Lincoln (2006: 7).[7] Fortier says that part of the problem with absentee voting was purely practical—should it be by proxy where someone votes for you, or should it be by mail? Fortier details a system of absentee balloting that ebbed and flowed with the advent of wars. He wrote that civilian absentee voting became possible in most states before World War II (WWII). For a good part of the twentieth century, a potential voter had to provide some sort of excuse in order to vote an absentee ballot. According to the National Conference of State Legislatures, in 1972, Tennessee and Idaho offered no-excuse absentee voting.[8] In 1978, California began offering no-excuse absentee voting (Fortier, 2006). Currently, about half of the states offer no-excuse absentee voting; some offer voters the ability to vote absentee in person, and some administer the process via mail.[9] In some states, there is a permanent absentee list where the state will simply send a ballot to the potential voter (for example, California).

Overseas voters (both domestic and military) have faced problems receiving and returning ballots in a timely manner in order to have that ballot counted toward the total. The *Washington Post* reported that more than one in four overseas ballots were lost in the 2008 election,[10] although apparently the rates of return have improved. In 2009, Congress passed the Military and Overseas Voter Empowerment Act (the MOVE Act), which required that states transmit ballots to overseas personnel 45 days in advance of elections (among other things states were required to do), and the Department of Justice has taken action against several states to enforce the law.[11] The US General Accountability Office (GAO) reports that Congress has added requests to several pieces of legislation for the Department of Defense (DOD) to have systems in place for secure electronic delivery of ballots. So, the GAO reports, since 2000, the DOD has been working on alternative methods for ballot delivery than just US mail (or the military mail). However, in 2007, the GAO reported several problems with the programs, which put not only the "secret ballot" in jeopardy, but also the basic right to vote. Not only that, but the DOD spent a lot of money for very few ballots.[12]

The variation in the implementation of absentee voting across the states provides the leverage needed to verify empirically whether the program accomplishes goals such as increasing turnout. Political scientist J. Eric Oliver (1996) conducted one of the first individual-level analyses of the effects of liberalized (no-excuse) absentee voting, in which he included the two states that voted "early" in person. He found that liberalized absentee voting did indeed increase voter turnout, but only when paired with partisan mobilization; in particular, he found that the availability of voter registration lists made a difference to voter turnout because it enabled the party mobilization efforts, in particular, the Republican Party efforts. Oliver wrote,

> Judging from my survey, state Republican party organizations are pursuing absentee mobilization campaigns with far more vigor than their Democratic counterparts. Consequently, the absentee electorate has become more upscale and Republican than the general electorate. The greater Republican absentee mobilization campaigns are likely to redefine American electoral politics, especially on the local level.[13]
>
> (page 511)

What is notable about Oliver's work is that it contrasts with more recent work on voting indicating that Democrats had an advantage.[14] However, it makes theoretical sense that mobilization efforts affect turnout levels. Political scientists Jan E. Leighley and Jonathan Nagler provide some of the most recent work on absentee voting and its effect on turnout. They make the argument that one cannot rely on just a survey during one year to infer that absentee voting increases turnout. Their evidence examining voter returns over a decade from all the states using several different statistical models provides evidence that absentee voting has increased voter turnout.

VOTING AT THE KITCHEN TABLE

As of this writing, three states run all elections by mail: Oregon, Washington, and most recently, Colorado. Voters can complete ballots and mail them in, or they can drop them off at designated locations. In California, precincts with fewer than 250 registered voters are required to vote by mail. Currently, then, other than those already noted, according to the National Conference of State Legislators, 15 states allow some elections to be conducted entirely by mail (19 in all). Policymakers have been experimenting with mail voting for a while. Public administration scholar Randy H. Hamilton stated that as of 1988 there had been at least 1,000 elections held just by mail. "In round numbers, approximately 80 elections by all-mail balloting have been held in Kansas, 400 in Oregon, 350 in California, 40 in Montana, 12 in Washington, 15 in Missouri, and 6 in Nebraska, the most recent state to adopt enabling legislation" (page 860).[15] Oregon began voting by mail (VBM) in 1981 for local elections without candidates and by 1993 used it completely for the first time. In 1998, voters passed a referendum adopting all VBM (Fortier, 2006: 14).

What does VBM mean for turnout? As it turns out, this is a complicated question empirically. Early research indicated the potential for increased voter turnout. Political scientists Patricia Southwell and Justin Burchett (2000) found about a 10 percent increase in turnout in VBM elections when looking at Oregon elections between 1960 and 1996. Southwell (2004) also analyzed Oregon residents to try to understand how people felt about all-mail ballots. Using a somewhat different approach than measuring actual turnout, she measured how people thought they voted. The majority believed that they voted the same as they had before all-mail voting had been adopted, and close to 30 percent felt they voted more often (Southwell, 2004).

More recent research uses statistical matching to analyze the effect of VBM in California in 2000 and 2002. Political scientists Thad Kousser and Megan Mullin compare the by-mail precincts in California that were similar to those that were not. Their research indicates that in general elections, turnout was actually lower in the by-mail jurisdictions. They speculate that the reason may be that either the voters moved (similar voters in precinct voting counties might still vote, where the VBM individuals never receive a ballot), or

> [b]allots that arrive in the proper mailbox might still get lost among glossy attack ads and other unsolicited mail. Rather than reduce the cost of participation, it is possible that all-mail elections make voting more difficult by presenting the ballot before voters are ready. As election day approaches and people begin to think about their vote decisions, their ballots might be long discarded.[16]
>
> (page 443)

Analyzing special elections, Kouser and Mullin are not able to conduct exactly the same analysis because the demographic data are not available at the precinct level, but they did follow a similar methodology. They found that turnout increased in the low-salience elections (that is, elections that were not as exciting as a presidential election—lower-profile or second-order elections—for example, than for a water district commissioner).[17]

In terms of other electoral values, although some early scholars (such as Hamilton) argued that VBM increased the integrity of the election. Hamilton also argued that the post office provided a "nearly foolproof" way to remove ineligible voters (who moved or died) from the voter registration list.

> In mail balloting, it becomes immensely more difficult for "tombstones" to vote. Such voting runs the risk of adding to violation of state election laws a federal crime of using the mails to defraud. Updating registration rolls is enhanced, more accurate records are established, election administration is improved, and elections are more "honest".
>
> (page 864)

Indeed, Oregon officials report that may be the case. According to the Election Assistance Commission *Alternative Voting Method Report* (2008: 17): "Oregon election officials claim that voter registration lists tend to be more accurate because the frequent mailing of nonforwardable ballots provides local election officials with updated information about the actual home addresses of the voters when mail is returned as undeliverable."[18] Note that the Pew Research Center reports that before the 2012 election, as many as one in eight voter registrations were inaccurate.[19] Yet states such as California do use returned mail to maintain the list.[20] Interestingly, not for voting by mail, but for voting more generally, voting rights advocates charge that Republicans are using returned mail lists to challenge voters—the practice is referred to as "voter caging."[21]

Further, one of the consequences of VBM is that the voters do not have access to voting equipment that will check for potential errors on the ballot. Because scholars who study elections cannot look over any particular person's shoulder and see how they voted, scholars analyze "residual votes" by geographic area. The term refers to the difference between how many voters turn out and the number of votes cast for a particular office. Political scientists R. Michael Alvarez, Dustin Beckett, and Charles Stewart III have long analyzed issues of voting equipment and tracked over the years the reduction of residual votes with the use of new voting equipment in California. Their conclusions are striking and sobering at the same time:

> Regardless of the race, increasing the percentage of voters in a county using the mail to vote is robustly associated with a rise in the residual vote rate in that county. The effect is so strong that we estimate that the rise of voting by mail has mostly wiped out all the reductions in residual votes that were due to improved voting technologies since the early 1990s.
>
> (page 23)

I find similar results examining North Carolina elections. Examining 2008 elections, I am able to separate out whether the votes were actually cast by mail (where there is no error notification), early, or at the precinct on Election Day. Ballots cast absentee by mail in North Carolina have statistically higher amounts of residual voting, controlling for the racial composition of a county, its (former) Section 5 status (Kropf, 2013).[22] In other words, the voter may have lost the right to vote, even if he or she gained it because of the easy access of VBM.

VOTING IN-PERSON BEFORE ELECTION DAY

In 1987, Texas began early voting programs with a version that was basically expanded in-person absentee voting, but by 1991, the state legislature created a program wherein multiple sites would be located in every county in Texas. More than half of the states offer early in-person voting.

Where early voting is concerned, the best studies of its effects take into account Valelly's institutional complementarity idea (see Chapter 5); no formal rule works alone—each interacts with structural inequalities and currently existing laws and institutional norms already in existence. An example of this is instructive; Oliver found that liberalized absentee voting increases voter turnout where political parties mobilize voters. Studies that examine a somewhat more comprehensive group of voting reforms across a longer period have found very little evidence that pre–Election Day voting increases turnout. Political scientist Mary Fitzgerald (2005) examined the so-called "convenience voting measures" used by states from 1972 to 2002, such as early voting and unrestricted absentee voting, and found they had little impact on turnout.[23] She found that the only significant policy factors to increase turnout were policies that made registration easier, like motor vehicle registration and Election Day registration (Fitzgerald, 2005). Gronke, Galanes-Rosebaum, and Miller (2007) examined the impact of voting reforms on turnout from 1980 to 2004. They found that none of the convenience voting reforms showed any increase in turnout except for VBM, which only slightly increased turnout in presidential elections (Gronke et al., 2007). Similarly, Leighley and Nagler (2014) examined absentee voting, Election Day registration, and early voting and found that perhaps scholars should analyze even more parts of the electoral institution.

> Early voting could increase turnout, given a long enough voting period. However, the length of the period required suggests that previous scholars who inferred that early voters are individuals who simply shifted the day on which they voted—rather than new voters who cast early ballots instead of staying home and not voting—may have been correct. The sensitivity of the result to the length of the early voting period suggests that we may need to more accurately model other aspects of implementation, such as the number and location of polling places available, to have a better understanding of the impact of early voting on turnout.[24]
>
> (page 118)

Finally, political science and public administration scholars Barry C. Burden, David T. Canon, Kenneth R. Mayer, and Donald P. Moynihan remind us that one cannot simply examine the formal rules—the "direct effects" of election laws.

> Yet an exclusive focus on direct effects leads to a misunderstanding of how election laws indirectly affect mobilization by nongovernmental actors such as the media, campaigns, interest groups, friends, and family. These actors indirectly raise or lower the costs of voting depending on how much information they provide and the social incentives for voting they generate.
>
> (page 95)

Using both individual- and geographic-level data from two different elections (2004 and 2008), as well as considering the varying reforms, including, for example, the effects of same-day (or Election Day) voter registration, Burden and his colleagues find that early voting actually decreases the likelihood of voter turnout.[25] What they conclude is consistent with previous studies, which show that early voting is a convenience for those planning to vote anyway—it is better as a program for voter "retention" rather than "stimulus."

One way to think about the idea of early voting (or other convenience voting) is to consider other behaviors that are socially desirable but may be "habitual" nevertheless. Given the context of the theory presented herein, I argue that one could compare voting to church attendance: one develops a habit for weekly churchgoing growing up, but what often happens when a churchgoer heads to college? Similarly, a variety of political science scholars have suggested that voting is "habit forming" (see Chapter 6)—what if some event caused a person to miss voting because he or she happened to be out of town on Election Day and did not have enough time to get an absentee ballot? For the person with a lower sense of civic norms,[26] the habit of voting may be broken. The real question is whether early voting may retain voters because the program allows voters to continue the habit of voting?

The study by Burden and colleagues does not necessarily measure the social effects of early voting, although their findings do comport well with the idea that convenience voting may have both an information effect and a social effect, which may result in lower turnout overall. They write, "It turns a large-scale social activity that once took place on a single election day into a weeks-long process that diffuses public visibility" (page 97). They continue,

> Rather than building up to a frenzied Election Day in which media coverage and interpersonal conversations revolve around politics, early voting makes voting a more private and less intense process. Social pressure is less evident, guidance on how and where to vote is less handy, and the prospect of positive social interactions at the polls is decreased. These reductions in stimulation—both strategic and nonstrategic mobilization—are greater than the modest positive benefits of additional convenience that accrue largely to those who would vote in any case.
>
> (page 98)

The idea is that voting at different times and away from the polls makes it more costly to obtain information mobilizing one to vote.

So what does happen when people are not voting in their own neighborhoods and seeing their neighbors when they vote? Consider two things: first, voting with one's neighbors may prevent fraud. Second, voting with one's neighbors may also provide a source of social benefits (or sanctions if one fails to vote in a particular election).

An illustration of fraud prevention is North Dakota, where there is no voter registration (which is the premier government program designed to reduce fraud). Here is what North Dakotans say about the system:

> North Dakota is a rural state and its communities maintain close ties and networks. North Dakota's system of voting, and lack of voter registration, is rooted in its rural character by providing small precincts. Establishing relatively small precincts is intended to ensure that election boards know the voters who come to the polls to vote on Election Day and can easily detect those who should not be voting in the precinct.[27]

In other words, when one votes with people one knows, that knowledge may reduce the prevalence of fraud. This would be a rather difficult hypothesis to test, even with the large amount of election data from all over the country. One might be able to show there is more potential election fraud in large jurisdictions, but it might be very difficult to tie that fraud to the idea that pollworkers do not know their neighbors. Still, this is not a possibility to dismiss; the question is really just this: Is the possibility of fraud bigger than the possibility that early voting may make voting easier?

Although the fraud hypothesis may be difficult to test, the idea that voting with one's neighbors makes it more likely that one will vote is not actually that difficult to examine and to provide evidence suggesting early voting may reduce social capital and voting in the long term. Some of my early research worked to address the social side of the equation, arguing that voting is a social activity; this is squarely in line with the theory presented throughout the book that institutions comprise both formal and informal rules (the law allowing early voting creates fewer social spaces for the enforcement of civic norms).[28] Along with David Swindell and Elizabeth Wemlinger (2009), we argued that partaking in the civic duty of voting is an important community activity and there are social sanctions for not voting and social rewards for voting. Such sanctions may only be effectively administered when one interacts with friends and neighbors, as one may do in one's polling place on Election Day. Although we did not directly measure the social sanctions (as did the Green and colleagues experimental research discussed at the beginning of Chapter 2), we utilized the American National Election Study Panel dataset spanning the years 2000–2004. We found that even using this short time span, those who voted before Election Day in 2000 had lower levels of "social capital" than those who voted in their precinct on Election Day in 2000. In turn, those who displayed behavior more consistent with social capital in 2004 were more likely to vote than those who displayed behavior that is less consistent.[29]

Public opinion toward early voting is the primary reason that early voting continues, but public opinion has not necessarily prevented limitations on early voting. Note that the McClatchy Newspapers and Marist College asked a national sample of people in July 2013, "Do you think it is a good thing or a bad thing if election laws were changed to do each of the following?) … Allow early voting in elections before Election Day?" Sixty-eight percent of Americans thought that was "a good thing."[30] The Marist Poll data do indicate that Democrats support early voting far more than do Republicans (78 percent versus 62 percent), but nevertheless, there is support for early voting within both parties.[31] Yet, several state legislatures have passed legislation that limits the amount of time during which early votes can be cast, which some scholars argue will limit voting rights, in particular, for minorities. In Florida, for example, political scientists Michael C. Herron and Daniel A. Smith argue that eliminating voting on Sunday was especially negative for African American, new and younger voters because they are the ones most likely to vote on Sunday.[32] My research with one of my former students, David Pezzella, shows that African American individuals who were members of a church were more likely to vote early in 2008, but not in 2000. We argue that African American voters were voting together on Sunday across the country, consistent with the National Association for the Advancement of Colored People (NAACP) mobilization effort, Souls to the Polls.

VOTING AT THE PRECINCT ON ELECTION DAY

For most of the twentieth century, individuals voted in precincts in their neighborhoods on Election Day. Scholars have learned quite a lot about precinct voting and its connection to voting rights. It is important to note that a polling place can be almost any sort of building: a school, a country club, a church, a laundry mat, a bowling alley, or even a car dealership.[33]

It is challenging for local election officials to ensure all of these places are accessible to those with disabilities. The General Accounting Office studied a scientifically selected sample of polling places in 2000, 2008, and 2012. In the 2012 report, the GAO report found,

> In comparison to our findings in 2000, the proportion of polling places with no potential impediments increased in 2008. In 2008, we estimated that 27 percent of polling places had no potential impediments in the path from the parking area to the voting

area—up from 16 percent in 2000. Specifically, polling places with four or more potential impediments decreased significantly—from 29 percent in 2000 to 16 percent in
2008 .... Potential impediments included a lack of accessible parking and obstacles en
route from the parking area to the voting area.

Many of the polling places that had potential impediments offered curbside voting
or other accommodations to assist voters who may have had difficulty getting to or
making their way through a polling place. Some polling places provided assistance
to voters by bringing a paper ballot or provisional ballot to a voter in a vehicle. The
percent of polling places that had potential impediments that did not offer curbside
voting remained virtually unchanged from 28 percent in 2000 to 27 percent in 2008.[34]

(pages 7, 10–11)

Scholars Lisa Schur, Meera Adya, and Douglas Kruse (2013) conducted the first
large-scale survey of those with disabilities compared to those without disabilities.
They note that the GAO study only focuses on mobility issues. In their study of
more than 3,000 people after the 2012 election, they found that about one-third
of peope with disabilities had problems voting, compared with less than 10 percent
of voters without disabilities. There were many more difficulties than simply
mobility. "Reading or seeing ballot" and "Understanding how to vote or use voting equipment" were the top issues. But importantly, other highly mentioned problems were "Finding or getting to polling place," "Getting inside polling place (e.g.,
steps)," and "Waiting in line."[35] Schur prepared a white paper for the Presidential
Commission on Election Administration summarizing the research of her team
and others. She wrote: "Twelve surveys over the 1992–2004 elections, using varying samples and definitions of disability, found that eligible citizens with disabilities were between 4 and 21 percentage points less likely to vote than were eligible
citizens without disabilities" (2013).[36] In considering the right to vote, the election
institution does present some unique challenges to those with disabilities. For some
individuals, they are able to vote "curbside" with a pollworker coming outside with
ballots and necessary affidavits; the GAO report stated that 23 states allowed curbside voting in 2008 for individuals with age or mobility issues (28 allowed curbside
voting in 2000).[37]

However, it is not just the physical impairments such as a set of stairs in a small
church (with no elevator) in the middle of urban Kansas City.[38] Something as seemingly simple as sufficient parking around the polling place can pose a problem, and
certainly for most voters who do not have any physical impairment. Political scientists Matt Barreto, Mara Cohen-Marks, and Nathan D. Woods (2005) conducted
one of the first systematic analyses of the quality of polling places. In examining
polling places in Los Angeles, the largest local election jurisdiction in the country,
they found that the lowest-quality polling places "are more likely to be found in low-
income and minority neighborhoods" (page 458).[39]

For example, several polling places in Los Angeles were hard to find, did not have
addresses clearly displayed, and offered limited parking. In addition, polling places varied widely in their size, comfort of the waiting area, the number of machines available,

and the knowledge of poll workers. Furthermore, there were some notable differences within the city based on the demographic profile of the precinct.

(page 447)

Clear address labeling and parking are a part of the US electoral institution, even if they do seem prosaic. If a voter is unable to find the polling place or is unable to park, in essence, the institution is playing a role in the loss of this person's vote, even if some citizens say those who get lost should try harder.

Similar polling place monitoring has become an important tool in the belt of non-profit organizations advocating for voting rights, especially because reports of long lines at polling places may have affected election outcomes. (President Barack Obama was responding to the issues of long lines during the 2012 election when he commissioned a nonpartisan study group to improve elections.)[40] For example, Demoracy North Carolina, a nonpartisan voting-rights organization, had more than 400 volunteers monitoring polls in 120 precints in about one-third of the counties in the state. As part of a consortium of nonprofit groups, they also collected data from more than 1,000 voter protection hotline calls. The group prepared a research study about their findings, estimating that voting law changes in North Carolina meant that some voters did not vote and outlined a number of issues with particular polling places.

> Monitor reported curbside voters had to wait for long periods and endure a slow process as the official was overwhelmed with other responsibilities inside the polling place.
>
> Poll Monitor reported inadequate parking, with spaces next to the building occupied by cars of election officials. At different times, the Monitor and two campaign volunteers complained to the election official in charge, but to no avail. The parking lot had "only one way in and out, so cars were jammed up frequently. To be honest, I spent a good bit of my time directing traffic."
>
> Poll Monitor said curbside voters had to endure very long waits (apparently the bell to alert precinct officials to the presence of curbside voters was broken), and the voting lines in the late afternoon were up to an hour long.[41]

The North Carolina Board of Elections did conduct a county-level survey in 2014 of how long the lines were at polling places that year. County election directors reported that there were waits of one hour or more at 45 out of 2,726 locations.[42] Nationwide, during the 2012 election, political scientists Stewart and Ansolabehere estimated that during the 2012 general election, there were 500,000 to 700,000 "lost votes due to long lines."[43]

Finally, it should be noted that as early voting has become more common, having fewer polling places (or precincts) seems like a logical reaction, given the high costs of elections.[44] Fewer polling places are highly likely to have effects on voter turnout. Political scientists Henry Brady and John McNulty build an important theory about the costs created for voters because of consolidation: one cost is the "transportation effect"—a new consolidated polling place is likely to be farther away. This effect will persist, no matter how familiar a voter may become with a new polling place.

The other cost may decrease over time: the "search effect" is the idea that a potential voter may not know where to go and may have to travel to an unfamiliar part of the city (this is also consistent with the idea that there may be a cost due to disrupting the context within which people continue the habit of voting). Brady and McNulty analyzed precinct consolidation in Los Angeles, California, in the 2003 recall election. Indeed, for voters whose polling place changed, voter turnout declined. Some voters did vote absentee, which somewhat reduced the negative effects. The scholars found that Democratic voters were more likely to be affected by changes, but those effects were small.[45] Political scientists Moshe Haspel and H. Gibbs Knotts provided further evidence that consolidation of precincts increased transportation costs of voting. Analyzing consolidation of precincts in the Atlanta area, they found that potential voters who had to travel farther than they had before were less likely to vote, controlling for other relevant factors known to affect voting.

VOTING CENTERS?

A limited number of local election jurisdictions utilize or have utilized Election Day vote centers. Instead of neighborhood polling places, a local election jurisdiction establishes several large centers, where any voter within the jurisdiction could go on Election Day. Today, Colorado has all-mail voting, as noted earlier in this chapter. Larimer County, Colorado, was the first county in the country to pilot this type of voting. According to political scientists Robert M. Stein and Greg Vonnahme (2008, 2012), Election Day vote centers are created around two ideas that make them different from neighborhood precincts—openness and centralization.

> Openness might increase turnout by lowering transportation and information costs as voters can go to any location that is most familiar and convenient for them, particularly for individuals traveling outside the home (e.g., commuting for work, school, shopping, or recreation) on Election Day.
>
> Centralization refers to polling locations that are fewer in number and located at larger and more visible sites. Centralization also exists to varying degrees in precinct based polling locations. Centralization may have several positive effects on voter participation (Stein and Vonnahme 2008). Larger and more visible sites can reduce informational costs that voters incur when attempting to find a polling location and offer more available parking at the site.[46]
>
> (page 293)

In 2008, Stein and Vonnahme published research comparing Larimer County, Colorado (which used vote centers) to Wald County, Colorado, and found that the most infrequent voters were the ones most encouraged to vote when there are vote centers.[47] The 2012 research examined other counties that had adopted vote centers (19 in Colorado and 1 in Texas). The results of the analysis of the 2006 and 2008 elections (using both individual-level data and county data) were consistent with the earlier research focusing on the two Colorado counties.[48] Several other states have passed legislation to allow local election jurisdictions to use vote centers, but do not require all of them to use it.[49]

Vote centers are an interesting example of the theory that suggests that the American electoral system is an institution comprising both formal and informal rules. Stein and Vonnahme suggest that the opportunity cost of voting plays a role in the output of increased voter turnout. Because the locations are open to anyone during Election Day, one can basically vote wherever it is most convenient (assuming one of the vote centers is convenient). This is especially important if one does not work near one's neighborhood polling place. Because the total cost of equipping a vote center is arguably lower, the local election authority could make the site more visible, reminding voters that "today is the day to vote!"

CONCLUSION

Formal rules can make it easier or more difficult to vote. However, what effect such laws have are at least in part dependent on informal rules and practices; if someone a potential voter respects asks him or her to vote early, that is important. The best evidence for the interaction of formal and informal rules appears to be in early in-person voting, which could be a reason why results are so uninspiring where turnout is concerned. There are reasons to believe that allowing voters to cast a ballot when it is more convenient for them would unambiguously lead to an increase in voter turnout. Yet studies to date appear to indicate that early voting may even have negative effects (Burden and his colleagues) or the results simply are not robust—whether or not early voting matters to turnout depends on the statistical model (Leighley and Nagler).

There is some evidence that in the 2008 and 2012 elections, early voting increased voter turnout, especially among minorities. However, it is important to note that President Barack Obama's mobilization team was particularly talented at on-the-ground mobilization and worked hard at it; other evidence in this chapter indicates mobilization matters. According to *The Boston Globe,*

> Obama's national field director, Jon Carson, said the campaign is pushing early voting everywhere the law allows. But he named a number of battleground states where he said the campaign has made early voting a "major focus," including Nevada, New Mexico, North Carolina, and Indiana. He said that while the trend does not necessarily help one political party, it does help the best-run campaign.[50]

In other words, it is not clear how to interpret the effects of early voting in total. It is not unreasonable to say that if done correctly, early voting mobilization could have strong and positive effects. However, the unintended consequence of the success in mobilization has created a political backlash wherein state legislatures are limiting the days on which early voting is offered.

Although race and voting is one of the more visible issues at this writing because some states have limited early voting periods and there are a number of lawsuits charging that these states are disenfranchising voters, the reader should not just focus on race. Local election jurisdictions play a large role in whether or not those who are disabled are able to vote. Budgets are tight and localities make trade-offs that sometimes limit the franchise for these voters.

CHAPTER 8

COUNTING THE VOTES

THERE ARE A NUMBER OF INSTANCES WHERE ELECTION scholars might simply say: "You just can't make this stuff up." Indeed, consider this real newspaper story about counting votes in a local election reported by Zachary K. Johnson in *The Stockton (CA) Record*:

> At the election office on Wednesday, two observers and two election workers tried to decipher the scrawl on one pink envelope. The numbers in the address were unclear; so were the letters in the voter's name. Best guesses led them through a search of the voter rolls before his signature came up on a computer screen.
>
> "That's Justin," said staffer Jeff Dale, matching it up to the signature on the envelope. After a few more steps, including checking to see if it was the only time the person voted, the envelope landed in the box for envelopes to be opened and counted.
>
> "He went to the correct (polling) place. He didn't return his absentee (ballot). We're good to go," elections supervisor Liz Orosco said before the group moved on to the next pink envelope.[1]

The real-life story of "Justin" was not in Florida in the year 2000 (although there were a number of stories one could not even imagine making up in Florida in 2000). This example was a local contest in a county in northern California—nearly 14 years after the notable presidential election and 12 years after the federal government passed the Help America Vote Act.

A close county supervisor's race in San Joaquin County, California, pitted two Stockton City Council members against each other. Only 357 votes separated the two candidates, and two election workers worked at validating about 2,100 provisional ballots—according to *The Stockton Record*, there were about 20,000 ballots that still had not been counted in this local contest on a warm June day. San Joaquin County is not the first case of a close election being determined via implementation of this particular election policy, nor would it be the last. Every single election is determined based on administration of election rules—formal and informal. Voters just don't usually notice, unless a race is close. It was close in San Joaquin County— just as close as it was in the Bush-Gore presidential contest in 2000.

The newspaper article cited earlier says that Justin cast a provisional ballot. As detailed in Chapter 4, there are a variety of situations under which Justin might have had occasion to cast a provisional ballot on Election Day. Most likely, he went to check in and his name was not on the list of registered voters. Justin probably explained to the pollworker that yes, indeed, he was sure he was registered (maybe it was a data entry error in the first place! After all, apparently, his handwriting was sloppy, and entering handwritten information from hundreds if not thousands of would-be voters is most assuredly a chore!). Eventually on Election Day, the pollworker allowed him to cast a provisional ballot. After the hustle and bustle of Election Day, election officials worked through all the provisional ballots (the provisional ballots are separated from the total), trying to verify whether the provisional voter was in fact a valid voter (registered, in the right place, etc.). Once validated, the provisional votes are counted as a vote. Sometimes the provisional votes matter to the outcome of the election. Most times they do not.

The parts of the institution of elections that affect how and whether votes are counted include more than simply provisional ballots. Little noticed by most voters before the 2000 election but causing stress for local election administrators, the institution also includes voting equipment and ballots,[2] which allow the voter to communicate his or her preference. The voting equipment includes some sort of interface with the would-be voter—a paper ballot and a pencil or an electronic screen. Those votes are transmitted to a central location where they are tabulated together to create "the voice of the people."

I argue that the "right to vote" does not stop at the entrance of the polling place (or the mailbox, for that matter). Voting is not a complete act until the votes are tabulated and publicized. In other words, there are parts of the process wherein a person could lose his or her right to vote while trying to communicate his or her preferences. Similarly, the voter could gain a right to vote—failsafe balloting procedures may mean a voter who is not on the registration list can vote and have it count. Further, having accessible voting equipment may mean that someone who is disabled or who is unable to read may vote, and vote in private. This chapter discusses examples of institutions—both informal and formal rules—that affect one's right to vote when one has made it through the door of the polling place: provisional votes, voting equipment, and ballots.

PROVISIONAL BALLOTS

Provisional ballots are separated from the other ballots cast during the election, until such time as local election officials can verify that the person is eligible to vote, which usually occurs after the other ballots have been tabulated. Pollworkers may require a potential voter to cast a provisional ballot when the he or she arrives at the precinct and the pollworker cannot locate this person on the list of eligible voters. A voter might have to cast a provisional vote because he or she did not have the correct proof of identification. For example, part of the Help America Vote Act (HAVA) was that every voter who registered by mail and did not provide photo identification had to come to the polling place with photo identification the first time he or she voted.) After completing some paperwork, the provisional voter is allowed to cast his or her vote. Then, after the local election officials check the voter's eligibility, HAVA requires that officials allow the voter to check whether or not his or her vote counted in the total. And, of course, as more and more states begin to pass legislation that requires all would-be voters to present government-issued photo identification, the proportion of voters who must cast a provisional vote will probably increase.

Scholars have extensively studied provisional votes because it is just one piece of evidence about the performance of the election system. A large or small number of provisional votes within a state (or county or precinct) is not inherently "bad." One may perceive more provisional votes as a good thing because one can argue that there were a number of individuals who would have lost their right to vote, would it not have been for this "failsafe" balloting. On the other hand, one can consider provisional votes negative, especially if the reason for them has something to do with administrative errors or poor educational programs about what identification to bring to the polls. What policymakers should consider potentially negative is if there are large differences in the number of provisional votes among counties or precincts. That might indicate the election officials in a particular jurisdiction are not implementing election programs in a fair or uniform manner. On the other hand, it could be the demographic composition of the precinct or county—if a lot of people have very low educational levels in a county, then the number who know they can cast a provisional ballot might be very small. Another possibility might be that a pollworker is not trained properly. Maybe the pollworker does not allow people to cast a provisional ballot. Using statistics—in particular regression analysis—to analyze what causes more provisional votes to be cast (or ultimately counted after Election Day) can highlight if there are administrative problems, controlling for the educational level, race, or partisanship of the people in the jurisdiction. Such grouped data about a jurisdiction do not allow scholars to make conclusions about any particular person who is casting a provisional vote, or any particular pollworker. However, scholars know to look at a jurisdiction more carefully if the number of provisional ballots cast and counted is related to a factor such as race, especially if there is a history of racial discrimination in a particular location.

Scholars have studied the reasons for higher numbers of provisional votes cast and counted in counties all over the country. For example, my colleagues David C. Kimball, Lindsay Battles, and I analyzed provisional votes cast and counted in the 2004 election in local election jurisdictions (townships and counties) nationwide. We also gathered data concerning the partisanship of the local election officials (is the person in charge a Democrat or a Republican?), as well as whether the person in charge of elections in the county was elected rather than appointed (or hired) to the post. One unique finding in this study was that counties with a Democrat administering elections had higher expected numbers of provisional votes cast and counted, but only when the jurisdiction was highly Democratic in voting (and fewer votes cast and counted in Republicans in terms of voting). Similarly, those jurisdictions with a Republican leading the election jurisdiction have higher numbers in highly Republican areas and fewer in Democratic areas.[3] In 2013, Kimball, our colleague Timothy Vercellotti, and I published an article that found that the number of provisional ballots cast and counted correlated with the attitudes of the local election official. We considered many other causes of provisional votes, including the amount of direction from the state election office and the demographic makeup of the jurisdiction. Our analysis also found that local election official partisanship was related to the attitudes, with Democrats being more supportive if more Democrats live in the jurisdiction.[4] Although one cannot necessarily say that provisional votes are "bad" or "good," one can certainly say that the administration of the program should not be related to partisanship. All in all, this is indicative of the idea that the election system is not just comprised of formal rules, but is, at a basic level, affected by informal expectations, in this case concerning partisanship.

CASE STUDY: PROVISIONAL VOTES IN NORTH CAROLINA

Scholars can leverage the hyperdecentralization of elections to diagnose election problems, assuming that data are available to do so; it becomes easier to home in on problems with data at smaller and smaller levels of aggregation of voters, votes, and ballots. For example, one can tell more from county data than from state data. Precinct data can allow us to see if there are problems within a county. Individual data can tell us if there is variation among individuals that may be related to something about the person (for example, did an African American person or a Republican cast a vote that counted?). Another way of expressing this idea is that individual data might be able to tell us whether women, minorities, or people of a certain age are more likely to have a certain outcome where it concerns election administration, in this case provisional voting.

The federal government's Election Administration and Voting Survey (EAVS) gathers a large amount of data, which helps scholars diagnose potential problems, such as variations in provisional balloting. But more valuable yet, the North Carolina State Board of Elections makes a variety of data, including individual data, available for analysis. EAVS can tell us how many voters cast a provisional ballot in each county and the state. Using the North Carolina data, we can identify the 51,192 people who cast a provisional ballot in the general election held in November 2012, along with the party they registered with at the time they cast the vote, their gender,[5] and for the majority of the voters, but not all, their race. These pieces of information are on the standard voter registration form in North Carolina, but not all voters provide race, ethnicity, and gender. Further, in these data, one can identify why each voted a provisional ballot, whether the whole ballot counted, whether the ballot partially counted (perhaps the voter was in the wrong precinct and therefore the wrong congressional jurisdiction on Election Day),[6] or whether the ballot did not count at all. Admittedly, the 51,192 number is rather small in comparison to the 4,542,488 who voted in North Carolina in 2012. However, consider North Carolina's history of racial discrimination where balloting is concerned. (Note racial discrimination in voting used to be a formal rule, then became an informal practice, and the question is whether racial discrimination in voting is still an informal practice Or even whether formal practices are related to discriminatory effects.) These data may be able to shed light on whether these are vestiges of North Carolina's past. These data could also tell us whether for individuals, partisanship may be statistically related to whether those of a certain party are more or less likely to have their ballots count. Is there any evidence of differential treatment of voters within the precincts?

Furthermore, these data can help us predict the effects of election law changes on voting in a presidential election. In the summer of 2013, the North Carolina General Assembly changed the provisional ballot law; in the past, if a voter was in the wrong precinct but the correct county, when he or she cast a ballot, then the local election boards would count as much of the ballot as the voter was eligible for. However, the new law stated that the voter had to be in the current correct precinct in order to vote—any votes cast (even those for which any North Carolina resident would be eligible to vote no matter where he or she lived) would not be counted toward the vote total. Such rules are potentially consequential; in the 2012 presidential election North Carolina was a battleground state—Obama barely won the state in 2008, but barely lost the state in 2012. In 2014, there was a highly competitive US Senate contest. In any case, the 2012 data can show us whose vote counted in 2012 but would not count in 2014. Does that vary by partisanship? By race? By gender?

Figure 8.1 indicates the various reasons why people cast provisional votes in North Carolina. The reader will note that consistent with the information provided in Chapter 3, the North Carolina State Election Board explains to local jurisdictions

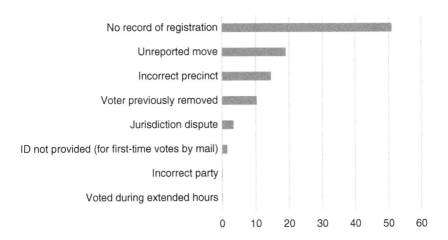

Figure 8.1   Reasons voted a provisional ballot

how to implement the laws created by a state legislature. It lays out detailed administrative procedures where it concerns provisional voting.[7]

The majority of the provisional voters were simply not listed on the voter registration list at the polling place (about 51 percent of the provisional ballots cast). This could occur for a variety of reasons; perhaps the county office had a last-minute rush of voter registrations or perhaps the Division of Motor Vehicles or other public offices did not transmit the registrations to the county office on time. Perhaps the official entering the voter registration applications prior to Election Day could not read someone's handwriting. Approximately 19 percent of potential voters moved but did not report the move (the voter could vote in his or her old jurisdiction for up to 30 days after the move). Another 15 percent were simply in the wrong precinct; perhaps the voters found it easier to try to cast a vote closer to where they worked. Less than four percent of voters had a "jurisdiction dispute" wherein according North Carolina's Administrative Procedures,

> [f]or instance, the voter may be offered the ballot to vote in the County Commissioner District One race but believes that their residence is in fact in County Commissioner District Two. In that case, the voter may vote a provisional ballot on County Commissioner Two, the ballot will count in the District Two race if it is determined that the voter is in fact eligible to vote in District Two. The voter shall not be allowed to cast ballots in both District One and District Two.

Although it affected very few voters, "incorrect party" should not matter for a general election—only for primaries when a voter actually needs a ballot for a certain party. Still, a little fewer than 100 people voted a provisional ballot because they were not registered to the correct party. Seemingly, administrative errors do occur, and elections are not perfect.

The next step for this analysis: How many of those ballots counted? First, I ask the reader to consider what might have happened had a provisional voter cast his or her vote in 2016 rather than 2012. Votes cast outside the "correct precinct" would not count. Table 8.1 shows that African American and White voters are about equally likely to cast a vote in the wrong precinct—Africans Americans are actually a bit less likely than Whites. The year 2012 is not a perfect case of what would happen in

Table 8.1   Whites and African Americans just as likely to vote out of precinct

Race	Number out of precinct	Provisional votes voted	Percent of provisional votes
Black/African American	2,203	12,045	18.3%
White/Caucasian	3,930	19,305	20.4%
Native American	155	887	17.5%
Asian/Pacific Islander	79	333	23.7%
Multiracial	89	471	18.9%
Other	222	800	27.8%

Table 8.2   Provisional vote status, 2012

Status of provisional	Number	Percent
Approved	18,041	35.2%
Not Counted	27,830	54.4%
Partial	5,321	10.4%

2016 because voters knew they were allowed to cast a vote outside the precinct (at least many likely did), so perhaps this led to many doing so, even though part of their ballots would not count.

Table 8.2 tells us what happened to the provisional ballots once they were cast. Of the ballots cast, 54 percent of the provisional ballots cast did not count toward the total. Ten percent counted only partially; only one-third of provisional votes counted. If those same votes had been cast after North Carolina changed its laws, then 6,708 votes that had partially or fully counted, even though they were cast outside the correct precinct, would not count.

Note that according to EAVS, 12,490 individuals had registered by mail and were voting for the first time in the jurisdiction on Election Day. Yet, according to the reasons why people cast provisional votes, more than 700 people failed to show the correct identification—in 2012, the only ID requirement was that the voter tell the pollworker his or her name and address; an exception is first-time voters who registered by mail. It seems 757 people did not bring a photo ID to the polls with them, the purported reason they cast a provisional vote. In order for these votes to count, the voter simply needed to provide the proper ID to the election board later. According to the data, 691 individuals never did this.

Figure 8.2 indicates the reasons why votes did not count. Justin (from this chapter's introduction) would be gratified to know he is not the only one with messy handwriting. In fact, 265 people across the state of North Carolina either did not complete the provisional ballot paperwork or did so in illegible handwriting. Maybe it is hard to imagine that a voter's handwriting is part of the electoral institution, but clearly it is.

Finally, I evaluated the likelihood of a person's provisional vote counting, taking into consideration race, gender, whether the person lives in a county with a past history of voting discrimination (VRA Section 5 status), and partisanship (Democrats compared with unaffiliated and Republican voters; Libertarians compared with unaffiliated and Republican voters). I also take into consideration the turnout on Election Day in the county where the potential voter lives (pollworkers may be tempted to solve a difficult problem with a provisional ballot even when a provisional ballot is not the correct solution). Not surprisingly, African Americans' votes are significantly less likely to count toward the total number of votes; African Americans in Section 5 counties are statistically significantly less likely to have their provisional vote count. If one is a typical provisional voter in a Section 5 county (woman, Democrat), and one is White, the chance of one's vote counting is 38.5 percent and if one is Black, the chance is 29.4 percent. Another surprise is that those provisional voters who report being Democrat are more likely to have their vote count than Republicans or unaf-filiated voters. Interestingly, women's votes are much more likely to count toward the total than men's votes (perhaps women cast provisional votes because of name change, which would presumably not be difficult to sort out). Those counties with a higher total turnout on Election Day see fewer provisional votes counted.

Provisional ballots do mean that voters who are not on the voter registration list still receive an opportunity to vote where they otherwise would not. However, it seems clear that there are a number of individuals who ultimately do not have a ballot counted and, in likelihood, never realize that is the case, even though HAVA requires that voters be able to look up the status of their ballots. The ability to cast a provi-sional vote is an unambiguous blessing for those who might be victims of administra-tive mistakes, because some number will count. As noted, more or fewer provisional votes is neither good nor bad, but clearly, the implementation of the provisional vote law depends on both the way in which the formal rules are written and the infor-mal rules. And clearly, even someone's handwriting might affect their right to vote. In North Carolina, the evidence indicates that provisional votes cast and counted are related to race and whether the county is a Section 5 county, which raises the question of whether the history of voting discrimination is over or not. Perhaps that "informal rule" remains in some way or another, even if those holding the attitudes are not aware of it.

FUTURE QUESTIONS

An interesting question to address in the future is whether technologies such as online voter registration and electronic pollbooks will help minimize provisional votes. According to the National Conference of State Legislatures (NCSL), only 20 states have online voter registration as of April 2015, and another 6 have adopted but not imple-mented it.[8] The first to implement online registration was Arizona in 2002. With online registration, there is not a person who tries to read the potential registrant's handwriting who may have been entering voter registrations for eight hours. In other words, there is less probability of an administrative error, and thus potentially fewer provisional votes cast. Without the data entry costs (and paper costs), there is also a long-term cost reduction for jurisdictions, although implementing such a system has a high startup cost. The trade-off for the convenience is accessibility; only those with a driver's license can register online to vote at this time.[9] In terms of security and privacy, according to the Pew Charitable Trusts and the NCSL, no state has reported fraud in online registration, although there are occasional reports of potential vulnerabilities.[10]

Most precincts in the United States use paper pollbooks on Election Day. However, the number of those using electronic pollbooks is growing. E-pollbooks could reduce the number of provisional votes. If a voter is not on the list, the pollworker could look up a voter on an e-pollbook and send that voter to the proper location (and per-haps even print out a map and directions). According to the National Conference of State Legislatures, the e-pollbook could also include a picture of the voter to reduce the probability of fraud. Of course, there are worries that e-pollbooks may be vulnerable to hacking as well.[11]

VOTING EQUIPMENT AND BALLOTS

Formal election rules determine the mode by which individuals communicate their voting preferences. The rules determine whether someone or something tabulates the votes and what exactly counts as a vote. Either a person (with inherent values, expectations, and biases) or a machine (chosen by people with inherent values, expectations, and biases) could tabulate the votes. Computers or other voting machines might themselves be neutral, but choices involved in the counting method may require trade-offs. Considering the machines, there are values inherent in the equipment itself (accuracy, reliability, security, auditability) and problems inherent in the voter interaction with the equipment and the ballot (usability and accessibility to those with disabilities of various types). From the standpoint of gaining the right to vote and actually participating, these are values that the public did not often consider before the 2000 election. What has remained constant since the passage of laws requiring the Australian ballot is the value of privacy: there has long been a concern that a person casts a vote for his or her preference and is not coerced in any way (Keyssar, 2000). These values are reflected in the creation of legislation about vote-casting technology.

ACCURACY MEASURED BY RESIDUAL VOTES

Accuracy in terms of whether the voter could cast his or her ballot as intended took center stage soon after the 2000 election. Political science scholars have examined the idea that people may not vote for certain contests on purpose (for example, Martin P. Wattenberg and his colleagues, 2000),[12] but what the country appeared to see were "lost votes" due to poor voting equipment. Scholars developed a measure of voting equipment accuracy called "residual votes." This measure evolved because scholars cannot look over someone's shoulder to see if the person voted correctly (value of privacy) or even ask if the person voted correctly. In all likelihood, a person would think he or she had voted as intended. The person may lose a vote, either in a contest or for all the contests, because the equipment was faulty or poorly designed. Thus, scholars measure residual votes by ascertaining how many people cast ballots in a jurisdiction such as a county and subtract the number of votes for a given contest (to obtain a residual vote rate, one can divide that number by the total number of ballots cast). The measure is called "residual votes" because scholars cannot know whether the missing votes were intended or not. What scholars do know is that residual votes should not be higher in jurisdictions that use a certain type of voting equipment or style of ballot (Kimball and Kropf, 2008, 501). However, depending on the availability of data, scholars may also consider "overvotes" (voting for too many candidates—this is mostly likely unintentional and is not considered "good") or "undervotes" (not voting for any candidate at all, which may be intentional—thus scholars cannot judge whether the undervote is a problem of voting equipment, usability or no vote was cast on purpose).

After the infamous 2000 election, policymakers, pundits, and policy scholars alike blamed punchcard ballots for causing more of the residual votes (see Table 8.3 for a listing of the general types of voting equipment used in the 2012 election compared with 1996). Research has consistently shown that counties that use punchcard ballots have among the highest residual vote rates; as a result, one can see that the use of punchcard ballots has declined dramatically, although in 2012, Idaho still had some voters who used punchcard voting.

However, the rate of residual votes tends to differ depending on where on the ballot the contest appears and what kind of user interface the equipment has. For example, Kimball and Kropf (2008) show that there are some electronic (ATM style) voting machines that show all the contests at once (full-face direct recording electronics [DREs]). Ballot propositions that are listed at the bottom of the ballot have a much higher residual vote rate than DREs with a feature that allows the voter to scroll through each contest. Scholars have also shown that when using the scrolling DREs, if election officials program more than one contest on a screen, it can be confusing. Political scientists Laurin Frisina, Michael C. Herron, James Honaker, and Jeffrey B. Lewis (2008) found that the way in which two contests were listed on the DRE screen caused a "high undervote rate in the November 2006 13th Congressional District race in Florida", which most likely changed the results of the election (page 40).[13]

A "user interface" is not just a screen on an electronic machine; it is also the ballot— a ballot is a mode of communication, which can vary across jurisdictions in terms of ease of use. With my coauthor David C. Kimball, we analyzed the various features of paper ballots used with optical scan systems. Given the decentralization of elections, our research from 2002 and 2004 found great diversity in the graphic design of ballots across jurisdictions. A variety of ballot features can trip up a voter. For example, clutter around the candidate choices; complicated and or poorly placed instructions; and poor placement of ovals, squares, or arrows on a ballot can be sources of voter mistakes on ballots. Having candidates listed in two columns, as they were in the 2000 election in Palm Beach County, can increase the expected percent change in residual votes by 373 percent. Connect-the-arrow ballots increase the expected change in residual ballots by 21 percent (Kropf and Kimball, 2012: 85). Figure 8.2 is an example from Iowa in the 2004 election. It is notable for the poor placement of connect-the-arrow response options.

With ballot design, there are some aspects that are formal rules—state statutes dictate, for example, whether or not the state has a straight party ticket feature. The order of the candidates on the ballot is also dictated by formal rules. In addition, voting technology (determined by formal rules) constrains ballots. Federal law (the Voting Rights Act) determines that some ballots need to be in different languages. Yet custom and informal rules play a role. Many states such as Oklahoma and North Carolina do have a standard ballot design, but in many others, local election officials still design ballots. In 2007, the Election Assistance Commission (EAC) issued voluntary election design guidelines (design of polling places, election signs, and ballots).

Table 8.3 Availability of types of voting equipment used for regular in-precinct balloting, 2012

Technology	Description	Use in 2012	Use in 1996
Punchcard	Voter inserts aprescored computer data card into a ballot holder. Voter uses a stylus to punch the card to vote for choice.[a]	0.05% of voters	42.44% of voters[b]
Lever machine	Voter flips small levers next to choice. Voter sees all contests at once. Flipping one large lever at the end casts the vote and resets the machine for the next voter. Machine keeps track of votes.	Used only in small school district elections and special district elections in New York. This is not reflected in the EAC data because the study only examines election districts.	21.74% of voters
Hand-counted paper	Voter completes paper ballot. Votes are counted by hand.	0.61% of voters	1.34% of voters[c]
Direct recording electronic	Voter selectschoices on an electronic ballot much like an ATM (some machines have a touchscreen interface; some have buttons; some have wheels; and some have a printed log the voter can verify). The DRE will not allow the voter to overvote, or vote for more than the required number of candidates. Machine alerts voter of undervotes. Votes tallied in computer memory; transferred to election office	39.99% of voters	5.89% of voters
Optical scan, central count	Voter darkens an oval or square OR completes an arrow on a paper ballot next to choice. Ballot counted using a scanner in central location (county or town office).	8.32% of voters	14.99% of voters

(continued)

Table 8.3 Continued

Technology	Description	Use in 2012	Use in 1996
Optical scan, precinct Count	Voter darkens an oval or square OR completes an arrow on a paper ballot next to choice. Voter inserts ballot into scanner at the polling place. Scanner may alert voter if ballot is over- or undervoted. Vote tallied at precinct.	46.96% of voters	3.98% of voters[d]
Hybrid	Electronic system that prints voter choices on an optical scan ballot (hybrid of a DRE and an optical scan system)[e]	4.07% of voters	0% of voters
Mixed	More than one type of equipment used in a county	No comparable category	9.63% of voters

Notes: [a] A voter uses a stylus to punch the card to vote for candidates, and the "chad" drops into a small chamber under the ballot holder (unless the pollworkers have not emptied the chamber in which case the stylus often cannot completely push the "chad" out because the disposed chads are in the way).

[b] I include the Datavotepunchcard machines herein; they are similar, except with Datavote, the choices were printed directly on the card instead of in a book. They are no longer used.

[c] In 1996, my research with Stephen Knack aggregated townships into counties. It is probable that there are more in townships in Maine, Wisconsin, and Vermont who used hand-counted paper and fewer who used "mixed."

[d] Some states such as North Carolina had precinct count machines, but chose not to activate the precinct count function. North Carolina is classified as central count in 1996.

[e] Quote taken directly from the EAVS 2012 Survey instrument, at http://www.eac.gov/assets/1/Documents/2012%20Election%20Administration%20and%20Voting%20Survey_2.6.2012.pdf, last accessed May 11, 2015.

Source of utilization data: Election Administration and Voting Survey, 2012; and Election Data Services, 1996. State reports of in-precinct regular ballot voting. Excludes American Samoa, Puerto Rico, and Guam. Frequencies are weighted by the total number who cast ballots in the 2012 general election (2012 EAVS #QF1a). For 1996, the data are weighted by the total number of voters who cast a ballot in 1996.[14]

Includes by-mail-only counties (coded as central count optical scan).

Voting equipment missing from EAVS completed using state websites (Kentucky, Utah, South Dakota, some Arkansas counties).

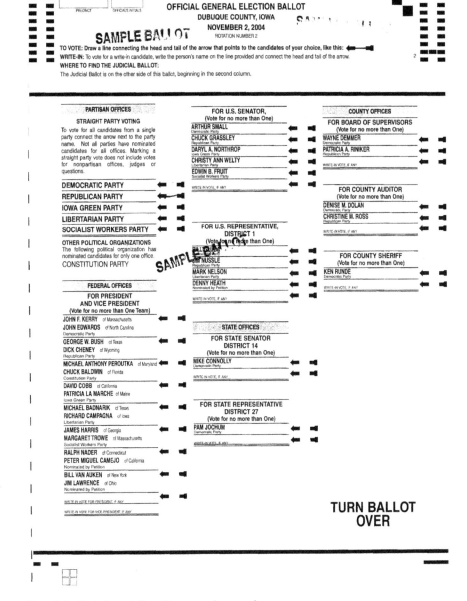

Figure 8.2 Optical scan ballot with connect-the-arrow feature

124

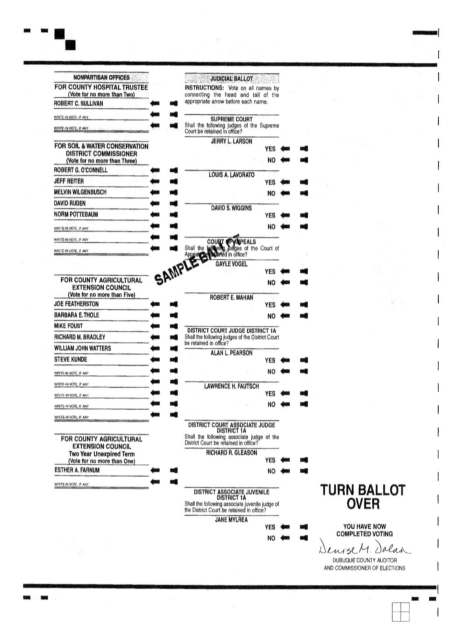

Figure 8.2   Continued

The EAC recommendations come from the AIGA's Design for Democracy initiatives (see Lausen, 2007). However, a report from the Brennan Center for Justice notes that Voluntary Voting System Guidelines have not "required vendors to fully support the ballot design recommendations made in *Effective Designs for the Administration of*

Federal Elections.[15] My research on ballot design in five states in 2010 indicated that only about 10 percent of the ballots followed the advice of the EAC and Design for Democracy (Kropf, 2014).[16] However, graphic design experts such as Dana Chisnell and Whitney Quesenbery have worked tirelessly to make election-related graphic design as useful as possible for local election officials. Using a Kickstarter campaign, they published a series of pamphlets called "Field Guides to Ensuring Voter Intent" (later some foundations also kicked in funds to publish the field guides). The first one was called *Designing Usable Ballots.*[17]

THE JUMP TO "MODERN" EQUIPMENT (ACCESSIBILITY, ACCURACY ... SECURITY?)

Shortly after the 2000 elections, several jurisdictions moved quickly to using "modern" technology. Georgia was the first to make a move, adopting all DRE equipment, followed by Florida, which adopted a mix of DREs and optical scan. There are many different types of DREs, but all have an electronic ballot (some have a touchscreen interface, some have buttons, and some have wheels; some have a printed log the voter can verify). The DRE will not allow the voter to overvote, or vote for more than the required number of candidates. As for optical scan machines, this voting format is similar to taking a standardized test in that the voter is supposed to darken an oval or square or complete an arrow. If it is a precinct count machine, there will be a scanner in the precinct into which the voter feeds the ballot. The scanner can alert the voter if he or she has overvoted or not voted in one of the contests (undervoted). Some scanners emit an audible beep and kick the ballot back, which may compromise the privacy of the voter.[18] ADRE may be easily adapted to provide accessible and independent voting for those with visual disabilities. Further, hybrid optical scan machines may also provide such accessible voting (Automark). Having accessible equipment became part of HAVA in 2002—the law required every precinct to have one.

However, according to some, gaining accessibility and increasing accuracy sacrificed security. Not long after the 2000 election and the rush to modern equipment, a number of reports were released concerning the security of the DRE machines— reports indicated it was not rocket science to hack into one and change the results.[19] Further, DRE equipment came under fire because officials could not double-check the election results (audit them) with a DRE because there was no paper trail. States such as Florida and Maryland backtracked on the decision to buy (or allow counties to buy) DRE equipment and purchased optical scan equipment. However, as reports later in the decade indicated, obviously, optical scan machines used computers to tabulate results; but because optical scan machines could be audited later (the voter does use a paper ballot which is—or at least should be—kept under lock and key).[20] However, for some states, the quick decision to move to DREs was costly. And even today, questions about the security of DREs persist.[21]

WHERE ARE WE TODAY?

According to election expert Kimball Brace, prior to 1980, no one kept track of what kind of voting equipment was used in all jurisdictions in the United States.[22] For a long time, state laws provided some parameters for the type of voting equipment that is allowed in a state. However, the final decision has traditionally been left to local election administrators (which, of course, follows from the history of voting as discussed in earlier chapters). Today, many more states are centralized in choices, or at least in certifying choices. Furthermore, in HAVA (see Chapter 4), the US government provided more than $3 billion dollars following the 2000 election for local election jurisdictions and states to replace old technology. Currently, optical scan machines and DRE machines are the predominant machines used in jurisdictions in the United States (although there are a few that have not moved to "modern" equipment—more in a minute). According to the EAVS Survey, as of 2012, approximately 56 percent of voters used optical scan equipment and 39 percent use DREs. About half of the jurisdictions that use DREs also use a voter-verified paper trail. In other words, as the voter is selecting choices, a printer prints the choices, and the voter can choose to verify from the printed recording whether his or her vote was cast as intended. The record is sealed inside the machine, and any record cannot be associated with any particular voter.

Although having a paper record sounds initially like a good solution for security, there are a couple of trade-offs to consider. First, disability rights groups have objected to the paper records because it makes it impossible for those who are blind (or unable to read) to cast a vote independently—they are not able to verify their own records. Second, research indicates that voters do not even check the paper records often. A team of scholars led by political scientist Paul S. Herrnson (2008) studied the usability of several different electronic voting machines. By usability, the scholars meant "the degree to which individuals find it easy to use systems and perform the expected tasks accurately and within a reasonable amount of time" (page 3). The team made systematic observations of how people voted on different voting systems, including voter-verified paper trails. Their research indicated that only a small proportion of their sample looked at the paper trail. Third, they found that paper trails added complexity. The authors noted,

> [t]he number of voters needing help is almost certain to increase, as is the time required for others to vote or to the number of voting systems needed. Vote verification units would create a significantly more complex task for voters who correct errors or who have become so confused by the voting and vote verification process they feel the need to start them all over again. Such added complexity may require more attention by poll workers.[23]
>
> (page 135)

The level of complexity and disability access issues did not stop about half the states from adopting the paper trail requirement, even though the similar federal legislation did not make it very far, according to political scientists Daniel Palazzolo, Vincent G. Moscardelli, Meredith Patrick, and Doug Rubin (2008).

> While VVPR legislation stalled in Congress, the idea swept across the states. Two states—New Hampshire and South Dakota—had adopted paper trail requirements prior to the enactment of HAVA, but between 2003 and 2007 legislatures and executive officials in twenty-nine states adopted VVPR requirements, most of them after the 2004 election ... Three states—Illinois, Michigan, and Nevada—adopted VVPR

policies in 2003, and in two of those cases (Michigan and Nevada), the Secretary of
State issued orders implementing paper ballots. Five states adopted the VVPR in 2004
(one, Missouri, by executive fiat), sixteen more in 2005, two in 2006, and three in
2007. VVPR legislation has been proposed but not passed in nine states and no such
legislation has been introduced in ten other states.[24]

(pages 524–525, notes removed)

There is, then, a trade-off if policymakers want paper trails. However, if few people
are examining the paper record, does it really help? Does it provide more security?

THE FUTURE?

Election officials worry that voting machines purchased in the wake of HAVA are
reaching the end of their usable lives; it is unclear who will pay for new equipment.
Furthermore, the Election Assistance Commission, whose job it was to set voluntary
standards, has been handicapped for many of the past few years because of the Senate's
refusal to confirm new commissioners.[25] The Presidential Commission on Election
Administration called the upcoming equipment replacement an "impending crisis":

> Well-known to election administrators, if not the public at large, this impending crisis
> arises from the widespread wearing out of voting machines purchased a decade ago,
> the lack of any voting machines on the market that meet the current needs of election
> administrators, a standard-setting process that has broken down, and a certification pro-
> cess for new machines that is costly and time-consuming. In short, jurisdictions do not
> have the money to purchase new machines, and legal and market constraints prevent
> the development of machines they would want even if they had the funds.[26]

(page 62)

The expense will potentially be quite large—for example, New Mexico just spent
around $12 million to replace its voting machines, according to the *Albuquerque
Journal*.[27] It should be noted that as the future unfolds, it appears that states are still
moving away from electronic voting. Some states—such as North Carolina—will move
away from DRE voting and use optical scan–only voting. Such a move was a part of
its large-scale 2013 voting reform bill.

However, research on new systems continues. Computer scientists have conducted
research into creating voting systems with different ways to provide security and ver-
ifiability, while at the same time, maintaining privacy. In particular, these scholars
have been working on "end to end" voting systems (e2e) that allow the voter to cast
a vote then verify it later on an official (government, in the case of an election) website. Computer scientists Claudia Z. Acemyan, Philip Kortum, Michael D. Byrne,
and Dan S. Wallach (2014) explain how the system works and attempts to make it
impossible for someone to sell their vote:

> In order to protect the identity and preferences of the voter, information that could iden-
> tify the voter is never associated with the ballot. Instead, e2e systems use a unique ballot
> identifier (such as a code associated with each ballot), allowing a voter to find and identify
> their own ballot while preventing others from being able to tell that the specific ballot

belongs to that individual. In addition, when a voter goes through the verification process to check that their ballot was cast and recorded, their actual ballot selections are never revealed. Rather, the voter may be shown another type of information that confirms that their ballot selections are recorded without disclosing the actual selections.[28]

(page 27)

The operation of these systems almost sounds like a spy novel. For example, the Scantegrity II system requires the use of a "paper bubble ballot, enhanced by traceable confirmation codes that can be revealed by invisible ink decoder pens" (Acemyan et al., 2014: 29). The systems are built to be similar to the ones that are used now, such as paper ballots. Not only are scholars working to create these e2e systems, but research is also continuing on how one might attack the system and, in some cases, provide an attacker with proof that the coerced voter is voting how the attacker intends, so a potential attacker could be foiled (Kelsey, Regenscheid, Moran, and Chaum, 2010).[29]

These types of systems have been used in real elections, but very few. In November 2009, Takoma Park, Maryland, used it for mayoral and city council elections. A team of voting technology experts assisted the city with testing the equipment (an Arbor Day election for the voters' favorite trees) and implementing the election. The team both observed and timed the voters and administered an exit survey concerning the experience.

> Quite a few voters did not understand that they could verify their votes on-line and that, to do so, they had to write down the codenumbers [sic] revealed by their ballot choices. Some explained that they intentionally did not read any instructions because they "knew how to vote." Others failed to notice or understand instructions on posters along the waiting line, in the voting booth, on the ballot, and in the Takoma Park Newsletter.[30]

(page 15)

Takoma Park used the system again in 2011. Again a team studied the elections using many different methods. Voters reported they were confident that the vote counted as cast. Takoma Park appears to be the only jurisdiction that has used the verifiable method of voting, although this equipment has been studied for its usability and continues to be studied. And e2e systems continue to be used for other elections that are not legally binding government elections. For example, one system, Helios is used for Princeton undergraduate elections.[31]

As it has been since the 1960s, voting equipment is still sold as separate technology in that local jurisdictions, for the most part, have technology produced by particular companies for voting and voting alone. That is to say, a local election jurisdiction generally cannot buy or rent laptops (or ask people to use their own) that are used for many purposes and install software on them. However, there are some experiments with commercial off-the-shelf technology such as iPads. According to the National Conference of State Legislatures (2012),

> [i]n 2011, Oregon voters in long-term health care facilities used iPads to select their choices. The iPad sent the selections to a portable wireless printer, and from there the printed ballot was handled like any other. The iPad is easier than paper for people with dexterity issues, and for those with poor vision. Colorado is running a similar experiment in its June primary.[32]

Many scholars and policymakers alike point out that the technology used for voting is far outpaced by the technology people hold in their hands. People are using smartphones and other advanced technology; as of late 2014, approximately two-thirds of Americans owned a smartphone.[33]

THOSE LEFT BEHIND?

However, the 2000 election did not force all jurisdictions to move to new technology. In the 2014 midterm election, 13 counties in Idaho used hand-counted paper ballots and 3 used punchcard ballots,[34] although as of May 2015, the Idaho Secretary of State's webpage indicates that no more counties use punchcard ballots. According to the EAC's Election Administration and Voting Survey, there were also more than 1,300 small townships in Maine and Wisconsin that used hand-counted paper ballots for Election Day voting; this represents fewer than 5 percent of voters in the United States.

Most people think that the old lever machines are completely phased out, but they are not. In 2010, the state of New York officially switched to optical scan from lever machines, but in the 2012 election, there were a number of administrative challenges with the optical scan machines, including handling voters displaced due to Hurricane Sandy. Those challenges must have left the New York City Election Board worried because they brought a proposal to the state legislature asking them to move the 2013 mayoral primary. The principal worry was over the speed with which they could determine if there had to be a primary election runoff (if one of the party candidates did not receive more than 40 percent of the vote, law requires a runoff).

> legislative leaders were unable to come to an agreement on how to respond to the city's request to move the primary to June from September, to allow more time for a hand recount of results if needed. But lawmakers decided that the electronic voting machines, bought after Congress required states to upgrade their voting systems to avoid a repeat of the Florida recount in the 2000 presidential election, had to be used in November.[35]

Not only that, but several New York villages, school districts, and special districts have (or can have) elections that are *not* run by county boards of election.[36] In such cases, the board of election "*may* permit towns, villages, school districts, fire, ambulance, water, sanitation, police and other special districts within the county to use voting machines [emphasis added]."[37] In 2012, more than three-quarters of the school districts were still using lever equipment, according to the New York State School Board Association.[38] The New York state legislature has voted more than once to extend the deadline for changing voting equipment for these districts. One of the sponsors[39] of the bill stated,

> Rather, the only way to ensure the integrity of every person's vote is to allow for lever machines when scanners are not available. This bill does that." Senator Martins continued, adding that original legislation provides "significant relief to local school districts, villages and special districts from the HAVA (Help America Vote Act) mandate that was intended to apply only to federal elections that have higher voter turnout and less annual costs to administer elections using optical scan voting machines."[40]

In other words, the state legislator was saying that the nonfederal elections did not have to comply with the federal law (the US Congress cannot regulate local elections), but that the voting equipment the counties did acquire was owned only by the counties. Lever machine parts are no longer manufactured. And although early research indicated that jurisdictions that used lever machines had lower levels of residual votes, the lower levels were at the top of the ballot. Toward the bottom—where bond issues might appear—lever machines had much higher levels of residual votes.[41] The most recent extension, as of this writing, was until the end of 2015.

CONCLUSION

It may be strange to think about graphic design or handwriting as a part of the electoral institution. Indeed they are. And, indeed, handwriting on voter registration forms or provisional ballot applications, as well as usability of voting equipment and ballots, can affect one's right to vote. Voting equipment and ballot design is where we really see many of the trade-offs in values. For example, some worry that computerized electronic equipment is not secure. Yet, electronic equipment helps ensure accessibility—not just to those who are blind or who never learned to read, but also to those who have conditions that make it difficult to complete an oval on an optical scan form or comprehend the words on a page. Furthermore, DREs can store multiple ballot forms, making it easier and more cost efficient to provide multiple types of ballots and to provide ballots in multiple languages. Research does continue apace on how to make equipment for a voting interface more usable, accessible, private, and secure.

The decentralization of voting and elections in the United States makes it possible to study and diagnose problems in the system. Scholars need to continue to study metrics such as provisional ballots, particularly if more states provide individual data. The 2012 North Carolina individual-level provisional vote data presented here are suggestive that there are racial differences. The provisional votes cast by African Americans are significantly less likely to count toward the total number of votes; African Americans in Section 5 counties are statistically significantly less likely to have their provisional vote count. However, at this point, these results are suggestive rather than definitive. One can and should study those data over time and across jurisdictions.

But finally, and most importantly, this chapter points to an apparent disjuncture in the way that Americans regard elections and what elections really are. As noted in Chapter 2, Americans regard the country, elections, and our democracy with a reverence that is something like religion. Such a view would point to the idea that elections should be pure and perhaps perfect. Every vote should count. Yet, Americans use imperfect methods to tabulate results of elections. The fact that failsafe methods such as provisional voting are necessary shows the imperfection of the system. Can this country do better? Yes: there are always ways to improve, but in an enterprise as large and unwieldy as a national election—or even a local election—votes can be lost. Nobody wants it to be their vote. However, as long as enough people believe in the legitimacy of the government and have confidence that their vote will count, that may be enough.

CHAPTER 9

CHOOSING VOTERS: REDISTRICTING AND RE-APPORTIONMENT

IF THERE IS ANY ELECTORAL INSTITUTION in the United States where the rules affect outcomes, it is in redistricting and reapportionment, yet it is one of the least understood parts of the electoral institution. The formal rules created in every state in the nation (each of the 50 states create districts in varying ways with varying laws) also affect citizen participation in electoral decisions. Citizen votes translate into public policy via representation at the federal, state, and local levels. Within states, congress members represent approximately equal numbers of individuals, but not between states.[1] Within states, state houses and senates are typically divided into equally populated geographic districts.

In the 1960s, a series of Supreme Court decisions determined that legislative bodies at all levels should be equally sized in terms of population. Thus, somebody must draw the lines to determine geographic districts of equal population size from which representatives are elected. Within cities and counties, legislative bodies are often also drawn into districts. One can probably imagine how policymakers may draw legislative lines to benefit themselves or hurt the electoral prospects of the minority political party: simply move the lines such that more core voters are in one district rather than another.

When our framers created this arrangement, they probably expected some clashes over choosing representatives. And, relatively recently, observers have called redistricting the "blood sport of politics" (see Engstrom, 2001, citing Aleinikoff and Issacharoff, 1993: 588), but perhaps hand-to-hand combat is not what is meant by that. The history of the United States does include occasional gun duels, but a voter in 2015 should reasonably expect that to be a thing of the past. Yet, bitter races can lead to bitter emotions.

The bitter race for a San Fernando Valley congressional district took a bizarre turn Thursday when Rep. Howard L. Berman (D-Valley Village) and Rep. Brad Sherman

(D-Sherman Oaks) got into a near-altercation during a forum at Pierce College. Video of the event in Woodland Hills shows the candidates exchanging words and Sherman at one point putting his arm around Berman, saying: "Do you want to get into this?" A uniformed officer then came onto the stage and appeared to ask that they move away from each other. Both men are vying for a newly drawn congressional district in what is considered one of the nation's nastiest congressional races.[2]

The framers and contemporary observers probably did not expect that public officials would be drawn into physical battles over the drawing of district lines. National Public Radio reported that these two incumbents were redistricted into the same district (double-bunked) got "nose to nose" at a candidate forum before "a shrieking college crowd."[3] In most states, state legislators draw the lines that create congressional districts, but in California, voters had decided through a pair of initiative petitions that a bipartisan citizen commission would draw the lines with consideration of communities of interest, which the second initiative petition defined. Yet, when all was said and done, members of the Republican Party filed four different legal challenges against the new district lines.[4] Why did that happen, and why did candidates nearly come to blows during an election year? Do the institutional decisions affect the ability and desire of citizens to participate in the relationship between representative and citizen? The goal of this chapter is show how our citizen representation is affected by the process and institutions public policymakers have created to ensure representation. Ultimately, it is a set of laws and rules surrounding redistricting that determines whether citizen votes really count or even whether a citizen chooses to vote. As such, this is probably one of the most important chapters in this book, practically speaking.

WHY REDISTRICTING?

The process of redistricting exists because we must have a way of translating voter turnout and voter choices into representation and actual policymaking. Because, for the most part, we do not have direct democracy, we must have a person "standing for" us when it comes to policy decisions. The rules dictate that representatives "stand for" the citizens that live in a particular geographic location, which has a given population. However, scholars have written vast amounts about representation, suggesting, for example, that there is descriptive representation (where a representative shares some trait with those who do not necessarily, but may, live in his or her district) or even that some individuals are not necessarily "represented" in a substantive way (individuals living in a district may not share the representative's policy views).[5] Typically in the United States the representative chosen is the one who wins the most votes in the district (single-member districts with first-past-the-post representation). The Constitution says we must do it after every Census. Our nation is a mobile one, so naturally some shifting of the boundaries is likely to occur every ten years; some states have begun to initiate the process even more often.

Yet, research indicates that these same decisions may affect the relationship between citizens and representatives: when redistricting, policymakers are naturally moving some people out of one district and into another. Districting decisions may affect citizens' knowledge about the decisions of the person representing them and therefore the ability of citizens to hold a politician accountable for his or her decisions in the ballot box. The quality of both substantive and descriptive representation may be disrupted, and ultimately, a citizen a citizen may choose not to vote in the contest because the cost of obtaining information is too high.

Incumbents do win. A lot. An often-cited problem with redistricting is the lack of competition in congressional races that results. The blame for the lack of competition is placed with partisan gerrymandering that benefits incumbent politicians and those who are members of the majority political party in a state legislature and who, in most states, have disproportionate influence over the process.

Despite the fact that the process of translating citizens' votes into representation lies at the heart of our republic (our indirect democracy), it is one shrouded in mystery for most citizens. Further, the process is plagued by politics, and the political elites who do not "win" in the process of redistricting have often used the courts to argue that they were treated unfairly. Sometimes, those in court really were *not* treated fairly … depending on how one defines fairness. Of course, with most election-related processes, redistricting appears to have had historical issues with race and racism. Consider North Carolina: it did not have an African American representative in Congress for nearly 100 years—from the 1890s to 1992, when district drawing allowed two: Eva Clay and Mel Watts.[6] It was application of the Voting Rights Act, in combination with court decisions that created two minority-majority districts, that allowed their election.

Thus, process seems to pit a variety of values we have in our representative democracy against each other. Because we are a republic, the first key value is representation. Citizens expect that their member of Congress (or state legislator or school board member) will articulate their views in decision-making bodies—this is substantive representation (Pitkin, 1967). Yet, as noted earlier in this book, a history of discrimination has resulted in some minority groups having very little say over who makes decisions. But others would go further and say that it is not just one's personal representative sharing one's views, but also sharing one's race. This "descriptive" representation expands beyond the simple geographic district, and the actions of minority representatives may also protect the minority from the majority and raise key concerns that the majority may not have considered.[7] The ability to elect a representative of one's choice is a vital part of citizenship in the United States.

> The redistricting process has enormous influence upon who is allowed full participation in the United States political system—it is centrally about the allocation of power in society, and it therefore should be analyzed to determine if constraints are embedded in its current structure that prevent some segments of the electorate from enjoying the "virtues of citizenship".
>
> (Webster, 2012: 2–3)

But also of key importance is being able to hold politicians accountable for the decisions they make; yet if citizens do not have enough information about the new person representing them, how can they hold the representative accountable? Still, even with some measure of accountability and ability to make decisions about one's representative in the voting booth, many observers point to the simple lack of competition in legislative races. In Congress, fully 98 percent of incumbents win, and there is seemingly little individuals can do about that. Because citizens also do not understand the process or even seem to care how the lines are drawn, Americans seldom influence the process that arguably should ensure that they have adequate representation.

TRADITIONAL PRINCIPLES DETERMINING REDISTRICTING

Congressional districts, which are not equal in size, violate principles of fairness that many citizens would articulate today. Yet, prior to the *Baker v. Carr* decision (1960) and a variety of other decisions (*Reynolds v. Sims, Westbury v. Sanders*, etc.), the equal-population standard was not necessarily a given; redistricting in state governments did not necessarily take place after every Census. Furthermore, the decisions stemming from *Baker v. Carr* indicated that courts had a place in determining the district boundaries (Cox and Katz, 2002). The rather ironic decision was that courts had a place in making a "political decision"—courts had rejected redistricting claims on those grounds prior to the 1960s cases. A redistricting "revolution" has taken place since the 1960s, when the US Supreme Court issued a decision concerning district lines.

A patchwork of different and seemingly contradictory values has emerged from the various court battles (Arrington, 2010). Most Americans probably think that "gerrymander" is a bad word, but creating districts that benefit one side or another or meet one or more goals has been the story of redistricting for the past 50 years.

One technical criteria of redistricting, contiguity, was implicitly intended to reduce gerrymandering and was widely viewed as a "race-neutral" criteria (Webster, 2012). For contiguity to be present, one must be able to travel to all parts of the district from any other part; there can't be a piece of one district inside of another. Webster relates that

> [a] district is contiguous if all of its parts are connected whether by land or water. For example, if a community of interest develops on either side of a river, a district could be delineated to include both banks even if there is no bridge physically located along the course of the river within the district.
>
> (Webster, 2012: 5)

Sometimes the connections between parts of a district are very narrow. According to the National Conference of State Legislatures, only 23 states required congressional districts to be contiguous; 47 required state legislative districts to be contiguous (NCSL, 2009; see also Webster, 2012).

Another technical criterion is often confounded with contiguity: compactness, which is the idea that a district is as efficiently drawn as possible (in essence, not weirdly shaped), which is one of the oldest criteria of redistricting, according to Webster (2012), and is there to prevent racial and partisan gerrymandering. Approximately 36 states require compactness of state legislative districts, and 17 require it of house districts. Court cases through the 1990s suggested that perhaps compactness could take a lesser role if the government had a compelling interest to advance, such as avoiding a violation of Section 2 of the Voting Rights Act (Tokaji, 2008; see also Chapter 4 in the present work). In the 1990s, the Justice Department first rejected the North Carolina General Assembly's plan, which had just one majority-minority congressional district, so legislators went back to the drawing board and created two majority-minority precincts. More than 20 percent of the state's population was African American and was scattered throughout the state, particularly in smaller urban areas up and down Interstate 85 in the center of the state (Canon, 1999; Tokaji, 2008). Scholars note that the North Carolina General Assembly (the majority of which was Democratic) also wanted to preserve Democratic control of the congressional delegation (Tokaji, 2008).

It was not surprising that the newly drawn plan was taken to court. According to political scientist David Canon, "The new 'I-85' black majority district was literally the width of the interstate in some places" (Canon, 1999: 111). South of the city of Charlotte, I-85 drivers would be in the twelfth district—until they exited the highway on either side (Morrill and Trevor, 1992; Canon, 1999). Journalists Jim Morrill and Greg Trevor wrote in *The Charlotte Observer* about the announcement of the new majority-minority districts, including the idea that it was hardly compact and the adjoining ninth district was barely contiguous. The ninth district was connected by the home of one voter:

> The 85-year-old woman is among 1,578 voters in a south Mecklenburg County precinct— but the only one not moving from the 9th Congressional District to the new 12th. ... She lives in a white house on Nations Ford Road a half-mile from the S.C. line. She votes in Precinct 77. But while the rest of her precinct shifts to the new, black-majority 12th District, her home and surrounding land will remain a bridge linking two sides of the 9th.[8]

Although state lawmakers had to yet again redraw the congressional districts during the 1990s, the final twelfth district still snaked down I-85, but was just a bit fatter in the middle (Tokaji, 2008). Ultimately, the result of the jurisprudence was that districting should be color blind and lawmakers could still take race into account, but any districts that appeared to do so would be inherently suspicious.

Another consideration is that "communities of interest" should—and in some cases must—be kept together; in other words, people who are alike should be in the same districts. Many states have elevated "communities of interest" into state law. According to the National Conference of State Legislatures, 20 states made this a criterion for state legislative districts in the 2010 round of redistricting; another 11 states considered it a criterion for congressional districts (Webster, 2012). However, policymakers have not clearly defined the meaning of this standard either. Political scientist Theodore Arrington suggests that "communities of interest" is "clearly the most elusive, of the conflicting redistricting criteria" (2010: 5) and argues that the courts "butcher" this concept. Communities of interest could be defined in many different ways—are people alike because they have similar ethnicity, jobs, incomes, education, social interests, cultural interests, media markets (watch the same TV, read the same newspapers), occupations, religious values, or maybe just shop at the same grocery store or stores (e.g., Arrington, 2010; Levitt, 2011)? Of course, many such interests transcend geographic community, especially with the rise in media sources such as social media and cable television.[9]

The final "traditional" criteria is that regarding preservation of the already-existing political geographic boundaries. That is to say, the boundaries of the district should be as consistent as possible with the boundaries of existing counties, townships, and cities. There is a traditional belief that geographies can be represented; those who share geography probably share political interests as well. Political geographer Weber (2012) notes that a justification for the standard is that elections are organized by local governments (counties or townships, as noted in Chapter 3 of this book). Furthermore, districts organized around existing boundaries are also more familiar to citizens and therefore are more recognizable. According to the National Conference of State Legislatures, at least 20 states articulate this standard for districting for Congress; 43 articulate this standard for state legislative districts. Weber (2012: 7) indicates this standard is often eschewed for "higher order and often contradictory goals." Weber argues that "compliance with the equal population or racial equity criteria is often of greater constitutional necessity than including whole cities or counties in districts" (page 7).

IMPLICATIONS

THE RELATIONSHIP BETWEEN THE REPRESENTATIVE AND REPRESENTED

All of the issues discussed so far are important, but what does the drawing of the lines have to do with citizens and voting? A growing body of evidence indicates that the way in which the lines are drawn may have powerful implications for those choosing to vote—at least in the contest for members of Congress. Consider this: Are voters able to hold their representative accountable for votes? Do voters know who is representing them? Does the process of redistricting disrupt voter turnout or engagement in the process of electing a representative? In terms of the themes proposed in this book, these issues should be front and center. Scholarship indicates that the institutions created for redistricting have a strong effect on citizen engagement. Interestingly, a great deal of research focuses on the prospects of incumbent candidates winning elections or the electoral advantage imparted to one party or another as a result of redistricting.

Some critiques of the current redistricting process highlight the idea that current institutions actually decrease competition and protect incumbents (particularly in the 2000s). This is one of the key arguments of those who advocate for nonpartisan redistricting, or at least redistricting that is not in the hands of partisan actors. Political scientists Antoine Yoshinaka and Chad Murphy explore the idea that redistricting may "foster electoral competition (which many find desirable) ... but also sever representational ties between constituents and their representatives (which many may find undesirable)" (Yoshinaka and Murphy, 2011: 435). Overall, they note that 92 percent of incumbents sought re-election in 2002. If the state had a partisan-redistricting institution (and the member of Congress was in the "out-party" not in control), 85 percent sought re-election, compared with 95 percent of in-party members of Congress). The 2002 data the authors examine are interesting. For bipartisan institutions, 94 percent sought reelection; for neutral plans, 90 percent sought re-election (page 441). Their results also show that, "[o]ut-party MCs were more likely to face a competitive reelection than were in-party MCs and MCs under bipartisan plans in 2002. It certainly does not appear that all MCs were equally protected by redistricting" (Yoshinaka and Murphy, 2011: 442).

However, there is contrasting evidence about competition and whether districting has an effect on candidate decisions to run; it may depend on the level of districting one examines and whether one examines the legislators over time or in one year (longitudinally or cross-sectionally). In examining both state legislative districting schemes over time in California and in two separate legislative sessions in state legislatures, political scientists Seth E. Masket, Jonathan Winburn, and Gerald C. Wright show that redistricting effects are not as simple as "gerrymanders decrease competition" or certain plans decrease competition. With divided partisan control, there is more likely to be incumbent protection, thus reducing competition. The authors indicate that

> [h]owever, when legislators under unified partisan control draw the maps, their results often actually increase competition, at least initially. Furthermore, the bipartisan 'neutral' commissions that some states have appointed to redraw their districts have seen less-competitive elections immediately following redistricting. However, these trends do not appear to hold with subsequent elections; we do not find evidence of clear long-term trends in levels of competition.
>
> (Masket et al., 2012: 43)

Masket and his colleagues did not find evidence that redistricting schemes affected decisions to run.

The types of institutions may affect the relationship between the voter and the representative, but the not-so-simple process of drawing the lines may vitally affect participation. Normally, voters do not hold much information about their representatives. However, recent scholarship has provided telling evidence that the redrawing of districts is key to whether a voter knows who to hold accountable. Political scientist Seth McKee theorized that redrawing district lines raises the information costs for potential voters; with his colleague Danny Hayes, he notes that "[i]nformation costs are among the most formidable barriers to citizens' political decision making and participation" (Hayes and McKee, 2009: 1008). After analyzing a decade of American National Election Study public opinion survey data, political scientist Seth McKee (2008) concluded that citizens living in a new congressional district (with a new-to-them incumbent) were significantly less likely to recall (state the name of their incumbent representative) or even recognize their member of Congress (McKee, 2008). In 1992, considering relevant factors such as education, on average, those who were represented by the same person were twice as likely to recall their member's name than those in a new-to-them district (page 970). Although the vast majority of citizens could recognize the name of the incumbents, on average, the probability of a citizen recognizing the name was lower, considering factors such as education.

Although it is clear that the major effects of redistricting are on being able to recall the name of the incumbent who is serving the citizen, McKee then took his study a step further with fellow political scientist Hayes. Examining the same survey data as the McKee (2008) study, they found that voters who lived in redrawn districts were less likely to vote for a candidate for the House of Representatives, even though they did turn out to vote. And, further, those who could not recall their incumbent's name were more likely to report that they had not voted for a candidate for the House, even though they had turned out to vote. Furthermore, looking at total precinct votes in Texas precincts (Voting Tabulation Districts[10]), Hayes and McKee found that roll-off (the number who voted for president or another top office but not for a member of House of Representatives) was significantly higher for voting districts in new-to-them congressional districts. The roll-off in participation appears to be exacerbated because Texas redrew its district lines three times in the 2000s; in fact, Texas was one of six states to redistrict multiple times during the decade, according to the authors.

Hayes and McKee (2012) turn their examination to the effect on minority voters, particularly African American voters, and expand their data to five states and 11 elections. They found that for precincts within redrawn districts, those with greater percentages of African Americans had higher rates of voter roll-off. However, they also found that when there is a new-to-the-precinct African American incumbent, the "negative effects of redistricting on participation are mitigated" (Hayes and McKee, 2012: 127). In other words, depending on the political context, they note that redistricting can increase or decrease the gap in participation among African American and White voters. This is especially key because 15 out of 20 of the congressional districts in the Hayes/McKee examination were majority-minority districts.

IS OPENING THE PROCESS THE ANSWER?

Common Cause is a "good government" group that believes the redistricting process should be transparent, fair, comply with the Voting Rights Act, and ensure citizen engagement.[11] However, "[w]hile procedural fairness alone does not guarantee that everyone impacted by redistricting outcomes will embrace the results, those charged with redrawing the district maps must at least adhere to an established, accepted set of rules and procedural guidelines."[12] However, inasmuch as citizens know little about who is representing them, particularly after redistricting, citizens know even less about the complex process of redistricting, and appear not to care.

With redistricting comes the raft of problems that affect the quality of democracy as cited throughout this book. Note that citizens simply usually don't care or know much about the redistricting process, largely because the process is difficult to grasp, and a large majority of Americans do not even know who is responsible for drawing districts in their state. Scholars Joshua Fougere, Stephen Ansolabehere, and Nathaniel Persily cite a general-population public opinion survey administered by the Pew Center showing that 47 percent of Americans responded that they didn't know who was "in charge of drawing congressional districts in your state." Another 11 percent of respondents guessed wrongly in trying to answer that question (Fougere et al., 2010: 328).

Examining the November 2005 ballot initiatives voted on by California and Ohio voters concerning redistricting gives us insights into how voters think about institutional design where redistricting is concerned. Voters there had the chance to take redistricting out of the hands of the respective state legislatures and put it in the hands of nonpartisan redistricting commissions. Yet voters overwhelmingly rejected both ballot propositions. Political scientists Caroline J. Tolbert, Daniel A. Smith, and John C. Green show evidence that institutional change can be a game—losers support change in the method of drawing district boundaries, but winners probably won't. However, any voter can be a loser at the congressional level in redistricting but a winner where it concerns the state legislative boundaries. They note that

> district-level winners—a majority of voters in both California and Ohio—are far more likely to favor the status quo (keeping partisan gerrymandering) than are electoral losers. Furthermore, since voters can be winners and losers at two different levels (statewide and district), there are multiple potential blockage points for the adoption of redistricting reform.
>
> (Tolbert el al., 2009: 105)

In a low-information, complicated ballot measure concerning redistricting, voters would have been inclined to preserve the status quo and vote no. According to an Initiative and Referendum Institute report, California voters had rejected three other initiatives transferring redistricting power to independent commissions (1982, 1984 and 1990).[13]

Ultimately, however, Proposition 11—the Voters First Act—passed in 2008 created a citizens' commission to draw the lines for the state legislative districts. A second proposition passed in 2010 authorized the citizens' commission to draw the congressional districts as well (Kogan and McGhee, 2012). "Perhaps most importantly, the experience of the CRC has shown that a nonpartisan, participatory, and transparent process does not eliminate the zero sum nature of electoral competition" (Kogan and McGhee, 2012: 27). In other words, they note that in the process, there are still winners and losers.

DO VOTES TRANSLATE TO SEATS?

If, in fact, voters as a collective are holding representatives accountable or are "hiring" representatives that will represent the majority of Americans, one perhaps should expect that the majority party of voters will equate to the ultimate party of representatives as a collective. A neuroscientist penned an editorial for the *New York Times* in early 2013 entitled "The Great Gerrymander of 2012" that reflected this perspective. Sam Wang wrote that

> [n]ormally we would expect more seats in Congress to go to the political party that receives more votes, but the last election confounded expectations. Democrats received 1.4 million

more votes for the House of Representatives, yet Republicans won control of the House by a 234 to 201 margin. This is only the second such reversal since World War II.[14]

He argued that "gerrymandering is a major form of disenfranchisement."

As surprising as this point might be to some *New York Times* readers, the votes cast and seats won by particular political parties rarely match. Scholars of redistricting have published numerous articles concerning the "votes–seats" relationship— "characterization of the way in which the partisan allocation of legislative seats responds to changing vote totals" (Niemi and Deegan, 1978: 1304). And, in fact, political scientist Richard Engstrom writes that our system of single-member districts (where typically the candidate with the most votes wins) makes it unlikely that seats will be allocated according to the collective votes. "When district-based outcomes are added together, it is unlikely that political parties win seats in proportion to the votes their candidates receive. Indeed, there is a well-documented tendency within the system for the party whose candidates receive the most votes overall to win a proportion of the seats that significantly exceeds its proportion of the votes" (Engstrom 2001: 9). Of course, the Engstrom quote addresses the issue of the party that wins the majority of the vote winning a large proportion of the seats. Yet in 2012, Democrats won the majority of the votes.

However, political geography scholars critique the "naive" approach of the *New York Times* analysis, which does not take into account human geography's effect on political outcomes. Political scientists Jowei Chen and Jonathan Rodden (2013) contend that the pattern of residence of Democratic voters is "inefficient" such that "when districting plans are completed, Democrats tend to be inefficiently packed in homogenous districts" (page 3). In other words, what appears to be a pro-Republican gerrymander is more likely a natural result of the fact that Democrats tend to live in large urban centers or are aggregated together into industrial areas. The logic, then, is that there are several overwhelmingly Democratic areas, but because Republicans are more dispersed, the districts might be majority Republican, but with enough Republicans left over to create another majority Republican district nearby. Largely Democratic areas are so closely clustered that a Democratic majority is a super-majority if the district is contiguous and compact. The scholars consider an in-depth case study of Florida, which was basically tied in the 2000 presidential election:

> In addition to being more internally heterogeneous, Republican precincts tend to be located in heterogeneous suburban and rural areas of the state where their nearest neighbors are more diverse. ... If one strings together neighboring precincts until reaching the population threshold for a district, this will usually require the inclusion of some rather heterogeneous precincts, often including pockets of Democrats in small cities or towns and on the fringes of larger cities.
>
> (page 7)

Using the logic of simulating many different possible districts with certain set districting principles programmed into the computer and then examining what the vote outcome would have been if the votes had been cast like Florida voters did in the

2000 election for president (where more than 500 votes separated the two major candidates), the authors show pro-Republican outcomes—in spite of a tied-vote outcome—resulting from procedures using geography and population equality. The authors conclude that the "Democrats not only waste more votes in the districts they lose, but they also accumulate more surplus votes in the heavily Democratic districts they win" (Chen and Rodden, 2013: 15). The authors write that they have data for another 20 states that indicate the same pattern as Florida. The problem is not as severe for the Democrats in the West and in the South.[15]

SO WHAT DO WE DO?

PROCESS: COMPUTERS AND REDISTRICTING

We have seen personal computing advance to the point that even citizens may create proposed districts that meet whatever criteria they input. According to redistricting experts Micah Altman and Michael McDonald (2010), redistricting may be automated or semiautomated, but any process requires some inputs as to what the key criteria for redistricting are. In other words, policymakers must still decide what value or values they wish to maximize and how those "values" (such as contiguity) should be measured. Altman and McDonald note that computers have made the process of redistricting faster, but have not necessarily reduced gerrymandering. "A difficulty with this approach is that seemingly neutral criteria may lead to biased outcomes; indeed, criteria may be chosen with a specific political outcome in mind" (Altman and McDonald, 2010: 76). At best, the use of computers may make the process more transparent; the advent of redistricting plans that allow any citizen to create his or her own plans have opened the door to more public, as well as interest-group, participation (page 77).

CONCLUSION

Simply put, the process of translating our votes into public policy is not straight-forward. It is an institution that affects both representation and participation, just like every other aspect of election administration thus far mentioned. Professor of law Justin Levitt has written that redistricting is an American institution that is inherently political.

> It is political in the colloquial partisan sense, in that this is the arena in which competing Republican and Democratic partisans have conducted their most pitched battles, jousting with each other to divvy electoral turf in the most advantageous manner. And it is political in a more inherent sense, in that multiple complex tradeoffs are required along multiple goals, with no outcome that clearly serves all of the population equally.
>
> (Levitt, 2011: 518)

Indeed, the institution of redistricting is a complex process with multiple goals that political actors trade off in order to create the institutions that enable democracy.

This process has changed over time, especially as courts became involved.[16] And the "traditional" standards of redistricting, combined with relatively new attempts to protect voting rights for minorities, have certainly been in conflict at times.

Ultimately, what will arguably have one of the largest impacts in future redistricting is the idea of majority-minority districts. Given that the Supreme Court has struck down Section 4b of the Voting Rights Act, Southern states must no longer clear districts through the Justice Department or the District Court of the District of Columbia. Although many Republican state legislatures may find a benefit to bleaching out districts and creating minority-majority districts anyway (or those near it), the strike-down of Section 4b may mean the end of such districts. Political scientist Richard Engstrom writes,

> [g]iven the majority-minority districts have been the major medium for the election of minority representatives in this country, due to the persistence of racially polarized voting, a reduction in the number of such districts is likewise expected to result in fewer minority representatives on governing bodies across the country.
>
> (Engstrom, 2001: 5)

In the future, expect redistricting plans to continue to be challenged in court as the United States continues to struggle with issues of race and representation in our institution of elections.

CHAPTER 10

IMPLICATIONS OF INSTITUTIONALISM FOR DEMOCRACY

THE VARIOUS WORKS OF ELINOR OSTROM have many complexities, but the fundamentals of the framework and theory are not difficult to comprehend. A key part? Knowing the rules of the game makes a big difference. Scholars Larry Kiser and Ostrom write (2000):

> Individuals cannot play a game without coming to a common understanding of the rules. Players must share a similar view of the range of allowable actions or the distribution of rights and duties among players, of likely consequences, and of preferences among players for alternative outcomes. Common understanding, however, does not imply equal distribution of information among community members. Some common knowledge of the institutional constraints is necessary for interdependent decision making, but participants may vary in their level of knowledge. Incentives therefore, may differ among individuals (even individuals with similar preferences) choosing within similar decision situations.
>
> (page 73)

Imagine two small children playing a made-up card game—the one who makes up the game makes the rules and, of course, the rules constantly evolve so she or he can win. If you have ever observed children, what usually happens is the other child throws all his or her cards up in the air and leaves crying. This is not a recipe for institutional stability. Elections are not games, but they have formal and informal rules and arenas of action (kitchen table, precinct, county/township, state and nation), and sometimes people are simply not allowed to participate or are unable to participate. Sometimes, there are sore losers.

The election system in the United States is an institution. There are shared rules and understandings, both formal and informal. Those in power try to stay in power: the degree of trust we hold for the leaders and belief in the legitimacy of the system makes a difference to the stability of the institution. Those who hold power occasionally change the rules. The effects of the rules may vary depending on the context within which the rule is made. The distribution of knowledge among the members of the institution about the rules may vary, as well as the degree to which individuals hold norms and values.

VOTER IDENTIFICATION DEBATE IN THE INSTITUTION

Thus, this concluding chapter serves to re-emphasize the main themes concerning institutions and the right to vote. Right now, photo identification laws for voting are in the courts and being hotly debated. Where and when the laws apply are evolving. However, I conclude with this current event because it demonstrates many of these themes: informal norms concerning security and some evidence of racial motivations (if photo identification was a neutral issue five to ten years ago, it has definitely evolved, given the way the debate about it has). In particular, the photo ID debate and related lawsuits have become what some scholars call the "third generation" issues in voting rights—or, as legal scholar Daniel P. Tokaji put it, an example of one of many election administration laws that are "the new vote denial."[1] For some, the issue might be framed: it is vote denial because poor and minority communities are less likely to have photo identification, and those without transportation (or no need for it) may be particularly affected. The issue might be alternatively framed: there is fraud. Even a little fraud is bad because it either disrupts the purity of the election or it cancels out legitimate (your) votes.[2]

VOTER FRAUD

The best and most useful definitions of fraud distinguish among different kinds of fraud. Political scientist Stephen Ansolabehere and law professor Nate Persily assess public opinion about fraud, analyzing perceptions of and reaction to three different types of voter fraud. The first concerns "illegal casting of votes by noncitizens or the casting of more than one ballot by a voter" (2008: 1744). A second form of fraud occurs when one voter casts a vote using the name of another voter (voter impersonation). The third type they note is vote theft, which they define as occurring once a vote is cast. This suggests that we consider first that "election" fraud and "voter" fraud are different. Differentiating between the two is key. Political science professor Lorraine Minnite writes that "[v]oter fraud is a sub-category of election fraud, or the intentional corruption of the electoral process by voters" (2006: 6). In a related report, Minnite continues,

> [t]his covers knowingly and willingly giving false information to establish voter eligibility, and knowingly and willingly voting illegally or participating in a conspiracy to encourage illegal voting by others. Apparent acts of fraud that result from voter mistakes or isolated individual wrongdoing or mischief making not aimed at corrupting the voting process should not be considered fraud, though sometimes these acts are prosecuted as such.[3]

Her scholarship suggests that fraud requires intent to commit, so an important related point is why do some individuals commit fraud? The answer seems rather obvious: winning elections, of course, when one does not believe one can do so through honest means. And, furthermore, if a person weighs the costs and benefits of fraud, it would take a rather large and very risky operation to change elections (Alvarez and Hall, 2008). Thus, Mexican political scientist Fabric Lehoucq adds to the definition of fraud the reason as being "clandestine efforts to shape election results" (2003: 233).

FRAMING FRAUD?

How do policymakers and the media (elites) talk about voter identification? What are the main themes? This is the idea behind "framing" of public policy issues. Scholars know a lot about framing and the way in which it influences public opinion. For example, public policy scholars have shown that talking about capital punishment in terms of "innocent people wrongly being punished" rather than "capital punishment is immoral or unconstitutional" is more likely to affect public opinion.[4] The contemporary discussion about whether or not states should require government-issued photo identification for voting has been, to say the least, controversial and partisan. Numerous scholars and media public opinion polls have established the partisan divide on identification, with Republicans in support and with Democrats in opposition.[5] As should have become obvious from reading this book, there are numerous examples throughout history of the use of "integrity" or "fighting fraud" or "voter suppression" frames to pass (or not) legislation that may be of benefit to one party or another (see Keyssar, 2000).

A case study is women voting in New Jersey. In New Jersey, from 1776 until 1807, women had the right to vote (if they were "of full age, … worth fifty pounds of proclamation money, clear estate in the same, and have resided within the county in which they claim a vote for twelve months immediately preceding the election …").[6] Historian Edward Raymond Turner showed in 1916 how the occurrence of fraud was used to justify a change in election law: women were committing fraud and should not be allowed to vote.

> Vehicles were used to transport the voters quickly, and throngs of outsiders were brought in to swell the number, spies going meanwhile to Elizabethtown to learn how many votes were needed. During this carnival of fraud women vied with men, and seemed to contemporaries to excel them. Women and girls, black and white, married and single, with and without qualifications, voted again and again. And finally men and boys disguised as women voted once more, and the farce was complete …. The jubilation of the victors was surpassed by the agonized appeals from the defeated. Each side accused the other of beginning the fraud, but the outcries of the vanquished were more prolonged and vehement.[7]
>
> (pages 181–182, 183)

The story of women voting in New Jersey seems every bit as political as discussions of fraud seem to the "vanquished" today. Turner concludes his scholarly work by noting that "[i]t is true that exclusion was owing partly to the fraud and illegal practices of some women voters, but these women were not worse than the men among whom they voted" (1916: 187). Women did not get back the right to vote until the federal constitutional amendment was ratified in 1920. Today, no one would say (hopefully) that women commit more fraud than men and should not vote.

Compare that story to one from current times from Fact Checker columnist Glenn Kessler in the *Washington Post*:

> One state lawmaker famously declared: "We must have certainty in South Carolina that zombies aren't voting."
>
> It turns out the claims of 953 votes by dead people actually involved not one election but 74 elections over a seven-year period. ... The report confirms what the State Election Commission had found after preliminarily examining some of the allegations: The so-called votes by dead people were the result of clerical errors or mistaken identities.
>
> In other words, no zombie voters—just egg on the face of the politicians who promoted these "facts" across national television.[8]

Even though laws affect turnout at the margins, with today's polarized politics, it may seem to citizens and policymakers (politicians) alike that elections are close and that laws will make a difference to winning and losing. Hopefully at this point, readers who chose to read all of the chapters in this book so far have seen that the history of voting is not just ideological, but also about the battle for power: the battle to win elections. Institutional theory would suggest that politicians (not just Republicans, not just Democrats) have the incentive to stay in power once they are in office. Although ideological debates continue about access to the electoral institution of voting versus integrity of the electoral institution, a quick look at history gives the savvy reader insight into why politicians may want to effect change (or not) in electoral institutions.

Certainly, more than one scholar has suggested that voting changes and "reforms" often have political goals. Historian Alexander Keyssar argues that political advantage is a key reason for both expansion and contraction of the electorate in the United States. In discussing the design of ballots in North Carolina, public policy scholars James Hamilton and Helen Ladd (1996) argue "[s]ince institutions are designed by individuals who have preferences over political outcomes, the technologies of aggregation are likely to be chosen strategically" (page 260). They conclude their research by asserting

> [t]he bottom line for policymakers concerned with election law may simply be an acknowledgment that in a system where ballot formats may have an impact on voter choices, the ability to design ballot formats may simply be one of the electoral advantages of incumbency.
>
> (page 277)

It is not surprising, then, that there has been a profusion of scholarship concerning why state legislatures pass certain election reforms and changes, including most recently, photo identification for voters. Public policy scholars Keith G. Bentele and Erin E. O'Brien (2013) analyze both the proposal and passage of what they (and others) term "suppressive voter restriction legislation" from 2006 to 2011. Their careful collection of data and multiple tests for whether their results are valid clearly

> demonstrate that the emergence and passage of restrictive voter access legislation is unambiguously highly partisan, influenced by the intensity of electoral competition. The fact that in the context of heightened competition Republican control increases while Democratic control reduces, the rate of restrictions passed underlines the highly strategic nature of these efforts.
>
> (Bentele and O'Brien, 2013: 1103)

However, they make clear that this is not a recent phenomenon, but the evidence they marshal concerning the types of legislation passed and the racial and partisan characteristics of states serve to indicate that procedures and rules for voting can be manipulated in such a way as to suppress voter turnout. [9] There is a variety of evidence about photo identification laws and their effects on the probability of voters turning out. There is certainly evidence that minorities are less likely to have identification (Barreto, Nuño, and Sanchez, 2009).[10] Scholarship seems to indicate that voter identification laws reduce the likelihood of voter turnout, but not necessarily disproportionately among minorities (Hood and Bullock, 2012, but see Alvarez, et al., 2007.).

The debate has become at least partially about race and racial attitudes, which, of course, are consistent with our country's history—as much as people may deny it, and even if the racism is not as explicit as it once was. Political scientist David C. Wilson and communications scholar Paul R. Brewer (2013) examined the factors that affect public opinion toward photo ID laws, in particular whether "racial resentment" affected opinion. By that they meant "negative beliefs about Blacks are tied to perceptions that they receive unjustifiable or unfair advantages and opportunities at the expense of Whites" (page 965).

> Support for voter ID laws is strongest among Republicans, conservatives, and those with higher levels of racial resentment, as well as with regular Fox News viewers and those who perceive voting fraud as common. It is especially strong among those conservatives who are most familiar with voter ID laws. Opposition is strongest among Democrats, liberals—especially those with higher levels of familiarity with the laws— and those with lower levels of racial resentment, as well as those who see fraud as rare.
>
> (page 980)

Interestingly, Democrats with stronger feelings of racial resentment had more support for photo identification laws. They also conducted an experiment within their public opinion survey asking a question about support for voter ID laws, but framed the question in differing ways based on ideas about fraud (pro-ID) or eligible people will not be able to vote (anti-ID).[11] There were high levels of support for photo ID among the various ways of asking about fraud, but asking the question noting the people who can't vote decreased support. All in all, level of information and cues from policymakers and the media made a difference. Informal rules seemingly affect the propensity to change formal rules.

The mass public and state legislatures, however, are not the only arenas of action where voter identification is concerned. The Department of Justice has brought lawsuits in federal court charging violations of the Voting Rights Act in North Carolina and other states. What many do not consider is the rulemaking procedures at the state level as well. Such rules represent the bureaucracy's way of implementing the laws passed by the political bodies of states. For example, as of this writing, North Carolina has issued proposed rules that tell precinct workers how to interpret the photo identification law. For example, what should the pollworker do if the person appears to have gained a substantial amount of weight?

> Perceived differences of the following features shall not be grounds for the election official to find that the photograph appearing on the photo identification fails to depict the person presenting to vote: (A) weight; (B) hair features and styling, including changes in length, color, hairline, or use of a wig or other hairpiece; (C) facial hair; (D) complexion or skin tone; (E) cosmetics or tattooing; (F) apparel, including the presence or absence of eyeglasses or contact lenses; (G) characteristics arising from a perceptible medical condition, disability, or aging; (H) photographic lighting conditions or printing quality.[12]

The state board of elections asked for public comments about the rules and planned on having public meetings all over the state; at the time of this writing, these were draft rules and could change, but they do say the ID should be essentially interpreted toward allowing voting. In the meantime, voting advocacy groups have worked to mobilize participants. An email read: "Unfortunately, some anti-voter groups want to make those rules so strict that they would disenfranchise a lot of people—as the rules have done in Texas and other states."[13]

The perspective of institutionalism is useful because it should cause scholars to realize there are many moving parts where elections are concerned. When policymakers create formal rules, they are creating them in an environment that includes norms and values that may create unintended consequences. Any law takes effect in context with many other laws—the idea of institutional complementarity explains it well. Political scientist Richard Valelly wisely explained how the Australian ballot had the effect of disenfranchising voters—and that policymakers probably counted on that. Furthermore, there are arenas to effect change in laws on many levels.

Photo identification laws come with baggage. First, evidence seems to indicate that requiring photo identification will keep some people from voting. Thus, the institution changes the costs and benefits of voting. Some will simply give up—such as a college student who misplaced her or his driver's license (or who changed addresses and did not have time to get a new identification). If an individual has plenty of resources, then the law probably seems like a good idea. Yet more than 600 people were not able to vote in the 2012 election in North Carolina, presumably because they were not able to return to the election office and show an identification (they were first-time registrants by mail and did not show an ID at the polls). It is unclear, however, how much in-person fraud there is. I do make the argument that office holders want to keep power, but there are much less risky ways of doing so than committing fraud—estimating how many votes he or she needs and then making sure he or she can mobilize all the people necessary to vote illegally and thus win the election. Why not just mobilize legal voters to go and vote once for him or her? In a big operation, there are always weak links. One would think it would be too easy to get caught. There are examples of fraud, but not the widespread examples that some rhetoric would have the public believe.

It seems clear that politicians have found ways to affect the vote by changing laws or framing actions in terms of our norms and values. It also seems clear that some political groups have figured out how to mobilize voters—in perfectly legal ways that involve lots of door knocking and interpersonal contact.

CONCLUSION

Understanding norms and other informal rules will prove very useful in the future study of election administration. Understanding the local election director or the precinct worker under the hypothesis that these individuals have a sense of civic duty that can manifest in different ways is important. It can help us understand that training precinct workers more effectively can fight implicit bias and prejudices they might hold. Institutional theory would suggest that even pollworkers have a role to play in the institution, but it is shaped by their predispositions.

As I noted in Chapter 1, many might argue that only those who are well informed and completely cognitively-able should be able to vote. Perhaps. But who decides that? Institutional theory should tell us that politics may very well get in the way of the objective decision, as it does in most policy issues. Politics has mattered since the beginning, and it will continue to matter.

Notes

Chapter 1

1. http://bensguide.gpo.gov/6-8/citizenship/index.html, last accessed August 13, 2014.
2. http://disability-abuse.com/doj/stephen-statement-lr.pdf, last accessed 10 October 2014.
3. http://disability-abuse.com/doj/eric-holder-letter.pdf, last accessed October 10, 2014.
4. Native American Rights Fund. 2007. "Lawsuit Charges Native Voting Rights Violated." http://narfnews.blogspot.com/2007/06/lawsuit-charges-native-voting-rights.html, last accessed December 18, 2014. For information about the settlement, see http://www.narf.org/cases/nick-v-bethel/, last accessed February 11, 2016.
5. http://www.gotvoterid.com/proof-of-citizenship.html#evidence, last accessed August 13, 2014.
6. See, for example, Raskin, Jamin. 2004. "A Right-to-Vote Amendment for the U.S. Constitution: Confronting America's Structural Democracy Deficit." *Election Law Journal* 3(3): 559–573.
7. The phrase "who are eligible" may be only three words in parentheses here, but defining that eligibility has been a major source of conflict in the United States and in other countries.
8. Those representatives then go and vote for law and policy in place of all the US citizens (or in place of certain geographically defined citizens, depending on the level of government).
9. I suspect that there may be some who argue that a "system" and an "institution" are conceptually different.
10. Tyler cites political scientist Easton for this idea, bringing the idea of diffuse or affective support into consideration.
11. Pildes, Richard H. 2007. "What Kind of Right Is the 'Right to Vote'?" *Virginia Law Review* (April 23): 43–50.
12. I should note that the phrase "one man, one vote" was originally more about the idea of dilution of votes via redistricting plans, or lack thereof, in Supreme Court cases.
13. The focus of the present book is election administration and the development of the right to vote. Although political parties and campaigns are certainly a very important informal and formal part of the election institution, they are not covered herein.
14. "New institutionalism" is a theory that many have used—and abused. Political scientist B. Guy Peters offers an excellent summary of different intellectual approaches to the theory. Many of the theoretical analyses are related to that offered herein: using norms or incentives to improve the electoral system. See Richard L. Hasen's (2010) review of Heather Gerkin's *The Democracy Index: How Our Election System Is Failing and How to Fix It*.

CHAPTER 2

1. Reed, Tina. 2012. "Election day specials, discounts planned around Annapolis today." The Capital, November 6, 2012, page A11.
2. Christians, Lindsay. 2012. "Table Talk: Free Food for Voters." The Capital Times, Madison, Wisconsin, June 5, 2012, accessed via Lexis/Nexis. According to that same article, a representative from the Wisconsin Accountability Board said that local businesses could not offer more than $1 in exchange for a vote.
3. See, for example, Mani, Ankur, Iyad Rahwan, and Alex Pentland. 2013. "Inducing Peer Pressure to Promote Cooperation." *Nature* (3), Article number: 1735; DOI:10.1038/srep01735, at http://www.nature.com/srep/2013/130426/srep01735/full/srep01735.html, last accessed April 23, 2015.
4. Gerber, Alan S., Gregory A. Huber, David Doherty, and Conor M. Dowling. 2015. "Why People Vote: Estimating the Social Returns to Voting." *British Journal of Political Science*, FirstView Article/April 2015, pages 1–24 DOI: 10.1017/S0007123414000271, Published online: October 20, 2014.
5. See Rice, Tom W. and Jan L. Feldman. 1997. "Civic Culture and Democracy from Europe to America." *Journal of Politics* 59(4): 1143–1172.
6. In considering new institutionalism, scholars such as political scientist Donald Searing discuss "role theory," the idea that the formal rules in institutions define roles (he articulates various roles in the British Parliament). His article, "Roles, Rules and Rationality in the New Institutionalism," published in 1991 in the *American Political Science Review* (Volume 85, No. 4: 1239–1260), discusses why a motivational role framework is key to the theory of new institutionalism and why a more structural view of roles in institutions does not advance our understanding of roles and new institutionalism. To define roles briefly, one way to think about roles is that they are positions that individuals hold. The structural view suggests that "[i]ndividuals are presented with roles that are built into an institution's structure and will continue to exist whether or not these individuals choose to play them" (page 1245), but Searing argues that individuals who hold the various roles vary, as do expectations for the roles among others. To make the parallel, think about the norms varying based on individual predispositions and on location (political culture).
7. Pew Research Center for the People & the Press Values Survey, April 2012. iPOLL Databank, The Roper Center for Public Opinion Research, University of Connecticut, at http://www.ropercenter.uconn.edu.librarylink.uncc.edu/data_access/ipoll/ipoll.html, last accessed November 13, 2014. Also, The Pew Research Center for the People & the Press. 2012. Trends in American Values: 1987–2012: Partisan Polarization Surges in Bush, Obama Years, at http://www.people-press.org/files/legacy-pdf/06-04-12%20Values%20Release.pdf, last accessed November 14, 2014.
8. Associated Press/GfK Knowledge Networks Poll, July 2014. The iPOLL Databank, The Roper Center for Public Opinion Research, University of Connecticut, at http://www.ropercenter.uconn.edu.librarylink.uncc.edu/data_access/ipoll/ipoll.html, accessed November 13, 2014. The question wording is: "We all know that American citizens have certain rights. For example, they have the right to free public education and to police protection, the right to attend religious services of their choice, and the right to elect public officials. The following questions are about certain obligations that some people feel American citizens owe their country. For each, please indicate your own opinion on whether you feel it is a very important obligation, a somewhat

important obligation, or not an obligation that a citizen owes to the country ... First, to vote in elections?"

9. General Social Survey 1984 Supplement. February 1984. Retrieved November 13, 2014, from the iPOLL Databank, The Roper Center for Public Opinion Research, University of Connecticut, at http://www.ropercenter.uconn.edu.librarylink.uncc.edu/data_access/ipoll/ipoll.html, accessed November 13, 2014.

10. Lepore, Jill. 2008. "Rock, Paper, Scissors: How We Used to Vote." The New Yorker, October 13, 2008, at http://www.newyorker.com/magazine/2008/10/13/rock-paper-scissors, last accessed August 14, 2014.

11. Washington Times/JZ Analytics Poll. August 2012. Retrieved November 13, 2014, from the iPOLL Databank, The Roper Center for Public Opinion Research, University of Connecticut, at http://www.ropercenter.uconn.edu.librarylink.uncc.edu/data_access/ipoll/ipoll.html, last accessed November 13, 2014.

12. Learn-Andes, Jennifer. 2007. "Voting Privacy Still an Issue." Wilkes Barre Times Leader, September 14, 2007, page 14A, accessed via Newsbank.

13. Apparently, there has been a long and spirited debate about whether or not there are local jurisdictions that actually hold elections to elect a dogcatcher. See Bump, Phillip. 2014. "A Brief History of People Who Have Actually Been Elected Dogcatcher." The Washington Post, June 2, 2014, at http://www.washingtonpost.com/blogs/the-fix/wp/2014/06/02/a-brief-history-of-people-who-have-actually-been-elected-dog-catcher/, last accessed June 6, 2014.

14. According to the Vermont Secretary of State's website, there is a local elected office of "listers." The website indicates that listers "[a]ppraise property within the town for the purpose of property tax assessment. Should be able to be polite, yet firm, and not be oversensitive to criticism." 17 V.S.A. § 2646(5), at https://www.sec.state.vt.us/elections/candidates/local-office-descriptions.aspx, last accessed June 6, 2014.

15. Harris, Sarah. 2013. "Run for Coroner: No Medical Training Necessary." Weekend Edition, National Public Radio, at http://www.npr.org/2013/11/03/242416701/run-for-coroner-no-medical-training-necessary, last accessed June 6, 2014.

16. http://www.aoc.gov/capitol-hill/other-paintings-and-murals/apotheosis-washington, last accessed July 16, 2014.

17. CNN/Opinion Research Corporation Poll, February 2010. Retrieved November 13, 2014, from the iPOLL Databank, The Roper Center for Public Opinion Research, University of Connecticut, at http://www.ropercenter.uconn.edu.librarylink.uncc.edu/data_access/ipoll/ipoll.html, last accessed November 13, 2014. To be fair, George Washington is not the only president held in high regard; in the same survey 26 percent of Americans reported that Abraham Lincoln had never "lied to the American public while he was president."

18. Scripps Howard News Service/Ohio University Poll, July 1994. The iPOLL Databank, The Roper Center for Public Opinion Research, University of Connecticut, at http://www.ropercenter.uconn.edu.librarylink.uncc.edu/data_access/ipoll/ipoll.html, last accessed November 13, 2014.

19. Kohut, Andrew and Bruce Stokes. 2006. "The Problem of American Exceptionalism," at http://www.pewresearch.org/2006/05/09/the-problem-of-american-exceptionalism/, last accessed July 16, 2014.

20. Gallup Poll, June 2013. Retrieved November 13, 2014, from the iPOLL Databank, The Roper Center for Public Opinion Research, University of Connecticut,

http://www.ropercenter.uconn.edu.librarylink.uncc.edu/data_access/ipoll/ipoll.html, last accessed November 13, 2014.

21. PRRI/RNS Religion News Survey, June 2013. Retrieved November 13, 2014, from the iPOLL Databank, The Roper Center for Public Opinion Research, University of Connecticut, at http://www.ropercenter.uconn.edu.librarylink.uncc.edu/data_access/ipoll/ipoll.html, last accessed January 20, 2016.

22. See for example, Parry, Janine, Jay Barth, Martha Kropf, and E. Terrence Jones. 2008. "Mobilizing the Seldom Voter: Campaign Contacts and Effects in High-Profile Elections." *Political Behavior* 30(1): 97–113

23. Gallup Poll (AIPO), September 1963. Retrieved from the iPOLL Databank, The Roper Center for Public Opinion Research, University of Connecticut, at http://www.ropercenter.uconn.edu.librarylink.uncc.edu/data_access/ipoll/ipoll.html, last accessed November 13, 2014.

24. McConnaughy, Corrine M. 2013. *The Woman Suffrage Movement in America: A Reassessment.* New York: Cambridge University Press.

25. The reader familiar with election policy will probably wonder why I do not explicitly mention the value conflict best illustrated by the Help America Vote Act (see Kropf and Kimball, 2013). I argue that implicitly, the ideas of duty to vote and purity of the ballot box imply access and integrity, but also that my research indicates that the political parties use these terms, but ultimately use them because they want to win elections.

CHAPTER 3

1. http://www.scstatehouse.gov/code/t61c006.php, last accessed October 28, 2014.

2. Initiative and Referendum Institute at the University of Southern California, at http://www.iandrinstitute.org/South%20Carolina.htm, last accessed October 30, 2014.

3. "2012 Presidential Election Results." The Denver Post, at http://data.denverpost.com/election/results/president/2012/, last accessed October 30, 2014.

4. "Editorial: Block the Vote, Ohio Remix." The New York Times, June 7, 2006, at http://www.nytimes.com/2006/06/07/opinion/07wed1.html?_r=0, last accessed July 22, 2014.

5. Brace, Kimball. 2013. "Election Administration Basics: A Summary of Findings." Election Data Services, Inc., at https://www.electiondataservices.com/research-services/, last accessed January 29, 2015.

6. See Foley, Edward B. 2006. "The Legitimacy of Imperfect Elections: Optimality, Not Perfection, Should Be the Goal of Election Administration" in Andrew Rachlin (ed.) *Making Every Vote Count: Federal Election Legislation in the States.* Princeton: Princeton University Press.

7. Despite this language, Douglas notes that many state-level courts defer to the federal constitution (or are in lockstep) when it comes to the minimal federal protections of the "right to vote." Also, I should note that in 2014, Illinois voters considered a constitutional amendment guaranteeing the "right to vote" (more specifically, "… would prohibit any law that disproportionately affects the rights of eligible Illinois citizens to register to vote or cast a ballot based on the voter's race, color, ethnicity, status as a member of a language minority, national origin, religion, sex, sexual orientation, or income"). Observers believed that such language would prevent the state legislature from passing a strict voter photo identification law (see "Thumbs Up—And Down—For Five Questions on the Ballot." Chicago Sun Times, Web Edition, November 1, 2014. Accessed via Newsbank January 8, 2015.

8. http://reports.oah.state.nc.us/ncac.asp?folderName=\Title%2008%20-%20Elections, last accessed January 8, 2005.

9. See Gerken, Heather. 2009 and 2012. *The Democracy Index: Why Our Election System Is Failing and How to Fix It.* Princeton: Princeton University Press.

10. Pew Center on the States. 2014. Elections Performance Index, at http://www.pewtrusts. org/en/multimedia/data-visualizations/2014/elections-performance-index#indicator Profile-CPD, last accessed January 9, 2015.

11. Information about state rulemaking procedures can be found at the National Association of Secretaries of State, Administrative Codes and Registers Section, at http:// www.administrativerules.org/administrative-rules/, last accessed July 22, 2014.

12. 08 NCAC 04 .0305 INSTRUCTION OF PRECINCT OFFICIALS AND VOTERS IN THE USE OF VOTING SYSTEMS, AT HTTP://REPORTS.OAH.STATE. NC.US/NCAC/TITLE%2008%20-%20ELECTIONS/CHAPTER%2004%20-%20 VOTING%20EQUIPMENT/08%20NCAC%2004%20.0305.HTML, last accessed March 24, 2016.

13. "Editorial: Block the Vote, Ohio Remix." The New York Times, June 7, 2006, at http:// www.nytimes.com/2006/06/07/opinion/07wed1.html?_r=0, last accessed July 22, 2014.

14. Douglas, Joshua A. 2014. "The Right to Vote Under State Constitutions." *Vanderbilt Law Review* 67(1): 89–149.

15. Blythe, Anne. 2015. "Critics of NC's Voter ID Law to Present Their Case in Court Friday." *The Charlotte Observer*, January 29, 2015, at http://www.charlotteobserver. com/2015/01/29/5481074/critics-of-ncs-voter-id-law-to.html#.VNkLBU05CM8, last accessed February 9, 2015.

16. *Weinschenk v. State*, 203 S.W.3d 201 (Mo. 2006), at http://moritzlaw.osu.edu/electionlaw/ litigation/documents/Jackson_Opinion.pdf, last accessed February 10, 2015.

17. The Supreme Court struck down the formula which defined jurisdictions that had to receive pre-approval for voting law changes (because of a history of voter discrimination) in 2013. This research was conducted before that case. Please see Chapter 4.

18. The Pew Center on the States' Election Initiative staff examined the level of pollworker pay in the country's largest jurisdictions and found that pay in the most populous areas ranged from under $100 to up to $300, depending on experience of the pollworkers. See Dispatch: Pollworker Pay. October 17, 2012, at https://www.supportthevoter.gov/ files/2013/08/Poll-Worker-Pay-Election-Data-Dispatches.pdf, last accessed January 14, 2015.

19. U.S. Election Assistance Commission. 2013. *The 2012 Election Administration and Voting Survey: A Summary of Key Findings*, at http://www.eac.gov/assets/1/Page/ 990-050%20EAC%20VoterSurvey_508Compliant.pdf, last accessed January 14, 2015.

20. Burden, Barry C. and Jeffrey Milyo. 2013. "The Recruitment and Training of Pollworkers: What We Know From Scholarly Research." Report prepared for The Presidential Commission on Election Administration, September 6, 2013, at https://www.supportthevoter.gov/files/2013/09/The-Recruitment-and-Training- of-Poll-Workers-Burden-and-Milyo.pdf, last accessed January 14, 2015.

21. Seligson, Daniel. 2001. "Election Administrators Struggle with Workforce Problem," at http://www.pewtrusts.org/en/research-and-analysis/blogs/stateline/2001/04/24/election- administrators-struggle-with-workforce-problem, last accessed January 14, 2015; see also The National Commission on Federal Election Reform. "To Assure Pride and Confidence in the Electoral Process," at http://web1.millercenter.org/commissions/ comm_2001.pdf, last accessed January 14, 2015.

22. Federal law only says that first-time voters who registered by mail must show a picture ID, but state law determines the level of identification required beyond that.

23. Atkeson, L. R., L. A. Bryant, T. E. Hall, K. Saunders, and M. Alvarez. 2010. "A New Barrier to Participation: Heterogeneous Application of Voter Identification Policies." *Electoral Studies* 29(1): 66–73.

24. "Inactive" voters are defined in Massachusetts as those who have not voted recently and who did not respond to local census forms (see Cobb et al., 2010: 5). However, the perceptive reader will note that it is highly likely that every state has differing laws concerning what an "inactive voter" is.

25. Presidential Commission on Election Administration commissioner and former Maricopa County Election Department's federal compliance officer Tammy Patrick provided a detailed breakdown of the state law in Arizona and how the costs of elections are divided among various jurisdictions.

26. Hawkins, Ernest. 2001. "Cost and Finance of Elections." Paper presented to CalTech-MIT/Voting Technology Conference 2001, March 30, 2001, at http://people.hss. caltech.edu/~voting/hawkins_present.pdf, last accessed February 18, 2015.

27. Patrick, Tammy. 2010. "What Does an Election Cost and Why?" Maricopa County Elections Department Community Network Meeting, January 27, 2010. PowerPoint slides on file with author and available upon request.

CHAPTER 4

1. The Carter Center. Observing Kenya's March 2013 National Elections: Final Report, at http://www.cartercenter.org/resources/pdfs/news/peace_publications/election_reports/kenya-final-101613.pdf, last accessed April 6, 2013.

2. The Carter Center. Observing Elections, at http://www.cartercenter.org/resources/pdfs/factsheets/elections-facts.pdf, last accessed April 6, 2015.

3. Liptak, Adam. 2013. "Voting Rights Act Challenged as Cure the South Has Outgrown." *The New York Times*, February 17, 2013, at http://www.nytimes.com/2013/02/18/us/politics/supreme-court-to-hear-alabama-countys-challenge-to-voting-rights-act.html?_r=0, last accessed April 6, 2015.

4. Kirby, Brendan. 2013. "Evergreen Mayor Wins Re-Election, Racial Makeup of Council Stays the Same." Alabama Media Group, June 18, 2013, at http://blog.al.com/live/2013/06/evergreen_mayor_wins_re-electi.html, last accessed April 6, 2015.

5. Liptak, Adam. 2014. "Judge Reinstates Some Federal Oversight of Voting Practices for an Alabama City." The New York Times, January 14, 2014, at http://www.nytimes.com/2014/01/15/us/judge-reinstates-federal-oversight-of-voting-practices-for-alabama-city.html, last accessed April 6, 2014.

6. Brendan, Kirby. 2013. "Rejecting Race Allegations Evergreen to Oppose Continued Scrutiny in Municipal Elections." Alabama Media Group, August 6, 2013, at http://blog.al.com/live/2013/08/rejecting_race_allegations_eve.html, last accessed April 6, 2015.

7. There are actually different programs for observation and examination. See http://www.justice.gov/crt/about/vot/examine/activ_exam.php, last accessed April 22, 2015. See also http://www.usccr.gov/pubs/051006VRAStatReport.pdf, last accessed April 22, 2015.

8. Allen v. City of Evergreen, Alabama, Case No.: 1:12:CV-00496-CB-M. at http://www.gpo.gov/fdsys/pkg/USCOURTS-alsd-1_12-cv-00496/pdf/USCOURTS-alsd-1_12-cv-00496-0.pdf, last accessed April 6, 2015.

9. Office of Public Affairs, Department of Justice. November 3, 2014, at http://www.justice.gov/opa/pr/justice-department-announces-ground-monitoring-polling-places-18-states-election-day-0, last accessed April 6, 2015.

10. In Louisiana, the counties are called "parishes."

11. Evergreen, Alabama (Conecuh County); Alameda, California; St. Landry, Louisiana; Colfax, Nebraska (order expired March 30, 2015); and Orange County, New York and Port Chester, New York (Orange County). See Civil Rights Division, United States Department of Justice. About Federal Observers and Election Monitoring, at http://www.justice.gov/crt/about/vot/examine/activ_exam.php, last accessed April 6, 2015.

12. *United States v. Orange County (New York) Board of Elections*, Consent Decree, at http://www.justice.gov/usao/nys/pressreleases/April12/occ/usvorangecountyconsentdecree.pdf, last accessed April 6, 2015.

13. The reader will see later in this chapter that the Election Assistance Commission provided federal dollars for modernized equipment on which voters could cast ballots in the mid-2000s. However, as that equipment ages out, as of this writing, the federal government may not be providing such funding again. Furthermore, there have been a number of congressional efforts to eliminate the EAC. See Coleman, Kevin J. and Eric A. Fischer. 2015. "The Help America Vote Act and Election Administration: Overview and Issues." Congressional Research Service, at http://fas.org/sgp/crs/misc/RS20898.pdf, last accessed April 26, 2015.

14. Hale, Kathleen and Mitchell Brown. 2013. "Adopting, Adapting, and Opting Out: State Response to Federal Voting System Guidelines." *Publius: The Journal of Federalism* 43(3): 428–451. See also Hale, Kathleen, Robert Montjoy and Mitchell Brown. 2015. *Administering Elections: How American Elections Work*. New York: Palgrave.

15. See http://www.justice.gov/crt/about/vot/, last accessed January 22, 2015.

16. See Ewald, Alec C. 2009. *The Way We Vote: The Local Dimension of American Suffrage*. Nashville: Vanderbilt University Press.

17. Pildes, Richard. 2006. "Introduction" in David L. Epstein, Richard H. Pildes, Rodolfo O. de la Garza, and Sharyn O'Halloran (eds.) *The Future of the Voting Rights Act*. Russell Sage Foundation: New York.

18. This characterization was stated by President Ronald Reagan. See Ifill, Sherrilyn. 2015. "Celebrating Selma without Fixing the Voting Rights Act Dishonors the Sacrifices of Bloody Sunday." The New York Times, March 9, 2015, at http://www.latimes.com/opinion/op-ed/la-oe-ifill-voting-rights-act-amendment-bloody-sunday-20150310-story.html, last accessed March 11, 2015.

19. Grofman, Bernard, Lisa Handley and Richard G. Niemi. 1992. *Minority Representation and the Quest for Voting Equality*. Cambridge: Cambridge University Press: page 16.

20. Pildes, Richard. 2006. "The Future of Voting Rights Policy: From Anti-Discrimination to the Right to Vote." *Howard Law Journal* 49(3): 741–765, page 744.

21. Daniel P. Tokaji. 2006. "If It's Broke, Fix It: Improving Voting Rights Act Preclearance." *Howard Law Journal* 49(3): 785–842.

22. There had been previous attempts to enforce the Fourteenth and Fifteenth Amendments at the national level in the form of both court cases and legislation passed to implement the franchise for Black Americans.

23. The US Commission on Civil Rights. 2006. Voting Rights Enforcement and Reauthorization: The Department of Justice's Record of Enforcing the Temporary Voting Rights Act Provisions, at http://www.usccr.gov/pubs/051006VRAStatReport.pdf, last accessed April 23, 2015. The report quotes Department of Justice rulemaking implementing Section 5.

24. Hasen, Richard L. 2006. "Congressional Power to Renew Preclearance Provisions" in David L. Epstein, Richard H. Pildes, Rodolfo O. de la Garza, and Sharyn O'Halloran (eds.) *The Future of the Voting Rights Act*. New York: Russell Sage Foundation.

25. *South Carolina v. Katzenbach*, 383 U.S. 301 (1996).

26. Ansolabehere, Stephen, Nathaniel Persily, and Charles Stewart III. 2013. "Regional Differences in Racial Polarization in the 2012 Presidential Election: Implications for the Constitutionality of Section 5 of the Voting Rights Act." *Harvard Law Review Forum* 126: 205–220.

27. See House Bill 589/S.L. 2013-3681, VIVA/Election Reform, 2013–2014 Session, North Carolina General Assembly, at http://www.ncga.state.nc.us/gascripts/BillLookUp/BillLookUp.pl?Session=2013&BillID=h%20+589&submitButton=Go, last accessed April 26, 2015.

28. The Voting Rights Act of 1965, §2 42 U.S.C. § 1973.

29. For more discussion of this idea, see Stephanopoulos, Nicholas. 2013. "The South After Shelby County." The University of Chicago Law School Public Law and Legal Theory Working Paper No. 451, at http://chicagounbound.uchicago.edu/cgi/viewcontent.cgi?article=1436&context=public_law_and_legal_theory, last accessed April 24, 2015.

30. Katz, Ellen; with Margaret Aisenbrey, Anna Baldwin, Emma Bheuse, and Anna Weisbrodt. 2006. "Documenting Discrimination in Voting: Judicial Findings Under Section 2 of the Voting Rights Act Since 1982: Final Report of the Voting Rights Initiative, University of Michigan Law School." *University of Michigan Journal of Law Reform* 39(4): 643–772, Available at SSRN: http://ssrn.com/abstract=1029386.

31. Local governments often elect representatives on an at-large basis. That is, voters from all over the jurisdiction are able to vote for the representatives and typically have as many votes as there are seats on the local government body (see Engstrom, 2001)

32. Bureau of the Census, Department of Commerce. Federal Register / Vol. 76, No. 198 / Thursday, October 13, 2011 / Notices, at http://www.justice.gov/crt/about/vot/sec_203/2011_notice.pdf, last accessed April 6, 2015.

33. CNN Poll, June 2006. Retrieved from the iPOLL Databank, The Roper Center for Public Opinion Research, University of Connecticut, at http://www.ropercenter.uconn.edu.librarylink.uncc.edu/data_access/ipoll/ipoll.html, last accessed December 19, 2014.

34. Asian American Legal Defense and Education Fund. 2012. "Language Access for Asian Americans Under the Voting Rights Act in the 2012 Election," at http://aaldef.org/AALDEF%20Election%202012%20Interim%20Report.pdf, last accessed December 17, 2014, page 8.

35. Bovbjerg, Barbara. 2013. Voters with Disabilities: Challenges to Accessibility. Statement before the National Council on Disability, April 23, 2013, Washington, DC: General Accounting Office, at http://gao.gov/assets/660/654099.pdf, last accessed January 22, 2015.

36. Kansas and Arizona secretaries of state both filed suit against the Election Assistance Commission in 2013 because the federal voter registration form does not require proof that the person registering is a US citizen. In Kansas, more than 15,000 registrants would be only allowed to vote in federal races unless they could prove their citizenship. See Marso, Andy. 2013. "Kobach, Arizona Counterpart Sue Federal Commission." Topeka Capital-Journal, August 21, 2013, at http://cjonline.com/news/2013-08-21/kobach-arizona-counterpart-sue-federal-commission, last accessed January 7, 2015. The American Civil Liberties Union filed a countersuit challenging the system in November 2013. See "Kansas Group, Voters Sue Kobach Over Registration

Rules." The Kansas City Star, November 21, 2013, at http://www.kansascity.com/news/local/article332245/Kansas-group-voters-sue-Kobach-over-registration-rules.html, last accessed January 7, 2015. The EAC does list separate instructions for each state, but does not mention proof of citizenship provisions. See http://www.eac.gov/voter_resources/register_to_vote.aspx, last accessed January 7, 2015.

37. Piven, Frances Fox and Richard A. Cloward. 1988. "National Voter Registration Reform: How It Might Be Won." *PS: Political Science and Politics* 21(4): 868–875. Stable URL: http://www.jstor.org/stable/420026.

38. Hess, Douglas R. and Scott Novakowski. 2008. Neglecting the National Voter Registration Act, 1995–2007. Project Vote and Demos, at http://www.projectvote.org/images/publications/NVRA/Unequal_Access_Final.pdf, last accessed January 24, 2015.

39. Federal Voting Assistance Program. 1964. Post Election Survey Report to Congress (Fifth Report), at http://www.fvap.gov/uploads/FVAP/Reports/5threport.pdf, last accessed April 29, 2015.

40. According to the Election Assistance Commission, "UOCAVA covers voting by members of the seven uniformed services and their eligible dependents; members of the U.S. Merchant Marine and their eligible dependents; Commissioned Corps of the U.S. Public Health Service and the National Oceanic and Atmospheric Administration; and U.S. citizens residing outside the United States. Under UOCAVA, States and territories are to provide a means for these citizens to register and to vote in elections for Federal office using absentee procedures." See http://www.eac.gov/assets/1/Documents/508compliant_Main_91_p.pdf, last accessed December 15, 2014, page 1.

41. Coleman, Kevin T. 2014. The Uniformed and Overseas Citizens Absentee Voting Act: Overview and Issues, Congressional Research Service, April 21, 2014, at http://www.fas.org/sgp/crs/misc/RS20764.pdf, last accessed April 29, 2015.

42. For more information about overseas voting, see Pew Center on the States. 2012. "Pew: New Reforms in 47 States and D.C. Improve Military and Overseas Voting," at http://www.pewtrusts.org/en/about/news-room/press-releases/2012/01/27/pew-new-reforms-in-47-states-and-dc-improve-military-and-overseas-voting, last accessed January 9, 2015.

43. 20 U.S. Code § 1094(a)(23)(A).

44. The NVRA indicates that states may designate other state agencies such as colleges and universities as voter registration agencies, but the Higher Education Act specified that the schools must provide the forms if they wish to participate in federal aid programs. See http://www.justice.gov/crt/about/vot/nvra/nvra_faq.php, last accessed January 15, 2015.

45. For more information, see Kropf, Martha and David Kimball. 2012. *Helping America Vote? The Limits of Election Reform*. Routledge.

46. Hale and Brown (2013) explain the federal government has had a long-standing involvement with the standards for certification of voting equipment. From the mid-1970s until the establishment of the Election Assistance Commission, the Federal Election Commission and the National Association of State Election Directors worked together on certification and standards (see also Saltman, 2006).

47. See for example, Bartlett, Gary O. 2010. Health and Human Services Accessibility: HAVA Grants in North Carolina. North Carolina State Board of Elections, at https://www.ncsbe.gov/ncsbe/Portals/0/FilesP/HAVAAccessibilityNASED.pdf, last accessed February 26, 2015.

48.   Kropf and Kimball (2012) note that "the law also allowed grant funds to be used for such activities as recruiting and training election officials and poll workers; educating voters; and assuring access for voters with physical disabilities. The federal legislation also required states to establish an administrative grievance process to handle voters' complaints. In order to take advantage of the grants, states were required to appropriate a 5% match and submit a state plan detailing how the funds would be spent and how the state would meet the new federal requirements" (page 25).

49.   Coleman, Kevin J. and Eric A. Fisher. 2014. *The Help America Vote Act and Election Administration: Overview and Issues*, December 17, 2014, Congressional Research Service, at http://www.fas.org/sgp/crs/misc/RS20898.pdf, last accessed January 8, 2015.

50.   Because the policy deals mostly with registration problems, those states with Election Day registration or with no voter registration (North Dakota) were not required under federal law to have this program.

51.   Sherman, Jon. 2014. *Saving Votes: An Easy Fix to the Problem of Wasting Provisional Ballots Cast Out of Precinct*. Fair Elections Legal Network, at http://fairelectionsnetwork.com/sites/default/files/Provisional%20Ballot%20Rejection%20Memo%20FINAL.pdf, last accessed January 9, 2015.

52.   HAVA, Section 303a1B.

53.   See National Research Council. 2009. Improving State Voter Registration Databases, Final Report, at http://www.eac.gov/assets/1/Page/Improving%20State%20Voter%20Registration%20Databases.pdf, last accessed January 15, 2015.

54.   Such an effort would be similar to the National Driver Register, wherein states report "information about drivers who have had their licenses revoked or suspended, or who have been convicted of serious traffic violations such as driving while impaired by alcohol or drugs. State motor vehicle agencies provide NDR with the names of individuals who have lost their privileges or who have been convicted of a serious traffic violation." See http://www.nhtsa.gov/Data/National+Driver+Register+(NDR), last accessed January 20, 2015.

55.   National Research Council of the National Academies of Science. 2009. Improving State Registration Databases: Final Report, at http://www.eac.gov/assets/1/Page/Improving%20State%20Voter%20Registration%20Databases.pdf, last accessed January 20, 2015.

56.   Kobach, Kris W. 2013. "Interstate Voter Registration Crosscheck Program." Presented to the National Association of State Election Directors, at http://www.nased.org/NASED_Winter_2013_PP_Presentations/KANSAS.pdf, last accessed January 20, 2015 (also available from author).

57.   Pitzel, Mary Jo. 2012. "Arizona Makes Example Out of Few Caught Voting Twice." The Arizona Republic, December 29, 2012, at http://www.azcentral.com/news/politics/articles/20121226voting-twice-arizona.html, last accessed January 20, 2015.

58.   Bland, Gary and Barry Burden. 2013. Electronic Registration Information Center (ERIC), Stage 1 Evaluation Report to the Pew Charitable Trusts, at http://www.rti.org/pubs/eric_stage1report_pewfinal_12-3-13.pdf#page=27, last accessed January 20, 2015.

59.   The Election Assistance Commission does have some limited rulemaking authority where it concerns the National Voter Registration Act. Interestingly, that power has come under scrutiny in the form of the Arizona case concerning whether or not the federal registration form should have proof-of-citizenship information required on it (see *Arizona v. Intertribal Council of Arizona, Inc.*, No 12-71, slip op (June 17, 2013), online at http://www.supremecourt.gov/opinions/12pdf/12-71_7l48.pdf).

60. "EAC Requests Review of Voter ID, Vote Fraud and Voter Intimidation Research Projects." April 16, 2007, at http://www.eac.gov, last accessed June 18, 2007.

61. See for example, The Election Assistance Commission Termination Act, at https://www.govtrack.us/congress/bills/113/hr1994/text, last accessed February 23, 2015.

62. http://www.electionline.org/index.jsp?page=Newsletter%20May%2027%202004, last accessed December 30, 2004.

63. http://www.electionline.org/index.jsp?page=Newsletter%20Dec%2011%202003, last accessed December 30, 2004.

64. Moore, Martha T. 2014. "Lengthy Vacancy Ends for Election Commissioners." USA Today, December 17, 2014, at http://onpolitics.usatoday.com/2014/12/17/elections-assistance-commission-senate/, last accessed February 23, 2015.

65. Levinthal, Dave. 2013. "Kill the Election Assistance Commission? Two Commissioner Nominees Languish as Congress Mulls Axing Bedraggled Body," at http://www.publicintegrity.org/2013/12/12/13993/kill-election-assistance-commission, last accessed February 23, 2015.

66. Office of the Inspector General, Oversight and Review Division, Department of Justice. March 2013. A Review of the Operations of the Voting Section of the Civil Rights Division, at http://www.justice.gov/oig/reports/2013/s1303.pdf, last accessed April 26, 2015.

67. Hasen, Richard L. 2013. "The Voting Wars Within: Is the Department of Justice Too Biased to Enforce the Voting Rights Act?" Slate Magazine, March 18, 2013, at http://www.slate.com/articles/news_and_politics/politics/2013/03/justice_department_s_inspector_general_report_is_the_voting_rights_section.html, last accessed February 16, 2016

68. The reader will learn more about redistricting cases in Chapter 9.

69. Tokaji, Daniel P. 2007. "Leave It to the Lower Courts: On Judicial Intervention in Election Administration." Ohio State Law Journal 68: 1065–1095.

70. Stevens, John Paul. 2008. Crawford v. Marion County Election Board. 553 U.S. 181.

71. Brenner, Elsa. 2009. "Rich Ethnically, Poised for Change Politically." The New York Times, April 10, 2009, at http://www.nytimes.com/2009/04/12/realestate/12livi.html?n=Top%2FClassifieds%2FReal%20Estate%2FColumns%2FLiving%20In, last accessed April 23, 2015.

72. The reader will note the use of the term "Hispanic" even though a more accepted term is "Latino." However, I note that the complaints, testimony, and court documents refer to "Hispanics" so that is the terminology adopted here. See also Kimball, David C. and Martha Kropf. Forthcoming. "Voter Competence with Cumulative Voting." Social Science Quarterly.

73. See United States v. Village of Port Chester, NY (S.D.N.Y. 2006), at http://www.justice.gov/crt/about/vot/sec_2/portchester_comp.php, last accessed April 23, 2015.

74. Brenner, 2009.

75. See for example, Tokaji, Daniel P. 2006. "The New Vote Denial: Where Election Reform Meets the New Voting Rights Act." South Carolina Law Review 57(4): 689–733.

76. Bowler, Shaun, Todd Donovan, and David Brockington. 2003. Electoral Reform and Minority Representation: Local Experiments with Alternative Elections. Columbus: The Ohio State University Press.

77. See Engstrom, Richard. 2008. Report on Cumulative Voting for United States of America v. Village of Port Chester, at http://archive.fairvote.org/media/engstrom.pdf, last accessed May 14, 2015.

78. Kimball, David C. and Martha Kropf. Forthcoming. "Cumulative Voting: The Case of Port Chester, New York." *Social Science Quarterly*.

79. Fitzgerald, Jim. 2010. "Port Chester Election: New York Villagers Get SIX VOTES Each." Huffington Post, at http://www.huffingtonpost.com/2010/06/15/port-chester-election-new_n_612365.html, last accessed November 18, 2014.

CHAPTER 5

1. See US Department of Justice, Civil Rights Division, "Jurisdictions Previously Covered by Section 5 at the Time of the Shelby County Decision," at http://www.justice.gov/crt/about/vot/sec_5/covered.php, last accessed September 11, 2014.

2. See for example Raskin, Jamin. 2004. "A Right-to-Vote Amendment for the U.S. Constitution: Confronting America's Structural Democracy Deficit." *Election Law Journal* 3(3): 559–573.

3. See also Keyssar, Alexander. 2000. *The Right to Vote: The Contested History of Democracy in the United States*. New York: Basic Books.

4. Article 2 of the US Constitution.

5. It is important to note that the parties of the "First Party System" were different from contemporary Republicans. They were less likely to be elites than the Federalists and worried about strong national government. They were aligned with agricultural interests (see Bibby and Maisel, 2003).

6. Ratcliffe and Polgar are among early American history scholars who have utilized the database "A New America Votes" compiled over a 40-year period by Phillip Lampi, at http://elections.lib.tufts.edu/, last accessed January 29, 2015.

7. Polgar, Paul J. 2011. "'Whenever They Judge It Expedient': The Politics of Partisanship and Free Black Voting Rights in Early National New York." *American Nineteenth Century History* 12(1): 1–23.

8. Maine, New Hampshire, Vermont, and Massachusetts never denied African American suffrage. See http://www.pbs.org/wgbh/aia/part4/4p2957.html, accessed March 12, 2015.

9. James, Scott C. and Brian L. Lawson. 1999. "The Political Economy of Voting Rights Enforcement in America's Gilded Age: Electoral College Competition, Partisan Commitment and the Federal Election Law." *American Political Science Review* 93(1): 115–131.

10. McDuffie writes that the conservatives gradually "assumed the Democratic label" in the early 1870s (page 83). See McDuffie, Jerome A. 1979. *Politics in Wilmington and New Hanover County, North Carolina, 1865–1900: The Genesis of a Race Riot*, unpublished PhD dissertation, Kent State University.

11. Umfleet, LeRae. 2006. 1898 Wilmington Race Riot Report of the 1898 Wilmington Race Riot Commission, accessed at http://www.history.ncdcr.gov/1898-wrrc/report/front-matter.pdf, last accessed February 3, 2015.

12. Tyson, Timothy B. and David S. Cecelski. 1998. "Introduction" in David. Cecelski and Timothy B. Tyson (eds.) *Democracy Betrayed: The Wilmington Race Riot of 1898 and Its Legacy*. Raleigh: University of North Carolina Press.

13. For a particularly dramatic and recent report about racial terror/lynchings, please see Equal Justice Initiative. 2015. *Lynching in America: Confronting the Legacy of Racial Terror*, at http://www.eji.org/files/EJI%20Lynching%20in%20America%20SUMMARY.pdf, last accessed March 1, 2015.

14. *South Carolina v. Katzenback*, 383 U.S. 301 (1966), at https://supreme.justia.com/cases/federal/us/383/301/case.html, last accessed February 6, 2015.

15. Kaplan, Rebecca. 2015. "John Lewis Reflects on Selma Marches." CBS News, Face the Nation. February 15, 2015, at http://www.cbsnews.com/news/john-lewis-reflects-on-selma-marches/, last accessed April 26, 2015.

16. CBS News. CBS News Poll, February 2015 [survey question]. USCBS.030415. R07. CBS News [producer]. Storrs, CT: Roper Center for Public Opinion Research, iPOLL [distributor], accessed April 26, 2015. See also Dutton, Sarah, Jennifer De Pinto, Anthony Salvanto, and Fred Backus. 2015. "Have the Goals of the Civil Rights Movement been Achieved?" at http://www.cbsnews.com/news/have-the-goals-of-the-civil-rights-movement-have-been-achieved/, last accessed April 26, 2015.

17. CBS News. CBS News Poll, February 2015 [survey question]. USCBS.030415.R12. CBS News [producer]. Storrs, CT: Roper Center for Public Opinion Research, iPOLL [distributor], accessed April 26, 2015.

18. Dutton, Sarah, Jennifer De Pinto, Anthony Salvanto, and Fred Backus. 2015. "Have the Goals of the Civil Rights Movement Been Achieved?" at http://www.cbsnews.com/news/have-the-goals-of-the-civil-rights-movement-have-been-achieved/, last accessed April 26, 2015.

19. Von Spakovsky, Hans A. 2008. "The Threat of Non-Citizen Voting." The Heritage Foundation, Legal Memorandum #28, at http://www.heritage.org/research/reports/2008/07/the-threat-of-non-citizen-voting, last accessed February 15, 2015.

20. German Marshall Fund of the US, the Lynde and Harry Bradley Foundation of the US, the Compagnia di San Paolo, Italy, the Barrow Cadbury Trust, United Kingdom, and the Fundacion BBVA, Spain. Transatlantic Trends Immigration Survey, November 2010 [survey question]. USTNS.11IMMIG.R22. TNS Opinion and Social Institutes [producer]. Storrs, CT: Roper Center for Public Opinion Research, iPOLL [distributor], accessed February 13, 2015.

21. One scholar of immigration, Monica W. Varsanyi, argues that "the two primary qualifications for voting were residence in a particular place and not being a British citizen, with secondary (though no less important) property-owning, racial, religious and gender qualifications" (2005: 116). This appears to be a matter of emphasis of qualifications by various scholars. Monica W. Varsanyi. 2005. "The Rise and Fall (and Rise?) of Non-citizen Voting: Immigration and the Shifting Scales of Citizenship and Suffrage in the United States." *Space and Polity*, 9(2): 113–134, DOI: 10.1080/13562570500304956. See also Raskin, Jamin B. 1993. "Legal Aliens, Local Citizens: The Historical, Constitutional and Theoretical Meanings of Alien Suffrage." *University of Pennsylvania Law Review* 141: 1391–1470.

22. A *Washington Post* editorial endorsing noncitizen voting in local elections in Takoma Park, Maryland, cited the *Minor v. Happersett* case as a reason why there should be noncitizen voting: it was, in fact, the editorial stated, referred to "approvingly." See "Their Chance to Vote." The Washington Post, October 13, 1991, page C8. Available at http://www.lexisnexis.com.librarylink.uncc.edu/hottopics/lnacademic/?shr=t&sfi=AC01NBSimplSrch, last accessed February 16, 2015.

23. *Minor v. Happersett*, 88 U.S. 162 (1874). The case was presented before the court in 1874 and decided in 1875.

24. Aylsworth, Leon E. 1931. "The Passage of Alien Suffrage." *The American Political Science Review* 25(1): 114–116.

25. See also Hayduk, Ron. 2014. "Op-Ed: Give Noncitizens the Right to Vote—It's Only Fair." The Los Angeles Times, December 22, 2014, at http://www.latimes.com/opinion/op-ed/la-oe-hayduk-let-noncitizens-vote-20141223-story.html, last accessed February 16, 2015.

26. US Citizenship and Immigration Services. "Mass Immigration and WWI," at http://www.uscis.gov/history-and-genealogy/our-history/agency-history/mass-immigration-and-wwi, last accessed April 27, 2015.

27. "The U.S. Military Helps Naturalize Non-Citizens," at http://www.military.com/join-armed-forces/eligibility-requirements/the-us-military-helps-naturlize-non-citizens.html, last accessed April 27, 2015.

28. Rytina, Nancy. 2013. "Estimates of the Legal Permanent Resident Population in 2012." Department of Homeland Security, at http://www.dhs.gov/sites/default/files/publications/ois_lpr_pe_2012.pdf, last accessed February 13, 2015.

29. Passel, Jeffrey S. 2005. "Estimates of the Size and Characteristics of the Undocumented Population." Pew Hispanic Center Report, March 21, 2005, at http://music-editor.com/mns.morris.com/Special_Pages/Immigration/Hispanic-Estimate%20of%20Undocumented.pdf, last accessed April 26, 2015.

30. "18 U.S.C. §611.—Voting by Aliens." US Congress, at http://uscode.house.gov/view.xhtml?req=(title:18%20section:611%20edition:prelim)%20OR%20(granuleid:USC-prelim-title18-section611)&f=treesort&edition=prelim&num=0&jumpTo=true, last accessed February 13, 2013.

31. Curtain, Tom. 2014. "Municipal Elections." Municipal Maryland, April, page 4, at http://www.mdmunicipal.org/ArchiveCenter/ViewFile/Item/280, last accessed February 16, 2015.

32. "Amherst Voting Proposal Faces Struggle." 1997. Daily Hampshire Gazette, May 1, 1997, accessed via Newsbank, April 26, 2015.

33. http://www2.cambridgema.gov/cityClerk/policyOrder.cfm?item_id=41455&pv=Yes, last accessed April 26, 2015.

34. Hilliard, John. 2009. "Illegal Immigrant Voting a Reality in Some States." MetroWest Daily News, April 9, 2009, accessed via Newsbank, April 26, 2015. Although the headline here says "illegal immigrants," the ordinance from Cambridge says "non-citizen residents."

35. Silber, John. 2000. "Editorial—Op-ed: Non-Citizens Don't Deserve Voting Rights." Boston Herald, October 2, 2000, accessed via Newsbank, April 26, 2015.

36. Hilliard, John. "Proposal Would Allow Non-U.S. Citizens to Vote in Brookline Local Elections." Brookline Tab, September 7, 2010, accessed via Newsbank, last accessed April 26, 2015.

37. Constable, Pamela. 2015. "D.C., Other Cities Debate Whether Legal Immigrants Should Have Voting Rights." The Washington Post, February 9, 2015, at http://www.washingtonpost.com/local/should-legal-immigrants-have-voting-rightscontentious-issue-comes-to-dc-other-cities/2015/02/09/85072440-ab0f-11e4-ad71-7b9eba0f87d6_story.html, last accessed February 16, 2015.

38. Historian Kate Kelly (1991) notes there was a period when Virginia had established that men (including servants) above the age of 16 could vote. She theorized, "[s]killed craftsmen were needed in the community, and it [was] likely that early colonists were reluctant to disenfranchise those whose efforts could make or break the success of the enterprise" (page 8).

39. Gallup Organization. Gallup Poll, May 1939 [survey question]. USGALLUP.061239.RA01. Gallup Organization [producer]. Storrs, CT: Roper Center for Public Opinion Research, iPOLL [distributor], accessed April 27, 2015.

40. Gallup Organization. Gallup Poll, October 1942 [survey question]. USGALLUP.011543.R15. Gallup Organization [producer]. Storrs, CT: Roper Center for Public Opinion Research, iPOLL [distributor], accessed April 27, 2015.

41. Gallup Organization. Gallup Poll (AIPO), September 1970 [survey question]. USGALLUP.814.Q012. Gallup Organization [producer]. Storrs, CT: Roper Center for Public Opinion Research, iPOLL [distributor], accessed April 27, 2015.

42. http://www.law.cornell.edu/supremecourt/text/400/112, last accessed January 15, 2015.

43. This is separate from the issue about whether there should be early voting sites on college campuses. Local election administrators must make decisions based on the expected turnout to certain locations and might locate a poll on campus during presidential elections, but not midterm elections. The bottom line is that college student voting activists can view these decisions as partisan, but I argue that is a question that requires more research. The question of college student residency is a long-running and problematic issue.

44. See Ardoin, Phillip J., Charles S. Bell, and Michael Raggozzino. Forthcoming. "The Partisan Battle over College Student Voting: An Analysis of Student Voting Behavior in Federal, State, and Local Elections." *Social Science Quarterly*. See also Ardoin, Phillip J., Paul Gronke, and Martha Kropf. 2015. "Town v. Gown: College Students and Voting in College Towns." Paper presented at the 2015 Midwest Political Science Association Meeting, April 16, 2015, Chicago, IL.

45. North Carolina refers to early voting as "absentee one-stop" voting.

46. Apuzzo, Matt. 2014. "Students Joining Battle to Upend Laws on Photo ID." The New York Times, July 5, 2014, at http://www.nytimes.com/2014/07/06/us/college-students-claim-voter-id-laws-discriminate-based-on-age.html?_r=0, last accessed April 27, 2015.

47. Wallsten, Peter. 2011. "In States, Parties Clash Over Voting Laws That Would Affect College Students, Others." The Washington Post, March 8, 2011, at http://www.washingtonpost.com/wp-dyn/content/article/2011/03/06/AR2011030602662.html?sid=ST2011031002881, last accessed April 28, 2015.

48. For an excellent analysis of registration policies and history of easing registration, see Hanmer, Michael. 2009. *Discount Voting: Voter Registration Reforms and Their Effects.* Cambridge: Cambridge University Press.

49. See also Ansolabehere, Stephen and Charles Stewart. 2013. "Report on Registration Systems in American Elections," at https://www.supportthevoter.gov/files/2013/08/Registration-Systems-in-American-Elections-White-Paper-Ansolabehere_Stewart.pdf, last accessed February 17, 2016.

50. Ansolabehere, Stephen and Eitan Hersch. 2010. "The Quality of Voter Registration Records: A State-by-State Analysis," at http://www.gab.wi.gov/sites/default/files/publication/65/the_quality_of_voter_registration_records_harvard__10685.pdf, last accessed May 12, 2015.

51. See http://www.pewtrusts.org/en/projects/election-initiatives/about/eric, last accessed May 12, 2015.

52. Chung, Jean. 2014. Felony Disenfranchisement: A Primer. The Sentencing Project, at http://www.sentencingproject.org/doc/publications/fd_Felony%20Disenfranchisement%20Primer.pdf, last accessed March 24, 2015.

53. Belson, Ken. 2014. "Brain Trauma to Affect One in Three Players, NFL Agrees." The New York Times, September 12, 2014, at http://www.nytimes.com/2014/09/13/sports/football/actuarial-reports-in-nfl-concussion-deal-are-released.html?_r=0, last accessed April 28, 2015.

54. Bazelon Center for Mental Health Law & National Disability Rights Network. 2008, 2012. Vote: It's Your Right. A Guide to the Voting Rights of People with Mental Disabilities, at http://www.bazelon.org/LinkClick.aspx?fileticket=8GRTfqaH_Qc%3d&tabid=543, last accessed April 28, 2015. See also the testimony of Jennifer

Mathis, Director of Programs, Bazelon Center for Mental Health Law, Hearing of Presidential Commission on Election Administration September 4, 2013, at http://www. bazelon.org/LinkClick.aspx?fileticket=ErCZBTv2_xw%3d&tabid=543, last accessed April 28, 2015.

55. Voter Challenge Statutes by State, at http://www.bazelon.org/LinkClick.aspx?file ticket=cPAQ9Co3ahk%3d&tabid=543, last accessed April 28, 2015.

56. Link, Jessica N., Martha Kropf, Mark Alexander Hirsch, Flora M. Hammond, Jason Karlawish, Lisa Schur, Douglas Kruse, and Christine S. Davis. 2012. "Assessing Voting Competence and Political Knowledge: Comparing Individuals with Traumatic Brain Injuries and 'Average' College Students." *Election Law Journal* 11(1): 52–69.

57. Testimony of Jennifer Mathis, Director of Programs, Bazelon Center for Mental Health Law, Hearing of Presidential Commission on Election Administration, September 4, 2013, at http://www.bazelon.org/LinkClick.aspx?fileticket=ErCZBTv2_ xw%3d&tabid=543, last accessed April 28, 2015.

CHAPTER 6

1. Moretti, M. Mindi. 2014. "'**Vote shaming' grows in popularity for GOTV**: *Some Turned Off by What They See Is Invasion of Privacy.*" *ElectionlineWeekly, November 20, 2014*, at http://www.electionline.org/index.php/electionline-weekly, *last accessed November 20, 2014.*

2. Knoke, David. 1990. *Political Networks: The Structural Perspective.* Cambridge: Cambridge University Press.

3. A common criticism of rational-choice–based theory is that it is not falsifiable. The idea is that a theory is not useful unless you can empirically demonstrate there is or is not evidence to support the theory. Critics might say that the psycho-sociological approach to rational-choice theory means that scholars are simply adjusting the theory a bit whenever someone provides evidence that does not support the theory. My argument is that considering these theories provides variables we can measure. Moreover, the decentralization of elections in the United States gives us leverage to test varying hypotheses about election reform.

4. Leighley, Jan E. and Jonathan Nagler. 2014. *Who Votes Now? Demographics, Issues, Inequality, and Turnout in the United States.* Princeton: Princeton University Press.

5. Political scientist Katherine Tate's 1984 book is an intellectual leader in the area of Black empowerment, examining how Jesse Jackson's 1984 presidential bid affected voter turnout among African Americans.

6. Bobo, Lawrence and Franklin D. Gilliam, Jr. 1990. "Race, Sociopolitical Participation and Black Empowerment." *American Political Science Review* 84(2): 377–393.

7. The current discussion on social and political identity is by necessity brief. For some of the most important work in social identity theory, see the various works of Leonie Huddy, for example, her 2001 article: "From Social to Political Identity: A Critical Examination of Social Identity Theory." *Political Psychology* 22(1): 127–156.

8. Some more recent work conceptualizes identity not necessarily about just demographic or social groups to which one belongs, but also "lifestyle" groups. See Bennett, W. Lance. 2012. "The Personalization of Politics: Political Identity, Social Media, and Changing Patterns of Participation." *The Annals of the Academy of Political and Social Science* 644(1): 20–39.

9. Huddy, Leonie and Simo V. Virtanen. 1995. "Subgroup Differentiation and Subgroup Bias Among Latinos as a Function of Familiarity and Positive Distinctiveness." *Journal of Personality and Social Psychology* 68(1): 97–108.

10. The reader who is dissatisfied with the lack of explanation about how norms developed in the United States (listed in Chapter 2) may find some comfort in the idea that racial discrimination and stereotyping may, in part, have their genesis in the idea of social identity theory (see for example, Virtanen, Simo V. and Leonie Huddy. 1998. "Old Fashioned Racism and New Forms of Racial Prejudice." *Journal of Politics* 60(2): 311–332 and Samson, Frank L. and Lawrence D. Bobo. 2014. "Ethno-Racial Attitudes and Social Inequality" in J. D. McLeod et al. (eds.) *Handbook of the Social Psychology of Inequality. Handbooks of Sociology and Social Research.* DOI 10.1007/978-94-017-9002-4_21.

11. Huddy, Leonie and Nadia Khatib. 2007. "American Patriotism, National Identity and Political Involvement." *American Journal of Political Science* 51(1): 63–77.

12. A group of psychology scholars conducted field experiments using eating popcorn at the movies. David T. Neal, Wendy Wood, Mengju Wu, and David Kurlander. 2011. "The Pull of the Past: When Do Habits Persist Despite Conflict with Motives?" *Personality and Social Psychology Bulletin* 37(11): 1428–1437.

13. I argue that given the varying norms and values that citizens have concerning voting, as mentioned in this book, perhaps a better way of thinking about voting as a habit is to see it like attending church.

14. Aldrich, John H., Jacob M. Montgomery, and Wendy Wood. 2011. "Turnout as a Habit." *Political Behavior* 33(4): 535–563.

15. There is a vast array of excellent and interesting scholarship on habit and voting, including for example, Plutzer, Eric. (2002). "Becoming a Habitual Voter: Inertia, Resources, and Growth in Young Adulthood." *The American Political Science Review*, 96: 41–56 and Green, Donald P., and Shachar, Ron. (2000). "Habit Formation and Political Behaviour: Evidence of Consuetude in Voter Turnout." *British Journal of Political Science*, 30: 561–573.

16. Coleman, James S. "Social Capital in the Creation of Human Capital." *American Journal of Sociology* 94(supplement): S95–S120.

17. Portes cites Berman, Sheri. 1997. "Civil Society and the Collapse of the Weimar Republic." *World Politics* 49(3): 401–429. See Portes, Alejandro. 2014. "Downsides of Social Capital." *Proceedings of the National Academy of Sciences of the United States of America* 111(52): 18407–18408.

18. Klofstad, Casey A., Anand Edward Sokhey, and Scott D. McClurg. 2013. "Disagreeing About Disagreement: How Conflicts in Social Networks Affects Political Behavior." *American Journal of Political Science* 57(1): 120–134.

19. For a comprehensive discussion of the use of network analysis, see Stephen P. Borgatti, Ajay Mehra, Daniel J. Brass, and Giuseppe Labianca. 2009. "Network Analysis in the Social Sciences." *Science* 323(5916) (Feb. 13): 892–895.

20. Granovetter, Mark S. 1973. "The Strength of Weak Ties." *American Journal of Sociology* 78(6): 1360–1380.

21. Leighley, Jan E. 2001. *Strength in Numbers: The Political Mobilization of Racial and Ethnic Minorities.* Princeton: Princeton University Press.

22. Uhlaner, Carole. 1989. "Rational Turnout: The Neglected Role of Groups." *American Journal of Political Science* 33(2): 390–422.

CHAPTER 7

1. Attlesey, Sam. 1988. "Election Night Spotlights Texas Politicos, Voting Rule." Dallas Morning News, November 13, 1988, page 46A.
2. Rhee, Foon. 1996. "Cure Sought for Voter Apathy: NC Panel Looks for Ways to Boost Turnout at the Polls." The Charlotte Observer, January 28, 1996, page 1B, accessed via Newsbank.
3. Morrill, Jim. 2000. "Early Voters Can Bypass Election Day Lines." The Charlotte Observer, September 17, 2000, page 2M, accessed via Newsbank.
4. Becker, Jo. 2004. "Voters May Have Their Say Before Election Day." The Washington Post, August 26, 2004, at http://www.washingtonpost.com/wp-dyn/articles/A33796-2004Aug25.html, last accessed June 27, 2008.
5. The Pew Charitable Trusts. 2015. "New Survey Highlights the 2014 Voting Experience." February 10, 2015, at http://www.pewtrusts.org/en/about/news-room/news/2015/02/09/new-survey-highlights-the-2014-voting-experience, last accessed April 28, 2015.
6. See for example, Blythe, Anne. 2014. "Children Learn to Cast Ballots at Family Voting Celebration in Durham." The News & Observer, October 25, 2014, at http://www.newsobserver.com/news/local/counties/durham-county/article10107686.html, last accessed May 3, 2015.
7. Fortier, John C. 2006. *Absentee and Early Voting.* Washington, DC: American Enterprise Institute.
8. See "States and Election Reform." The Canvass: A Newsletter for Legislators, March 2011, XVIII, at http://www.ncsl.org/research/elections-and-campaigns/cnv-the-canvass-vol-xviii-march-2011.aspx#Pre, last accessed April 29, 2015.
9. Some states, such as North Carolina, call their no-excuse early voting "absentee one-stop" voting. For all intents and purposes, it is early voting, wherein voters have to apply in person for an absentee ballot and then vote.
10. O'Keefe, Ed. 2011. "Military Voting Jumped Last Year, Report Says." The Washington Post, October 18, 2011, at http://www.washingtonpost.com/blogs/federal-eye/post/military-voting-jumped-last-year-report-says/2011/10/18/gIQAymZxuL_blog.html, last accessed April 29, 2015.
11. See http://www.justice.gov/crt/about/vot/litigation/caselist.php#uocava_cases, last accessed April 29, 2015.
12. US General Accountability Office. 2007. Action Plans Needed to Fully Address Challenges in Electronic Absentee Voting Initiatives for Military and Overseas Citizens. Washington, DC, at http://www.gao.gov/assets/270/262023.pdf, last accessed April 29, 2015.
13. Oliver, J. Eric. 1996. "Absentee Voting and Overall Turnout." *American Journal of Political Science* 40(2): 498–513.
14. Oliver is not the only one who found mobilization effects with election reform. In an unpublished paper (that is still one of my favorites), Stein and his colleagues (2003) posited that early voting may only be effective in increasing turnout where there is strong party mobilization. Analyzing survey data from Texas, they found only limited mobilization effects and only for the Democratic Party. They posited that many Republican voters were likely to vote anyway (Stein et al., 2003: 20).
15. Hamilton, Randy H. 1988. "American All-Mail Balloting: A Decade's Experience." *Public Administration Review* 48(5): 860–866.
16. Kousser, Thad and Megan Mullin. 2007. "Does Voting by Mail Increase Participation? Using Matching to Analyze a Natural Experiment." *Political Analysis* 15: 428–445.

17. Another recent study leverages the idea that the state of Washington staggered its introduction of VBM. See Gerber, Alan S., Gregory A. Huber, and Seth J. Hill. 2013. "Identifying the Effect of All-Mail Elections on Turnout: Staggered Reform in the Evergreen State." *Political Science Research and Methods* 1(1): 91–116.

18. Election Assistance Commission. 2008. Alternative Voting Methods, at http://www.eac.gov/assets/1/workflow_staging/Page/54.PDF, last accessed April 29, 2015.

19. Pew Research Center. 2012. Election 2012: The State of Voter Registration, at http://www.pewtrusts.org/en/multimedia/data-visualizations/2012/the-state-of-voter-registration-in-the-2012-election, last accessed April 28, 2015.

20. California Research Bureau at the California State Library. 2013. Maintenance of Voter Registration Lists, at https://www.library.ca.gov/crb/13/S-13-013.pdf, last accessed April 29, 2015.

21. See for example, Obama Campaign Files Suit Over Voter "Caging" Allegations. CNN, September 16, 2008, at http://politicalticker.blogs.cnn.com/2008/09/16/obama-campaign-files-suit-over-voter-caging-allegations/, last accessed April 29, 2015.

22. Kropf, Martha. 2013. "North Carolina Election Reform Ten Years After the Help America Vote Act." *Election Law Journal* 12(2): 179–189. Note that half of the counties in North Carolina were covered jurisdictions under the Voting Rights Act. See Chapter 4.

23. Some may disagree with the organization of this particular section because the studies I cite often do not just examine early in-person voting. Those studies that examine early voting often consider early voting and absentee voting as similar phenomena (for example, the Burden, et al. study). Given Valelly's idea of institutional complementarity, I would make the argument that it is very difficult to separate out the effects of various programs.

24. Leighley, Jan E. and Jonathan Nagler. 2014. *Who Votes Now?* New York: Princeton University Press.

25. Even though this study defines early voting to include liberalized absentee voting as well, that is not an unreasonable way to operationalize early voting because so many states allow multiple voting options when they have early voting, such as Kansas, where one could vote early or mail in one's ballot. North Carolina is an interesting case because its early voting program started out as "absentee voting" and was for several years reported within the traditional absentee figures (most counties did not separate the modes), and the state still calls its early voting "absentee one-stop."

26. Aldrich and his colleagues suggest that there are two types of habitual voters—those with a weaker habit of voting but a strong sense of civic duty (or strong partisan intensity) that keep them voting. There are also those for whom voting is a conditioned habit.

27. https://vip.sos.nd.gov/pdfs/Portals/votereg.pdf, last accessed December 14, 2014.

28. See also Richey (2005) who studies voting by mail. He argues that voting at home allows a voter to discuss choices with family and friends and to deliberate. In an examination of the 1998 and 2000 data on US voters, he found that voters who vote by mail do engage in more political discussion than those who do not (Richey, 2005). In other words, voting away from the polls actually increased interaction, except the interaction he described was more political than social.

29. Kropf, Martha, David Swindell, and Elizabeth Wemlinger. 2009. "The Effects of Early Voting on Social Ties: Using Longitudinal Data." Presented at the Non-Precinct Place Voting Conference, Portland, OR.

30. McClatchy/Marist Poll, July 2013. Retrieved from the iPOLL Databank, The Roper Center for Public Opinion Research, University of Connecticut, at

http://www.ropercenter.uconn.edu.librarylink.uncc.edu/data_access/ipoll/ipoll.
html, last accessed November 20, 2014.

31. McClatchy/Marist Poll National Tables. 2013, at http://maristpoll.marist.edu/wp-
content/misc/usapolls/us130715/Voter%20Rights/Complete%20July%202013%
20USA%20McClatchy-Marist%20Poll%20Voter%20Rights%20Tables.pdf#page=6,
last accessed November 20, 2014.These data are also available from the author. The
margin of error on this poll is +/-4 percent.

32. Herron, Michael C. and Daniel A. Smith. 2012. "Souls to the Polls: Early Voting in
Florida in the Shadow of House Bill 1355." *Election Law Journal* 11(3): 331–347.

33. Bradley, Ryan. 2012. "10 Unusual Places to Vote This Election Day." Fortune,
October 19, 2012, at http://fortune.com/2012/10/19/10-unusual-places-to-vote-this-
election-day/, last accessed April 30, 2015. It is unclear whether anyone has conducted
research about how the type of polling place affects voter turnout.

34. Bovbjerg, Barbara. 2013. Voters with Disabilities: Challenges to Voter Accessibility.
Washington, DC: General Accountability Office, at http://gao.gov/assets/660/654099.
pdf, last accessed May 1, 2015.

35. Schur, Lisa, Meera Adya, and Douglas Kruse. 2013. "Disability, Voter Turnout, and
Voting Difficulties in the 2012 Elections," Report to Research Alliance for Accessible
Voting and U.S. Election Assistance Commission, Rutgers University, June 2013, at
http://smlr.rutgers.edu/research-centers/disability-and-voter-turnout, last accessed
May 1, 2015.

36. Schur, Lisa. 2013. "Reducing Obstacles to Voting for People with Disabilities White
Paper prepared for Presidential Commission on Election Administration." June 22,
2013, at https://www.supportthevoter.gov/files/2013/08/Disability-and-Voting-White-
Paper-for-Presidential-Commission-Schur.docx_.pdf, last accessed May 1, 2015.
See also Schur, Lisa and Meera Adya. 2012. "Sidelined or Mainstreamed? Political
Participation and Attitudes of People with Disabilities in the United States." *Social
Science Quarterly* 94(3): 811–839.

37. The report acknowledged that a reason for the reduction is that states were taking
other steps like expanding absentee voting to address disability issues.

38. When I voted in Kansas City, my elderly neighbor (with hip issues and a walker) had
a great deal of difficulty coming down the stairs at our voting location.

39. Barreto, Matt, Mara Cohen-Marks, and Nathan D. Woods. 2009. "Are All Precincts
Created Equal? The Prevalence of Low-Quality Precincts in Low-Income and
Minority Communities." *Political Research Quarterly* 62(3): 445–458.

40. I should note that although I organize this discussion based on the type of voting,
long lines are not just an issue for Election Day voting, but also for early voting.
However, when one leaves a long line during early voting, one can usually come back
another time, including on Election Day. On Election Day when one leaves the line,
one can come back to the line, but because it is the last day of voting, one must vote
on Election Day or not at all.

41. Hall, Bob and Isela Gutierrez. 2015. Memo to the North Carolina State Board of
Elections, Re: Feedback on the 2014 election and impact of H-589 on voter turnout.
Democracy NC Date: January 26, 2015, at http://www.democracy-nc.org/downloads/
SBEMemo2015.pdf, last accessed May 1, 2015.

42. Additionally, the report provided a footnote that there were "likely" one hour or longer wait times in Wake County (second most populous county and home to Raleigh,
the capital), but precinct-level information was not available. See North Carolina

State Board of Elections. Analysis of Voter Wait Times, at ftp://alt.ncsbe.gov/data/November%202014_%20State%20Board%20of%20Elections%20Analysis%20of%20Voter%20Wait%20Times/November%202014%20-%20State%20Board%20of%20Elections%20Analysis%20of%20Voter.pdf, last accessed May 1, 2015.

43. Stewart, Charles III and Stephen Ansolabehere. 2013. "Waiting in Line to Vote." July 28, 2013, at https://www.supportthevoter.gov/files/2013/08/Waiting-in-Line-to-Vote-White-Paper-Stewart-Ansolabehere.pdf, last accessed May 1, 2015.

44. For a discussion, see Kropf, Martha and David C. Kimball. 2012. *Helping America Vote: The Limits of Election Reform*, New York: Routledge, Chapter 4.

45. Brady, Henry E. and John E. McNulty. 2011. "Turning Out to Vote: The Costs of Finding and Getting to the Polling Place." *American Political Science Review* 105(1): 115–134.

46. Stein, Robert M. and Greg Vonnahme. 2012. "Effect of Election Day Vote Centers on Voters Participation." *Election Law Journal* 11(3): 291–301.

47. Stein, Robert M. and Greg Vonnahme. 2008. "Engaging the Unengaged Voter: Vote Centers and Voter Turnout." *Journal of Politics* 70: 1–11.

48. Two notes: In 2006, media reports did indicate long lines and related problems with voting centers. *The Denver Post* suggested the centers were "a total fiasco." The major problem was that there were apparently not enough electronic pollbooks to check voters into the large, centralized centers. See Whaley, Monte and Joey Bunch. 2006. "Vote Centers 'A Total Fiasco." The Denver Post, November 9, 2006, at http://www.denverpost.com/election/ci_4627496, last accessed May 3, 2015. Second, the reader should note that scholars Eric Gonzalez Juenke and Julie Marie Shepherd (2008) found differing results in their county-level analysis in 2006. The scholars found "turnout is a function of historical voting patterns and involves relatively few 'new' factors, including procedural changes" (page 63). See Juenke, Eric Gonzalez and Julie Marie Shepherd. 2008. "Vote Centers and Voter Turnout" in Bruce Cain, Todd Donovan, and Caroline Tolbert (eds.) *Democracy in the States*. Washington, DC: Brookings Institution Press, pages 55–67.

49. National Conference of State Legislatures. 2015. Vote Centers, at http://www.ncsl.org/research/elections-and-campaigns/vote-centers.aspx, last accessed May 3, 2015.

50. Helman, Scott. 2008. "Minds Made Up: Millions Voting Early." Boston Globe, September 30, 2008, at http://www.boston.com/news/nation/articles/2008/09/30/minds_made_up_millions_voting_early/, last accessed May 3, 2015.

CHAPTER 8

1. Johnson, Zachary K. 2014. "Ballots Validated Under Watchful Eyes." The Stockton Record, June 12, 2014, 20140612-SK-Ballots-validated-under-watchful-eyes-0612-20140612, accessed via Newsbank, March 12, 2015.

2. It should be noted, however, that the National Institute for Standards and Technology's Roy Saltman was one of the first to articulate rampant potential problems with punch-card balloting. See (among other publications), Saltman, Roy G. 2006. *The History and Politics of Voting Technology: In Quest of Integrity and Public Confidence*. New York: Palgrave Macmillan.

3. Kimball, David C., Martha Kropf, and Lindsay Battles. 2006. "Helping America Vote? Election Administration, Partisanship, and Provisional Voting in the 2004 Election." *Election Law Journal* 5(4): 447–461.

4. Kropf, Martha, Timothy Vercellotti, and David C. Kimball. 2013. "Representative Bureaucracy and Partisanship: The Implementation of Election Law." *Public Administration Review* 73(2): 242–252.

5. In the 2012 voter list, approximately 15,130 voters did not have a gender listed. Thus, I went through all the voter names to identify whether they were men or women. In order to avoid cultural bias, I referred to name websites in order to assess the probability that the voter was a man or woman. However, some names such as "Casey" or "Jamie" could not be identified. I also could not locate some international names. Special thanks to my colleague Beth Whitaker, an Africanist who focuses on Kenya, for providing help on a couple of African names.

6. In 2013, North Carolina changed the law regarding provisional votes—provisional votes cast outside the precinct within which the voter is assigned no longer count at all, even for contests upon which all voters vote. In 2012, local election boards counted as much of the ballot as possible, so votes for some contests may not count, but the entire ballot is not disqualified, just those votes (for example, for a city commissioner when the wrong precinct the voter cast a ballot in is not the correct commissioner for that voter's residence).

7. Administrative Division, North Carolina State Election Board. *Provisional Voting Administrative Procedures.*

8. National Conference of State Legislatures. 2015. "Online Voter Registration," at http://www.ncsl.org/research/elections-and-campaigns/electronic-or-online-voter-registration.aspx, last accessed May 10, 2015.

9. The Pew Charitable Trusts Brief. "Understanding Online Voter Registration." January 2014, at http://www.pewtrusts.org/~/media/legacy/uploadedfiles/pcs_assets/2013/UnderstandingOnlineVoterRegistrationpdf.pdf, last accessed May 10, 2015.

10. For example, see Davis, Aaron C. 2012. "Maryland's Online Voter Registration Vulnerable to Attack, Researchers Say." Washington Post, October 16, 2012, at http://www.washingtonpost.com/local/md-politics/marylands-online-voter-registration-vulnerable-to-attack-researchers-say/2012/10/16/acc24cf6-17c0-11e2-a55c-39408fbe6a4b_story.html, last accessed May 10, 2015.

11. Farkas, Karen. 2013. "Electronic Poll Books Seem Conceptually Simple But May Be Vulnerable to Hacking and Cyber Attacks, Experts Say." Cleveland Plain Dealer, March 16, 2013, at http://www.cleveland.com/cuyahoga-county/index.ssf/2013/03/electronic_poll_books_seem_conceptually_simple_but_may_be_vulnerable_to_hacking_and_cyber_attacks_ex.html, last accessed May 10, 2015.

12. Political scientists Martin P. Wattenberg, Ian McAllister, and Anthony Salvanto (2000) found that voters refrained from voting in some contests because they did not have enough information. See "How Voting Is Like Taking an SAT Test: An Analysis of American Voter Rolloff." *American Politics Research* 28(2): 234–250.

13. Frisina, Laurin, Michael C. Herron, James Honaker, and Jeffrey B. Lewis. 2008. "Ballot Formats, Touchscreens, and Undervotes: A Study of the 2006 Midterm Elections in Florida." *Election Law Journal* 7(1): 25–47.

14. See Knack, Stephen and Martha Kropf. 2003. "Voided Ballots in the 1996 Presidential Election: A County Level Analysis." *Journal of Politics* 65(3): 881–897.

15. Brennan Center for Justice citing *Voluntary Voting System Guidelines Recommendations to the Election Assistance Commission* (prepared at the direction of the Technical Guidelines Development Committee) (August 31, 2007), available at http://www.eac.gov/assets/1/Page/TGDC%20Draft%20Guidelines.pdf, last accessed February 19, 2016.

16. Kropf, Martha. 2014. "The Evolution of Ballot Design Ten Years After Bush v. Gore" in R. Michael Alvarez and Bernie Grofman (eds.) *Election Administration in the*

United States: The State of Reform Ten Years After Bush v. Gore, Cambridge: Cambridge University Press.

17. Chisnell, Dana. Field Guides to Ensuring Voter Intent, at http://civicdesigning.org/wp-content/uploads/2013/06/Field-Guide-Vol-01-20130620.pdf, last accessed May 11, 2015.

18. See Miller, Michael G. 2013. "Do Audible Alerts Reduce Undervotes? Evidence from Illinois." *Election Law Journal* 12(2): 162–178. There are two ways to think about privacy. The audible beep compromises privacy because others around the voter will know that he or she failed to mark an office or overvoted. Another privacy concern is that if others could see how a person voted, they could coerce a person to vote a certain way. The other privacy concern is more relevant here: that the voter might feel uncomfortable if others judged him or her as having made a voting mistake or as not being knowledgeable to vote in all the contests on the ballot.

19. See Rubin, Aviel D. 2006. *Brave New Ballot: The Battle to Safeguard Democracy in the Age of Electronic Voting.* New York: Morgan Road Books.

20. See for example, Antonyan, Tigran, Seda Davtyan, Sotirios Kentros, Aggelos Kiayias, Laurent Michel, Nicolas Nicolaou, Alexander Russell, and Alexander A. Shvartsman. 2008. Statewide Elections, Optical Scan Voting Systems, and the Pursuit of Integrity, at http://nicolaoun.com/pubs/Journals/PDF/VoTeR-IEEE09.pdf, last accessed February 19, 2016.

21. Portnoy, Jenna. 2015. "Virginia Board of Elections to Decertify Some Machines." Washington Post, April 14, 2015, at http://www.washingtonpost.com/local/virginia-politics/va-board-of-elections-votes-to-decertify-some-voting-machines/2015/04/14/4 6bce444-e2a6-11e4-81ea-0649268f729e_story.html, last accessed February 19, 2016.

22. Brace, Kimball. 2005. "Chapter 9: Voting Equipment Usage." 2014 Election Day Survey Results, at http://www.eac.gov/assets/1/AssetManager/2004%20EAVS%20Chapter%209.pdf, last accessed May 10, 2015.

23. Herrnson, Paul S., Richard G. Niemi, Michael J. Hanmer, Benjamin D. Bederson, Frederick G. Conrad, and Michael W. Traugott. 2008. *Voting Technology: The Not-So-Simple Act of Casting a Ballot.* Washington, DC: Brookings Institution.

24. Palazzolo, Daniel, Vincent G. Moscardelli, Meredith Patrick, and Doug Rubin. 2008. "Election Reform After HAVA: Voter Verification in Congress and the States." *Publius: The Journal of Federalism* 38(3): 515–537.

25. electionLine.org. 2015. "Meet the New Elections Commissioners." electionLineWeekly, May 7, 2015, at http://www.electionline.org/index.php/electionline-weekly, last accessed May 10, 2015.

26. Presidential Commission on Election Administration. 2014. *The American Voter Experience: Report and Recommendations of the Presidential Commission on Election Administration*, at https://www.supportthevoter.gov/files/2014/01/Amer-Voting-Exper-final-draft-01-09-14-508.pdf, last accessed May 10, 2015.

27. Boyd, Dan. 2014. "New Voting Machines Set for November 4 Election." Albuquerque Journal, August 29, 2014, at http://www.abqjournal.com/453733/news/new-voting-machines-set-for-nov-4-election.html, last accessed May 10, 2015.

28. Acemyan, Claudia Z., Philip Kortum, Michael D. Byrne, and Dan S. Wallach. 2014. "Usability of Voter Verifiable, End-to-End Voting Systems: Baseline Data for Helios, Prêt à Voter, and Scantegrity II." *USENIX Journal of Election Technology and Systems (JETS)* 2(3): 26–56, at www.usenix.org/jets/issues/0203.

29. See Kelsey, John, Andrew Regenscheid, Tal Moran, and David Chaum. 2010. "Attacking Paper-Based E2E Voting Systems." *Towards Trustworthy Elections*, LNCS

         6000: 370–387, at http://www.itl.nist.gov/div897/voting/attacking-e2e-voting-systems. pdf, last accessed May 9, 2015.

30. Sherman, Alan T., Richard Carback, David Chaum, Jeremy Clark, Aleksander Essex, Paul S. Herrnson, Travis Mayberry, Stefan Popoveniuc, Ronald L. Rivest, Emily Shen, Bimal Sinha, Poorvi Vora. 2010. "Scantegrity II Municipal Election at Takoma Park: The First E2E Binding Governmental Election with Ballot Privacy," at http://vote. caltech.edu/content/scantegrity-ii-municipal-election-takoma-park-first-e2e-binding-governmental-election-ballot, last accessed May 9, 2015.

31. https://princeton.heliosvoting.org/, last accessed May 9, 2015.

32. National Conference of State Legislatures. 2012. "Voting Technology: Current and Future Choices." *The Canvass*, Issue #31, June 2012, at http://www.ncsl.org/documents/ legismgt/elect/Canvass_June_2012_No_31.pdf, last accessed May 5, 2015.

33. Smith, Aaron. 2015. Smartphone Use in 2015, Pew Research Center, at http://www. pewinternet.org/2015/04/01/us-smartphone-use-in-2015/, last accessed May 4, 2015.

34. Idaho Votes: A Citizen's Guide to Participation, at http://www.nyssba.org/ news/2014/05/09/on-board-online-may-12-2014/mandate-microscopevoting-machine-exemption-due-to-expire-this-year/, last accessed May 4, 2015. If one examines the 2014 voter's guide, one can see that three counties were still using the punchcard ballot in the 2014 election. As of May 2015, all counties reported using optical scan or hand-counted paper ballots.

35. http://www.nytimes.com/2013/09/09/nyregion/lever-machines-briefly-replace-paper-ballots-and-optical-scanners.html, last accessed May 4, 2015.

36. See for example, Village Elections: Chapter 17 of the New York State Consolidated Election Laws, § 15–104.1.c "General village election" and § 3–224, "Voting machines; use of by other than the board of elections" and § 5–612. Registration records; use by town or village clerks and for school district, improvement district and fire district elections, at http://www.elections.ny.gov/NYSBOE/download/ law/2014NYElectionLaw.pdf, last accessed May 5, 2015.

37. Chapter 17 of the New York State Consolidated Election Laws § 3–224, "Voting machines; use of by other than the board of elections."

38. Woodruff, Cathy. 2014. "Voting Machine Exemption Due to Expire This Year," at http://www.nyssba.org/news/2014/05/09/on-board-online-may-12-2014/mandate-microscopevoting-machine-exemption-due-to-expire-this-year/, last accessed May 6, 2015.

39. Senator Jack M. Martins (R-Mineola) and Assemblywoman Michelle Schimel (D-Great Neck).

40. Kreitzman, Wendy Karpel. 2012. "State Legislators Fight to Avoid Costly Use of New Voting Machines—Schimel, Martins spearheaded push to allow villages, school districts and special districts to continue to use lever voting machines." Glen Cove Record Pilot, July 5, 2012, page 3, accessed via Newsbank.

41. Kimball, David C. and Martha Kropf. 2008. "Voting Technology, Ballot Measures and Residual Votes." *American Politics Research* 36(4): 479–509.

CHAPTER 9

1. This is a by-product of our federal system. Every state in the United States gets at least one representative in the House. Thus, Wyoming's one representative represents 568,300citizens, whereas each one of the 53 representatives in California represents 704,566 citizens. Thus, the districts within California must be equal to each other,

not the population of the state of Wyoming. See Congressional Apportionment: 2010 Census Brief, November 2011 at http://www.census.gov/content/dam/Census/library/publications/2011/dec/c2010br-08.pdf, last accessed February 20, 2016.

2. "Berman, Sherman Get Into Near Altercation at Forum." http://latimesblogs.latimes.com/california-politics/2012/10/berman-sherman-get-into-physical-altercation-at-forum-video.html, October 12, 2012, last accessed February 20, 2016.

3. Gonzales, Richard. 2013. "Political Battles Still Dog Redistricting in California." National Public Radio, May 29, 2013, at http://www.npr.org/blogs/itsallpolitics/2013/05/29/186939613/political-battles-still-dog-redistricting-in-california, last accessed June 11, 2013.

4. http://www.npr.org/blogs/itsallpolitics/2013/05/29/186939613/political-battles-still-dog-redistricting-in-california, last accessed June 11, 2013.

5. See for example Pitkin, Hannah Fenichel. 1967. *The Concept of Representation*. Berkeley: University of California Press.

6. Tokaji, Daniel P. 2008. "Representation and Raceblindness: The Story of Shaw v. Reno." Chapter 14 in Rachel F. Moran and Devon W. Carbado (eds.), *Race Law Stories*. New York: Foundation Press.

7. Although the history of suffrage should enable the reader easily to picture that "minorities" refer to African Americans or other Black Americans, the reader should also consider that minorities are Native Americans and Asian individuals. Not to diminish the struggles that these groups have experienced, but "minority" status expands beyond race and ethnicity as well. Consider the battles that women, gay and lesbian communities, and those who are disabled have experienced. Further, consider groups who may have unpopular views. At some point in time, those in the majority may be a member of the minority and should consider whether there are adequate protections to ensure the full participation of all in both voting and in representational bodies.

8. Morrill, Jim and Greg Trevor. 1992. "Districts a Land of Confusion: Contortions Show Politics at Work." The Charlotte Observer, January 27, 1992, page 1A. Accessed via Newsbank, June 19, 2013.

9. Communications scholar Alan G. Stavinsky (1994) criticizes the concept of "localism," or geographic community, in discussing US broadcasting policy. He argues that in broadcasting, the concept of community has become less spatial and more a concept based on "shared interests, tastes, and values" (page 19). Certainly, the mass media has—to a certain extent—changed our concept of community.

10. See Hayes and McKee (2009) for a discussion about the differences between VTDs and precincts (page 1014).

11. Common Cause. "Our Redistricting Values," http://www.commoncause.org/site/pp.asp?c=5nJCJQPvEhKUE&b=7501269, last accessed June 14, 2013.

12. http://www.commoncause.org/site/pp.asp?c=5nJCJQPvEhKUE&b=7501269, last accessed June 14, 2013.

13. Garrett, Elizabeth. 2005. *Redistricting: Another California Revolution?* Initiative & Referendum Institute Report, at http://www.iandrinstitute.org/REPORT%202005-1%20Redistricting.pdf, last accessed June 14, 2013. Garrett also writes that a fourth attempt at redistricting reform in 2000 was removed from the ballot in 2000 because it violated the California constitution's single-subject requirement for initiatives.

14. Wang, Sam. 2013. "The Great Gerrymander of 2012." The New York Times, February 2, 2013, at http://www.nytimes.com/2013/02/03/opinion/sunday/the-great-gerrymander-of-2012.html?pagewanted=all&_r=0, last accessed June 14, 2013.

15. Goedert, Nicholas. 2012. "Not Gerrymandering, but Districting: More Evidence on How Democrats Won the Popular Vote but Lost the Congress," at http://themonkeycage.org, last accessed June 14, 2013.

16. For a longer view, see Altman, Micah. 1998. "Traditional Districting Principles: Judicial Myths vs. Reality." *Social Science History* 22(2): 159–200.

CHAPTER 10

1. Tokaji, Daniel P. 2006. "The New Vote Denial: Where Election Reform Meets the New Voting Rights Act." *South Carolina Law Review* 57(4): 689–733.

2. The Heritage Foundation. 2014. Does Your Vote Count? Ensuring Election Integrity and Making Sure Your Vote Counts, at http://thf_media.s3.amazonaws.com/2014/pdf/Doesyourvotecount.pdf, last accessed May 14, 2015.

3. Minnite, Lorraine. 2006. The Politics of Voter Fraud. Report for Project Vote, at http://poli375engage.pbworks.com/f/Politics_of_Voter_Fraud_Final.pdf, last accessed June 20, 2014.

4. Dardis, Frank E., Frank R. Baumgartner, Amber E. Boydstun, Suzanna De Boef and Fuyuan Shen. 2008. "Media Framing of Capital Punishment and Its Impact on Individuals' Cognitive Responses." *Mass Communication & Society* 11: 115–140.

5. See for example, Wilson, David R. and Paul R. Brewer. 2013. "The Foundations of Public Opinion on Voter ID Laws: Political Predispositions, Racial Resentment and Information Effects." *Public Opinion Quarterly* 77(4): 962–984.

6. Turner (1916: 166) quoting the New Jersey constitution.

7. Turner, Edward Raymond. 1916. "Women's Suffrage in New Jersey: 1790–1807." *Smith College Studies in History* 1(4): 165–187.

8. Kessler, Glenn. 2013. "The Case of 'Zombie' Voters in South Carolina." The Washington Post, July 25, 2013, at http://www.washingtonpost.com/blogs/fact-checker/post/the-case-of-zombie-voters-in-south-carolina/2013/07/24/86de3c64-f403-11e2-aa2e-4088616498b4_blog.html, last accessed July 25, 2013, Special thanks to Aunt Arlene I. for her assistance in locating this quote.

9. Other studies recently have provided additional support for the Bentele and O'Brien study. See for example: Hicks, William D., Seth C. McKee, Mitchell D. Sellers, and Daniel A. Smith. 2015. "A Principle or a Strategy? Voter Identification Laws and Partisan Competition in the American States." *Political Research Quarterly* 68(1): 18–33.

10. Barreto, Matt A., Stephen A. Nuño, and Gabriel R. Sanchez. 2009. "The Disproportionate Impact of Voter-ID Requirements on the Electorate—New Evidence from Indiana." *PS: Political Science and Politics* January: 111–116. See also Democracy North Carolina. 2013. April 2013 SBOE-DMV ID Analysis, at http://www.democracy-nc.org/downloads/SBOE-DMVMatchMemoApril2013.pdf, last accessed May 14, 2015.

11. Gronke, Paul, William D. Hicks, Seth C. McKee, and Charles Stewart III. 2015. "Voter ID Laws: A View from the Public." Massachusetts Institute of Technology Political Science Department Research Paper No. 2015–13 (unpublished manuscript).

12. Draft rule of "08 NC, AC 17 .0101 DETERMINATION OF REASONABLE RESEMBLANCE AT CHECK-IN," May 1, 2015, at ftp://alt.ncsbe.gov/Rulemaking/Initial%20Correspondence%20re%20Draft%20Rules.pdf, last accessed May 14, 2015. (These are also available from the author.)

13. Email to author from Democracy North Carolina, "Voting ID Public Hearings Coming Across North Carolina." May 13, 2015.

Works Cited

Aldrich, John H., Jacob M. Montgomery and Wendy Wood. 2011. "Turnout as a Habit." *Political Behavior* 33(4): 535–563.

Aldrich, John. 1993. "Turnout and Rational Choice." *American Journal of Political Science* 37(1): 246–278.

Aldrich, John H. 1995. *Why Parties? The Origin and Transformation of Political Parties in America.* Chicago: University of Chicago Press.

Aleinikoff, T. Alexander and Samuel Issacharoff. 1993. "Race and Redistricting: Drawing Constitutional Lines After *Shaw v. Reno*." *Michigan Law Review* 92(3): 588–651.

Altman, Micah and Michael McDonald. 2010. "The Promise and Perils of Computers in Redistricting." *Duke Journal of Constitutional Law and Public Policy* 5: 69–111.

Alvarez, R. Michael and Thad Hall. 2006. "Controlling Democracy: The Principal-Agent Problems in Election Administration." *Policy Studies Journal* 34(4): 491–510.

Alvarez, R. Michael and Thad Hall. 2008. "Measuring Perceptions of Election Threats: Survey Data from Voters and Elites" in R. Michael Alvarez, Thad Hall and Susan D. Hyde (eds) *Election Fraud: Detecting and Deterring Electoral Manipulation.* Washington, DC: The Brookings Institution.

Alvarez, R. Michael, Delia Bailey and Jonathan N. Katz. 2007. "The Effect of Voter Identification Laws on Turnout." California Institute of Technology Social Science Working Paper, #1267R.

Alvarez, R. Michael, Dustin Beckett, and Charles Stewart. 2013. "Voting Technology, Vote-By-Mail, and Residual Votes in California." *Political Research Quarterly* 66(3): 658–670.

Alvarez, R. Michael, Thad Hall, and Morgan Llewellyn. 2008. "Are Americans Confident Their Ballots are Counted?" *Journal of Politics* 70(3): 754–766.

Ansolabehere, Stephen and Charles Stewart. 2013. "Report on Registration Systems in American Elections," at https://www.supportthevoter.gov/files/2013/08/Registration-Systems-in-American-Elections-White-Paper-Ansolabehere_Stewart.pdf.

Ansolabehere, Stephen and Eitan Hersch. 2010. "The Quality of Voter Registration Records: A State-by-State Analysis," at http://www.gab.wi.gov/sites/default/files/publication/65/the_quality_of_voter_registration_records_harvard__10685.pdf, last accessed May 12, 2015.

Ansolabehere, Stephen and Nathaniel Persily. 2008. "Vote Fraud in the Eye of the Beholder: The Role of Public Opinion in the Challenge to Voter Identification Requirements." *Harvard Law Review* 121(7): 1737–1774.

Ansolabehere, Stephen, Nathaniel Persily and Charles Stewart III. 2013. "Regional Differences in Racial Polarization in the 2012 Presidential Election: Implications for the Constitutionality of Section 5 of the Voting Rights Act." *Harvard Law Review Forum* 126: 205–220.

Ansolabehere, Stephen. 2009. "Effects of Identification Requirements on Voting: Evidence from the Experiences of Voters on Election Day." *PS: Political Science and Politics* 42(1): 127–130.

Antonyan, Tigran, Seda Davtyan, Sotirios Kentros, Aggelos Kiayias, Laurent Michel, Nicolas Nicolaou, Alexander Russell, and Alexander A. Shvartsman. 2008. Statewide Elections, Optical Scan Voting Systems, and the Pursuit of Integrity, at https://voter.engr.uconn.edu/voter/wp-content/uploads/ieee.pdf.

Appelbaum, Paul S., Richard J. Bonnie, and Jason H. Karlawish. 2005. "The Capacity to Vote of Persons With Alzheimer's Disease." American Journal of Psychiatry 162(11): 2094–2100.

Ardoin, Phillip J., Charles S. Bell and Michael Raggozzino. Forthcoming. "The Partisan Battle over College Student Voting: An Analysis of Student Voting Behavior in Federal, State, and Local Elections." *Social Science Quarterly.*

Ardoin, Phillip J., Paul Gronke and Martha Kropf. 2015. "Town v. Gown: College Students and Voting in College Towns." Paper Presented at the 2015 Midwest Political Science Association Meeting, April 16, 2015, Chicago, IL.

Arrington, Theodore S. 2010. "Redistricting in the US: A Review of Scholarship and a Plan for Future Research." *The Forum* 8(2).

Asian American Legal Defense and Education Fund. 2012. "Language Access for Asian Americans Under the Voting Rights Act in the 2012 Election," at http://aaldef.org/AALDEF%20Election%202012%20Interim%20Report.pdf, last accessed December 17, 2014, page 8.

Atkeson, Lonna Rae, Lisa Ann Bryant, Thad E. Hall, Kyle. Saunders, and Michael Alvarez. 2010. "A New Barrier to Participation: Heterogeneous Application of Voter Identification Policies." *Electoral Studies* 29: 66–73.

Aylsworth, Leon E. 1931. "The Passage of Alien Suffrage." *The American Political Science Review* 25(1): 114–116.

Barabas, Jason and Jennifer Jerit. 2009. "Estimating the Causal Effects of Media Coverage on Policy-Specific Knowledge." *American Journal of Political Science* 53(1): 73–89.

Barach, Peter and Morton S. Baratz. 1962. "Two Faces of Power." *American Political Science Review* 56(4): 947–952.

Barreto, Matt A., Stephen A. Nuño, and Gabriel R. Sanchez. 2009. "The Disproportionate Impact of Voter-ID Requirements on the Electorate--New Evidence From Indiana." *PS: Political Science and Politics* 42(1): 111–116.

Barreto, Matt, Mara Cohen-Marks, and Nathan D. Woods. 2009. "Are All Precincts Created Equal? The Prevalence of Low-Quality Precincts in Low-Income and Minority Communities." *Political Research Quarterly* 62(3): 445–458.

Bartlett, Gary O. 2010. Health and Human Services Accessibility: HAVA Grants in North Carolina. North Carolina State Board of Elections, at https://www.ncsbe.gov/ncsbe/Portals/0/FilesP/HAVAAccessibilityNASED.pdf, last accessed February 26, 2015.

Bennett, W. Lance. 2012. "The Personalization of Politics: Political Identity, Social Media, and Changing Patterns of Participation." *The Annals of the Academy of Political and Social Science* 644(1): 20–39.

Bentele Keith G. and Erin E. O'Brien. 2013. "Jim Crow 2.0: Why States Consider and Adopt Restrictive Voter Access Policies." *Perspectives on Politics* 11(4): 1088–1116.

Berelson, Bernard, Paul F. Lazarsfeld and William N. McPhee., 1954. *Voting: A Study of Opinion Formation in a Presidential Campaign.* Chicago: University of Chicago Press.

Berman, Sheri. 1997. "Civil Society and the Collapse of the Weimar Republic." *World Politics* 49(3): 401–429.

Bibby, John F. and Louis Sandy Maisel. 2003. Two Parties or More?: The American Party System, 2nd Edition. Boulder: Westview Press.

Bland, Gary and Barry Burden. 2013. Electronic Registration Information Center (ERIC), Stage 1 Evaluation Report to the Pew Charitable Trusts, at http://www.rti.org/pubs/eric_stage1report_pewfinal_12-3-13.pdf#page=27, last accessed January 20 2015.

Bobo, Lawrence and Franklin D. Gilliam, Jr. 1990. "Race, Sociopolitical Participation and Black Empowerment." *American Political Science Review* 84(2): 377–393.

Borgatti, Stephen P., Ajay Mehra, Daniel J. Brass, and Giuseppe Labianca. 2009. "Network Analysis in the Social Sciences." *Science* 323(5916) (Feb. 13, 2009): 892–895.

Borgida, Eugene, Christopher M. Federico, and John Sullivan. 2009. "Introduction: Normative Conceptions of Democratic Citizenship and Evolving Empirical Research" in Eugene Borgida, Christopher Federico and John L. Sullivan (eds.) *The Political Psychology of Democratic Citizenship*. Oxford: Oxford University Press.

Bovbjerg, Barbara. 2013. Voters with Disabilities: Challenges to Accessibility. Statement Before the National Council on Disability, April 23, 2013, Washington, DC: General Accounting Office, at http://gao.gov/assets/660/654099.pdf, last accessed January 22, 2015.

Bovbjerg, Barbara. 2013. Voters with Disabilities: Challenges to Voter Accessibility. Washington, DC: General Accountability Office, at http://gao.gov/assets/660/654099.pdf, last accessed May 1, 2015.

Bowler, Shaun and Gary M. Segura. 2012. *The Future Is Ours: Minority Politics, Political Behavior, and the Multiracial Era of American Politics*. Thousand Oaks, CA: Congressional Quarterly Press/Sage.

Bowler, Shaun, Todd Donovan and David Brockington. 2003. *Electoral Reform and Minority Representation: Local Experiments with Alternative Elections*. Columbus: The Ohio State University Press.

Brace, Kimball. 2005. "Chapter 9: Voting Equipment Usage." 2004 Election Day Survey Results, at http://www.eac.gov/assets/1/AssetManager/2004%20EAVS%20Chapter%209.pdf, last accessed May 10, 2015.

Brady, Henry E. and John E. McNulty. 2011. "Turning Out to Vote: The Costs of Finding and Getting to the Polling Place." *American Political Science Review* 105(1): 115–134.

Burden, Barry and Jeffrey Milyo. 2013. The Recruitment and Training of Pollworkers: What We Know from Scholarly Research." Report Prepared for The Presidential Commission on Election Administration, September 6, 2013, at https://www.supportthevoter.gov/files/2013/09/The-Recruitment-and-Training-of-Poll-Workers-Burden-and-Milyo.pdf, last accessed January 14, 2015.

Burden, Barry C., David T. Canon, Kenneth R. Mayer and Donald P. Moynihan. 2014. "Election Laws, Mobilization, and Turnout: The Unanticipated Consequences of Election Reform." *American Journal of Political Science* 58(1): 95–109.

Canon, David T. 1999. *Race, Redistricting, and Representation: The Unintended Consequences of Black Majority Districts*. Chicago: University of Chicago Press.

Carpenter, Vivian L. 2001. "Institutional Theory and Accounting Rule Choice: An Analysis of Four U.S. State Governments' Decisions to Adopt Generally Accepted Accounting Principles." *Accounting, Organizations and Society* 26(2001): 565–596.

Chen, Jowei and Jonathan Rodden. 2013. "Unintentional Gerrymandering: Political Geography and Electoral Bias in Legislatures." *Quarterly Journal of Political Science* 8: 239–269.

Chisnell, Dana. Field Guides to Ensuring Voter Intent, at http://civicdesigning.org/wp-content/uploads/2013/06/Field-Guide-Vol-01-20130620.pdf, last accessed May 11, 2015.

Chong, Dennis and James N. Druckman. 2007. "Framing Theory." *Annual Review of Political Science* 10: 103–126.

Chung, Jean. 2014. Felony Disenfranchisement: A Primer. The Sentencing Project, at http://www.sentencingproject.org/doc/publications/fd_Felony%20Disenfranchisement%20Primer.pdf, last accessed March 24, 2015.

Claudia Z. Acemyan, Philip Kortum, Michael D. Byrne and Dan S. Wallach. 2014. "Usability of Voter Verifiable, End-to-End Voting Systems: Baseline Data for Helios, Prêt à Voter, and Scantegrity II." *USENIX Journal of Election Technology and Systems (JETS)* 2(3): 26–56, at: www.usenix.org/jets/issues/0203.

Cobb, Rachael V., D. James Greiner, and Kevin M. Quinn. 2010. "Can Voter ID Laws Be Administered in a Race-Neutral Manner? Evidence from the City of Boston in 2008." *Quarterly Journal of Political Science* 7(1): 1–33.

Coleman, James S. "Social Capital in the Creation of Human Capital." *American Journal of Sociology* 94(supplement): S95–S120.

Coleman, James. 1990. *Foundations of Social Theory.* Cambridge: Belknap Press of Harvard University Press.

Coleman, Kevin J. and Eric A. Fisher. 2014. The Help America Vote Act and Election Administration: Overview and Issues, December 17, 2014, Congressional Research Service, at http://www.fas.org/sgp/crs/misc/RS20898.pdf, last accessed January 8, 2015.

Coleman, Kevin T. 2014. The Uniformed and Overseas Citizens Absentee Voting Act: Overview and Issues, Congressional Research Service, April 21, 2014, at http://www.fas.org/sgp/crs/misc/RS20764.pdf, last accessed April 29, 2015.

Corrigan, John D. and Thomas B. Cole. 2008. "Substance Use Disorders and Clinical Management of Traumatic Brain Injury and Posttraumatic Stress Disorder." *Journal of the American Medical Association* 300(6): 720–721.

Cox, Gary W. and J. Morgan Kousser. 1981. "Turnout and Rural Corruption: New York as a Test Case." *American Journal of Political Science* 25(4): 646–663.

Cox, Gary W. and Jonathan N. Katz. 2002. *Elbridge Gerry's Salamander: The Electoral Consequences of the Reapportionment Revolution.* Cambridge: Cambridge University Press.

Crawford, Sue E. S. and Elinor Ostrom. 1995. "A Grammar of Institutions." *American Political Science Review* 89(3): 582–600.

Creek, Heather M. and Kimberly A. Karnes. 2010. "Federalism and Election Law: Implementation Issues in Rural American." *Publius: The Journal of Federalism* 40(2): 275–295.

Daniel Palazzolo, Vincent G. Moscardelli, Meredith Patrick and Doug Rubin. 2008. "Election Reform After HAVA: Voter Verification in Congress and the States." *Publius: The Journal of Federalism* 38(3): 515–537.

Dardis, Frank E., Frank R. Baumgartner, Amber E. Boydstun, Suzanna De Boef and Fuyuan Shen. 2008. "Media Framing of Capital Punishment and Its Impact on Individuals' Cognitive Responses." *Mass Communication & Society* 11: 115–140.

Davenport, Tiffany C. 2010. "Public Accountability and Political Participation: Effects of a Face-to-Face Feedback Intervention on Voter Turnout of Public Housing Residents." *Political Behavior* 32(3): 337–368.

Dawson, Michael C. 1994. *Behind the Mule: Race and Class in African-American Politics.* Princeton: Princeton University Press.

Dennis, Jack. 1970. "Support for the Institution of Elections by the Mass Public." *American Political Science Review* 64(3): 819–835.

Douglas, Joshua A. 2014. "The Right to Vote Under State Constitutions." *Vanderbilt Law Review* 67(1): 89–149.

Downs, Anthony. 1957. *An Economic Theory of Democracy*. New York: Harper.

Dyck, Joshua J. and James G. Gimpel. 2005. "Distance, Turnout, and the Convenience of Voting." *Social Science Quarterly* 86(3): 531–548.

Easton, David. 1965. *A Systems Analysis of Political Life*. Chicago: University of Chicago Press.

Engstrom, Richard L. 2001. "The Political Thicket, Electoral Reform, and Minority Voting Rights" in Mark E. Rush and Richard Lee Engstrom (eds.) *Fair and Effective Representation: Debating Electoral Reform and Minority Rights*. Lanham, MD: Rowman and Littlefield Publishers.

Ewald, Alec C. 2009. *The Way We Vote: The Local Dimension of American Suffrage*. Nashville: Vanderbilt University Press.

Fischer, Eric A. and Kevin J. Coleman. 2008. Election Reform and Local Election Officials: Results of Two National Surveys. Washington, DC: Congressional Research Service, at http://assets.opencrs.com/rpts/RL34363_20080207.pdf.

Fishkin, Joseph. 2011. "Equal Citizenship and the Individual Right to Vote." *Indiana Law Journal* 86: 1289–1360.

Fitzgerald, Mary. 2005. "Greater Convenience But Not Greater Turnout, The Impact of Alternative Voting Methods on Electoral Participation in the United States." *American Politics Research 33*(6): 842–867.

Foley, Edward B. 2006. "The Legitimacy of Imperfect Elections: Optimality, Not Perfection, Should Be the Goal of Election Administration" in Andrew Rachlin (ed.) *Making Every Vote Count: Federal Election Legislation in the States*. Princeton: Princeton University Press.

Fortier, John C. 2006. *Absentee and Early Voting*. Washington, DC: American Enterprise Institute.

Fougere, Joshua, Stephen Ansolabehere and Nathan Persily. 2010. "Partisanship, Public Opinion and Redistricting." *Election Law Journal* 9(4): 325–347.

Franklin, Charles H. and Liane C. Kosacki. 1989. "Republican Schoolmaster: The U.S. Supreme Court, Public Opinion, and Abortion." *American Political Science Review* 83(3): 751–771.

Frisina, Laurin, Michael C. Herron, James Honaker, and Jeffrey B. Lewis. 2008. "Ballot Formats, Touchscreens, and Undervotes: A Study of the 2006 Midterm Elections in Florida." *Election Law Journal* 7(1): 25–47.

Gerber, Alan S. and Donald P. Green. 2000. "The Effects of Canvassing, Telephone Calls, and Direct Mail on Voter Turnout: A Field Experiment." *American Political Science Review* 94(3): 653–663.

Gerber, Alan S. and Todd Rogers. 2009. "Descriptive Social Norms and Motivation to Vote: Everybody's Voting and So Should You." *Journal of Politics* 71(1): 178–191.

Gerber, Alan S., Donald P. Green and Christopher W. Larimer. 2008. "Social Pressure and Voter Turnout: Evidence from a Large-Scale Field Experiment." *American Political Science Review* 102(1): 33–48.

Gerber, Alan S., Donald P. Green and Christopher W. Larimer. 2010. "An Experiment Testing the Relative Effectiveness of Encouraging Voter Participation by Inducing Feelings of Pride or Shame." *Political Behavior* 32(3): 409–422.

Gerber, Alan S., Gregory A. Huber and Seth J. Hill. 2013. "Identifying the Effect of All-Mail Elections on Turnout: Staggered Reform in the Evergreen State." *Political Science Research and Methods* 1(1): 91–116.

Gerber, Alan S., Gregory A. Huber, David Doherty and Conor M. Dowling. 2015. "Why People Vote: Estimating the Social Returns to Voting." *British Journal of Political Science*,

FirstView Article/April 2015, pages 1–24 DOI: 10.1017/S0007123414000271, Published online: October 20, 2014.

Gerken, Heather. 2009 and 2012. *The Democracy Index: Why Our Election System Is Failing and How to Fix It*. Princeton: Princeton University Press.

Giles, Michael W. and Marilyn K. Dantico. 1982. "Political Participation and Neighborhood Social Context Revisited." *American Journal of Political Science* 26(1): 144–150.

Gimpel, James G., Joshua J. Dyck, and Daron R. Shaw. 2006. "Location, Knowledge and Time Pressures in the Spatial Structure of Convenience Voting." *Electoral Studies* 25(1): 35–58.

Goedert, Nicholas. 2012. "Not Gerrymandering, but Districting: More Evidence on How Democrats Won the Popular Vote but Lost the Congress," at http://themonkeycage.org, last accessed June 14, 2013.

Goren, Paul. 2013. *On Voter Competence*. Oxford: Oxford University Press.

Granovetter, Mark S. 1973. "The Strength of Weak Ties." *American Journal of Sociology* 78(6): 1360–1380.

Green, D. and Shachar, R. (2000). "Habit Formation and Political Behaviour: Evidence of Consuetude in Voter Turnout." *British Journal of Political Science* 30: 561–573.

Grofman, Bernard, Lisa Handley, and Richard G. Niemi. 1992. *Minority Representation and the Quest for Voting Equality*. Cambridge: Cambridge University Press.

Gronke, Paul, Eva Galanes-Rosenbaum, and Peter Miller. 2007. "Early Voting and Turnout." *PS: Political Science and Politics* 40(4): 639–645.

Gronke, Paul, Eva Galanes-Rosenbaum, and Peter Miller. 2008. "Convenience Voting." *Annual Review of Political Science* 11: 437–455.

Gronke, Paul, William D. Hicks, Seth C. McKee, and Charles Stewart III. 2015. "Voter ID Laws: A View from the Public." Massachusetts Institute of Technology Political Science Department Research Paper No. 2015–13.

Hale, Kathleen and Mitchell Brown. 2013. "Adopting, Adapting, and Opting Out: State Response to Federal Voting System Guidelines." *Publius: The Journal of Federalism* 43(3): 428–451.

Hale, Kathleen, Robert Montjoy and Mitchell Brown. 2015. Administering Elections: How American Elections Work. New York: Palgrave.

Hale, Kathleen and Ramona McNeal. 2010. "Election Administration Reform and State Choice: Voter Identification Requirements and HAVA." *Policy Studies Journal* 38(2): 281–302.

Hall, Bob and Isela Gutierrez. 2015. Memo to the North Carolina State Board of Elections, Re: Feedback on the 2014 Election and Impact of H-589 on Voter Turnout. Democracy NC Date: January 26, 2015, at http://www.democracy-nc.org/downloads/SBEMemo2015. pdf, last accessed May 1, 2015.

Hall, Thad E., J. Quin Monson and Kelly D. Patterson. 2009. "The Human Dimension of Elections: How Pollworkers Shape Public Confidence in Elections." *Political Research Quarterly* 62(3): 507–522.

Hall, Thad. 2013. "US Voter Registration Reform." *Electoral Studies* 32(4): 589–596.

Hamilton, James and Helen Ladd. 1996. "Biased Ballots: The Impact of Ballot Structure on North Carolina Elections in 1992." *Public Choice* 87(3/4): 259–280.

Hamilton, Randy H. 1988. "American All-Mail Balloting: A Decade's Experience." *Public Administration Review* 48(5): 860–866.

Hanmer, Michael. 2009. *Discount Voting: Voter Registration Reforms and Their Effects*. Cambridge: Cambridge University Press.

Harwin, Veronica. 2013. "A Tale of Two States: Challenges to Voter ID Ballot Measures in Missouri and Minnesota." *Washington Journal of Law & Policy* 42(1): 203–234.

Hasen, Richard L. 1996. "Voting Without Law." *University of Pennsylvania Law Review* 144(5): 2135–2179.

Hasen, Richard L. 2005. "Beyond the Margin of Litigation: Reforming U.S. Election Administration to Avoid Electoral Meltdown." *Washington & Lee Law Review* 62(3): 937–999.

Hasen, Richard L. 2006. "Congressional Power to Renew Preclearance Provisions" in David L. Epstein, Richard H. Pildes, Rodolfo O. de la Garza, and Sharyn O'Halloran (eds.) *The Future of the Voting Rights Act*. New York: Russell Sage Foundation.

Hasen, Richard L. 2012. *The Voting Wars: From Florida 2000 to the Next Election Meltdown*. New Haven: Yale University Press.

Hasen, Richard L. 2013. "The Voting Wars Within: Is the Department of Justice too Biased to Enforce the Voting Rights Act?" Slate Magazine, March 18, 2013, at http://www.slate.com/articles/news_and_politics/politics/2013/03/justice_department_s_inspector_general_report_is_the_voting_rights_section.html.

Haspel, Moshe and H. Gibbs Knotts. 2005. "Location, Location, Location: Precinct Placement and the Costs of Voting." *Journal of Politics* 67(2): 560–573.

Hayduk, Ron. 2006. *Democracy for All: Restoring Immigrant Voting Rights in the United States*. New York: Routledge.

Hayduk, Ron. 2014. "Op-Ed: Give Noncitizens the Right to Vote—It's Only Fair." *The Los Angeles Times*, December 22, 2014, at http://www.latimes.com/opinion/op-ed/la-oe-hayduk-let-noncitizens-vote-20141223-story.html, last accessed February 16, 2015.

Hayes, Danny and Seth C. McKee. 2012. "The Intersection of Redistricting, Race, and Participation." *American Journal of Political Science* 56(1): 115–130.

Hayes, Danny and Seth C. McKee. 2009. "The Participatory Effects of Redistricting." *American Journal of Political Science* 53(4): 1006–1023.

Herrnson, Paul S., Michael J. Hanmer and Richard G. Niemi. 2012. "The Impact of Ballot Type on Voter Error." *American Journal of Political Science* 56(3): 716–730.

Herrnson, Paul S., Richard G. Niemi, Michael J. Hanmer, Benjamin D. Bederson, Frederick G. Conrad, and Michael W. Traugott. 2008. *Voting Technology: The Not-So-Simple Act of Casting a Ballot*. Washington, DC: Brookings Institution.

Herron, Michael C. and Daniel A. Smith. 2012. "Souls to the Polls: Early Voting in t Florida in the Shadow of House Bill 1355." *Election Law Journal* 11(3): 331–347.

Hess, Douglas R. and Scott Novakowski. 2008. Neglecting the National Voter Registration Act, 1995–2007. Project Vote and Demos, at http://www.projectvote.org/images/publications/NVRA/Unequal_Access_Final.pdf, last accessed January 24, 2015.

Hicks, William D., Seth C. McKee, Mitchell D. Sellers, and Daniel A. Smith. 2015. "A Principle or a Strategy? Voter Identification Laws and Partisan Competition in the American States." *Political Research Quarterly* 68(1): 18–33.

Hood, M.V. III and Charles S. Bullock. 2012. "Much Ado About Nothing? An Empirical Assessment of the Georgia Voter Identification Statute." *State Politics & Policy Quarterly* 12(4): 394–414.

Huckfeldt, Robert, Paul E. Johnson, and John Sprague. 2004. *Political Disagreement: The Survival of Diverse Opinions Within Communication Networks*. Cambridge: Cambridge University Press.

Huckfeldt, Robert. 1979. "Political Participation and the Neighborhood Context." *American Journal of Political Science* 23(3): 579–592.

Huckfeldt, Robert and John Sprague.1995. *Citizens, Politics, and Social Communication*. Cambridge: Cambridge University Press.

Huddy, Leonie and Nadia Khatib. 2007. "American Patriotism, National Identity and Political Involvement." *American Journal of Political Science* 51(1): 63–77.

Huddy, Leonie and Simo V. Virtanen. 1995. "Subgroup Differentiation and Subgroup Bias Among Latinos as a Function of Familiarity and Positive Distinctiveness." *Journal of Personality and Social Psychology* 68(1): 97–108.

Hurme, Sally Balch and Paul S. Appelbaum. 2007. "Defining and Assessing Capacity to Vote: The Effect of Mental Impairment on the Rights of Voters." *McGeorge Law Review* 38: 931–979.

Idaho Votes: A Citizen's Guide to Participation, at http://www.nyssba.org/news/2014/05/09/on-board-online-may-12-2014/mandate-microscopevoting-machine-exemption-due-to-expire-this-year/, last accessed May 4, 2015.

Issacharoff, Samuel. 2013. "Beyond the Discrimination Model on Voting." New York University Public Law and Legal Theory Working Papers. Paper 416, at http://lsr.nellco.org/nyu_plltwp/416, last accessed June 9, 2015.

Iyengar, Shanto and Donald Kinder. 1987. *News That Matters: Television and American Opinion.* Chicago: The University of Chicago Press.

James, Scott C. and Brian L. Lawson. 1999. "The Political Economy of Voting Rights Enforcement in America's Gilded Age: Electoral College Competition, Partisan Commitment and the Federal Election Law." *American Political Science Review* 93(1): 115–131.

Jennings, M. Kent and Richard Niemi. 1981. *Generations and Politics.* Princeton: Princeton University Press.

Karpowitz, Christopher F., J. Quin Monson, Lindsay Nielson, Kelly D. Patterson, and Steven A. Snell. 2011. "Political Norms and the Private Act of Voting." *Public Opinion Quarterly* 75(4): 659–685.

Katz, Ellen; with Margaret Aisenbrey, Anna Baldwin, Emma Bheuse and Anna Weisbrodt. 2006. "Documenting Discrimination in Voting: Judicial Findings Under Section 2 of the Voting Rights Act Since 1982: Final Report of the Voting Rights Initiative, University of Michigan Law School." *University of Michigan Journal of Law Reform* 39(4): 643–772, available at SSRN: http://ssrn.com/abstract=1029386.

Kelly, Kate. 1991. *Election Day: An American Holiday, An American History.* Bloomington, IN: ASJA Press.

Kelsey, John, Andrew Regenscheid, Tal Moran, and David Chaum. 2010. "Attacking Paper-Based E2E Voting Systems." *Towards Trustworthy Elections, LNCS* 6000: 370–387, at http://www.itl.nist.gov/div897/voting/attacking-e2e-voting-systems.pdf, last accessed May 9, 2015.

Kerwin, Cornelius. 2003. *Rulemaking: How Government Agencies Write Law and Make Policy,* 3rd Edition. Washington, DC: Congressional Quarterly Press.

Kerwin, Cornelius and Scott R. Furlong. 2010. *Rulemaking: How Government Agencies Write Law and Make Policy,* 4th Edition. Washington, DC: Congressional Quarterly Press.

Key, V.O. 1949. *Southern Politics in State and Nation.* New York: A.A. Knopf.

Keyssar, Alexander. 2000. *The Right to Vote: The Contested History of Democracy in the United States.* New York: Basic Books.

Kimball, David C. and Martha Kropf. 2005. "Ballot Design and Unrecorded Votes on Paper-Based Ballots" *Public Opinion Quarterly* 69(4): 508–529.

Kimball, David C. and Martha Kropf. 2006. "The Street-Level Bureaucrats of Elections: Selection Methods for Local Election Officials." *Review of Policy Research* 23: 1257–1268.

Kimball, David C. and Martha Kropf. 2008. "Voting Technology, Ballot Measures and Residual Votes." *American Politics Research* 36(4): 479–509.

Kimball, David C. and Martha Kropf. Forthcoming. "Voter Competence with Cumulative Voting." *Social Science Quarterly*.

Kimball, David C., Martha Kropf and Lindsay Battles. 2006. "Helping America Vote? Election Administration, Partisanship, and Provisional Voting in the 2004 Election." *Election Law Journal* 5(4): 447–461.

Kimball, David C., Martha Kropf, Donald Moynihan, Carol L. Silva, and Brady Baybeck. 2013. "The Policy Views of Partisan Election Officials." *University of California-Irvine Law Review* 3: 551–574.

King, Gary, Robert O. Keohane and Sidney Verba. 1994. *Designing Social Inquiry: Scientific Inference in Qualitative Research*. Princeton: Princeton University Press.

Kiser, Larry L. and Elinor Ostrom. 2000. "The Three Worlds of Action: A Metatheoretical Synthesis of Institutional Approaches" in Michael D. McGinnis (ed.) *Polycentric Games and Institutions: Readings from the Workshop of Political Theory and Policy Analysis*. Ann Arbor: University of Michigan Press.

Klofstad, Casey A., Anand Edward Sokhey and Scott D. McClurg. 2013. "Disagreeing About Disagreement: How Conflicts in Social Networks Affects Political Behavior." *American Journal of Political Science* 57(1): 120–134.

Knack, Stephen and Martha Kropf. 1998. "For Shame! The Effect of the Community Cooperation Context on the Probability of Voting." *Political Psychology* 19: 585–599.

Knack, Stephen and Martha Kropf. 2003. "Invalidated Ballots in the 1996 Presidential Election: A County-Level Analysis." *Journal of Politics.* 65(3): 881–897.

Knack, Stephen. 1992. "Civic Norms, Social Sanctions and Voter Turnout." *Rationality and Society* 4(2): 133–156.

Knoke, David. 1990. *Political Networks: The Structural Perspective*. Cambridge: Cambridge University Press.

Kogan, Vladimir and Eric McGhee. 2012. "Redistricting California: An Evaluation of the Citizens Commission Final Plans." *The California Journal of Politics & Policy* 4(1). DOI: 10.1515/1944-4370.1197.

Kohut, Andrew and Bruce Stokes. 2006. "The Problem of American Exceptionalism," at http://www.pewresearch.org/2006/05/09/the-problem-of-american-exceptionalism/, last accessed July 16, 2014.

Kousser, Thad and Megan Mullin. 2007. "Does Voting By Mail Increase Participation? Using Matching to Analyze a Natural Experiment." *Political Analysis* 15: 428–445.

Kropf, Martha. 2005. "Dogs and Dead People: Incremental Election Reform in Missouri." In *Election Reform: Politics and Policy*, (pp. 157–173). Edited by Daniel J. Palazzollo and James W. Ceaser. Lanham: Lexington Books.

Kropf, Martha, David Swindell, and Elizabeth Wemlinger. 2009. "The Effects of Early Voting on Social Ties: Using Longitudinal Data." Presented at the Non-Precinct Place Voting Conference, Portland, OR.

Kropf, Martha and David C. Kimball. 2012. *Helping America Vote: The Limits of Election Reform*. New York: Routledge.

Kropf, Martha, Janine Parry, Jay Barth and E. Terrence Jones. 2008. "Pursuing the Early Voter: Does the Early Bird Get the Worm?" *Journal of Political Marketing* 7(2): 131–150.

Kropf, Martha and Stephen Knack. 2003. "Viewers Like You: Community Norms and Contributions to Public Broadcasting." *Political Research Quarterly* 56(2): 187–195.

Kropf, Martha, Timothy Vercellotti, and David C. Kimball. 2013. "Representative Bureaucracy and Partisanship: The Implementation of Election Law." *Public Administration Review* 73(2): 242–252.

Kropf, Martha. 2009. "Won't You Be My Neighbor? Norms of Cooperation, Public Broadcasting and the Collective Action Problem." *Social Science Quarterly* 90(3): 538–552.

Kropf, Martha. 2012. "Does Early Voting Change the Socio-Economic Composition of the Electorate?" *Poverty & Public Policy* 4(1): 1–19.

Kropf, Martha. 2013. "North Carolina Election Reform Ten Years After the Help America Vote Act." *Election Law Journal* 12(2): 179–189.

Kropf, Martha. 2014. "The Evolution of Ballot Design Ten Years After Bush v. Gore" in R. Michael Alvarez and Bernie Grofman (eds.) *Election Administration in the United States: The State of Reform Ten Years After Bush v. Gore*, Cambridge University Press.

Lau, Richard and David P. Redlawsk, 2006. *How Voters Decide: Information Processing in Election Campaigns*. Cambridge: Cambridge University Press.

Lausen, Marcia. 2007. *Design for Democracy: Ballot and Election Design*. Chicago: University of Chicago Press.

Lazarsfeld, Paul Felix, Bernard Berelson and Hazel Gaudet. 1944. *The People's Choice: How the Voter Makes Up His Mind in a Presidential Campaign*. New York: Columbia University Press.

Lehoucq, Fabrice. 2003. "Electoral Fraud: Causes, Types, and Consequences." *Annual Review of Political Science* 5: 233–256.

Leighley, Jan E. 2001. *Strength in Numbers: The Political Mobilization of Racial and Ethnic Minorities*. Princeton: Princeton University Press.

Leighley, Jan E. and Jonathan Nagler. 2014. *Who Votes Now? Demographics, Issues, Inequality, and Turnout in the United States*. Princeton: Princeton University Press.

Leighley, Jan E. and Arnold Vedlitz. 1999. "Race, Ethnicity and Political Participation: Competing Models and Contrasting Explanations." *Journal of Politics* 61(4): 1092–1114.

Leonie Huddy. 2001. "From Social to Political Identity: A Critical Examination of Social Identity Theory." *Political Psychology* 22(1): 127–156.

Lepore, Jill. 2008. "Rock, Paper, Scissors: How We Used to Vote." *The New Yorker*, October 13, 2008, at http://www.newyorker.com/magazine/2008/10/13/rock-paper-scissors, last accessed August 14, 2014.

Levitt, Justin. 2011. "Weighing the Potential of Citizen Redistricting." *Loyola of Los Angeles Law Review* 44: 513–544.

Levitt, Justin and Michael P. McDonald. 2006. "Taking the 'Re' out of Redistricting: State Constitutional Provisions on Redistricting Timing." *The Georgetown Law Journal* 95(1): 1247–1285.

Lijphart, Arend. 1999. *Patterns of Democracy: Government Forms and Performance in Thirty-Six Countries*. New Haven: Yale University Press.

Link, Jessica N., Martha Kropf, Mark Alexander Hirsch, Flora M. Hammond, Jason Karlawish, Lisa Schur, Douglas Kruse and Christine S. Davis. 2012. "Assessing Voting Competence and Political Knowledge: Comparing Individuals with Traumatic Brain Injuries and 'Average' College Students." *Election Law Journal* 11(1): 52–69.

Lipsky, Michael. 1980. *Street-Level Bureaucrats: Dilemmas of the Individual in Public Services*. New York: Russell Sage Foundation.

Manza, Jeff, Clem Brooks and Michael Sauder. 2005. "Money, Participation and Votes: Social Cleavages and Electoral Politics." Chapter 10 in Thomas Janowski, Robert Alford, Alexander Hicks, and Mildred A. Schwartz (eds.) *The Handbook of Political Sociology*. Cambridge: Cambridge University Press.

March, James G. and Johan P. Olsen. 1983. "The New Institutionalism: Organizational Factors in Political Life." *American Political Science Review* 78(3): 734–749.

March, James G. and Johan P. Olsen. 1989. *Rediscovering Institutions: The Organizational Basis of Politics*. New York: The Free Press.

Masket, Seth E., Jonathan Winburn and Gerald C. Wright. 2012. "The Gerrymanderers are Coming! Legislative Redistricting Won't Affect Competition or Polarization Much, No Matter Who Does It." *PS: Political Science and Politics* January 2012: 39–43.

McClurg, Scott D. 2006. "The Electoral Relevance of Political Talk: Examining Disagreement and Expertise Effects in Social Networks on Political Participation." *American Journal of Political Science* 50(3): 737–754.

McConnaughy, Corrine M. 2013. *The Woman Suffrage Movement in American: A Reassessment.* Cambridge: Cambridge University Press.

McDuffie, Jerome A. 1979. *Politics in Wilmington and New Hanover County, North Carolina, 1865–1900: The Genesis of a Race Riot,* Unpublished Ph.D. Dissertation, Kent State University.

McKee, Seth. 2008. "Redistricting and Familiarity with U.S. House Candidates." *American Politics Research* 36(6): 962–979.

McKee, Seth. 2008. "The Effects of Redistricting on Voting Behavior in Incumbent U.S. House Elections, 1992–1994." *Political Research Quarterly* 61(1): 122–133.

Miller, Michael. 2013. "Do Audible Alerts Reduce Undervotes? Evidence from Illinois." *Election Law Journal* 12(2): 162–178.

Minnite, Lorraine C. 2010. *The Myth of Voter Fraud.* Ithaca: Cornell University Press.

Montjoy, Robert S. 2005. "The Public Administration of Elections." *Public Administration Review* 68(5): 788–799.

Montjoy, Robert S. 2005. "HAVA and the States" in Daniel J. Palazzolo and James W. Ceaser (eds.) *Election Reform: Politics and Policy.* Landham: Lexington Books.

National Conference of State Legislatures. 2012. "Voting Technology: Current and Future Choices." The Canvass, Issue #31, June 2012, at http://www.ncsl.org/documents/legismgt/elect/Canvass_June_2012_No_31.pdf, last accessed May 5, 2015.

Neal, David T., Wendy Wood, Mengju Wu and David Kurlander. 2011. "The Pull of the Past: When Do Habits Persist Despite Conflict with Motives?" *Personality and Social Psychology Bulletin* 37(11): 1428–1437.

Niemi, Richard G. and John Deegan, Jr. 1978. "A Theory of Political Districting." *American Political Science Review* 72(4): 1304–1323.

Niemi, Richard G., Michael J. Hanmer, and Thomas H. Jackson. 2009. "Where Can College Students Vote? A Legal and Empirical Perspective." *Election Law Journal* 8(4): 327–348.

Nou, Jennifer. 2013. "Sub-Regulating Elections." *The Supreme Court Review* 2013(1): 135–182.

O'Loughlin, Michael and Corey Unangst. 2006. *Democracy and College Student Voting,* 3rd Edition. The Institute for Public Affairs and Civic Engagement, Salisbury University, at https://www.salisbury.edu/pace/publications/reports/dcv7-25-06.pdf, last accessed June 5, 2015.

Oliver, J. Eric. 1996. "Absentee Voting and Overall Turnout." *American Journal of Political Science* 40(2): 498–513.

Ostrom, Elinor. 1990. *Governing the Commons: The Evolution of Institutions for Collective Action.* Cambridge: Cambridge University Press.

Ostrom, Elinor. 1998. "A Behavioral Approach to the Rational Choice Theory of Collective Action: Presidential Address." *American Political Science Review* 92(1): 1–22.

Panagopoulos. Costas. 2010. "Affect, Social Pressure and Pro-Social Motivation: Field Experimental Evidence of the Mobilizing Effects of Pride, Shame and Publicizing Voter Behavior." *Political Behavior* 32(3): 369–386.

Passel, Jeffrey S. 2005. "Estimates of the Size and Characteristics of the Undocumented Population." Pew Hispanic Center Report, March 21, 2005, at http://music-editor.com/mns.morris.com/Special_Pages/Immigration/Hispanic-Estimate%20of%20Undocumented.pdf, last accessed April 26, 2015.

Peters, Guy B. 2012. *Institutional Theory in Political Science: The "New Institutionalism,"* 2nd Edition. New York: The Continuum International Publishing Company.

Pezzella, David and Martha Kropf. 2011. "The Celebration of Enfranchisement: Coming Together to Vote on Election Day." Unpublished Manuscript, University of North Carolina at Charlotte.

Pildes, Richard H. 2007. "What Kind of Right is the 'Right to Vote'?" *Virginia Law Review* (April 23): 43–50.

Pildes, Richard. 2006. "Introduction" in David L. Epstein, Richard H. Pildes, Rodolfo O. de la Garza, and Sharyn O'Halloran. Russell (eds.) *The Future of the Voting Rights Act.* New York: Sage Foundation.

Pildes, Richard. 2006. "The Future of Voting Rights Policy: From Anti-Discrimination to the Right to Vote." *Howard Law Journal* 49(3): 741–765.

Pitkin, Hanna Finichel. 1967. *The Concept of Representation.* Berkeley: University of California Press.

Piven, Frances Fox and Richard A. Cloward. 1988. "National Voter Registration Reform: How It Might Be Won." *PS: Political Science and Politics* 21(4): 868–875. Stable URL: http://www.jstor.org/stable/420026.

Plutzer, Eric. 2002. "Becoming a Habitual Voter: Inertia, Resources, and Growth in Young Adulthood." *American Political Science Review* 96(1): 41–56.

Polgar, Paul J. 2011. "'Whenever They Judge it Expedient': The Politics of Partisanship and Free Black Voting Rights in Early National New York." *American Nineteenth Century History* 12(1): 1–23.

Portes, Alejandro and Erik Vickstrom. 2011. "Diversity, Social Capital, and Cohesion." *Annual Review of Sociology* 37: 461–479.

Portes, Alejandro. 1998. "Social Capital: Its Origins and Applications in Modern Sociology." *Annual Review of Sociology* 24: 1–24.

Portes, Alejandro. 2014. "Downsides of Social Capital." *Proceedings of the National Academy of Sciences of the United States of America* 111(52): 18407–18408.

Prior, Markus. 2013. "Media and Political Polarization." *Annual Review of Political Science* 16: 101–127.

Putnam, Robert D. 1966. "Political Attitudes and the Local Community." *American Political Science Review* 60(3): 640–654.

Putnam, Robert. 2000. *Bowling Alone: The Collapse and Revival of American Community.* New York: Simon & Schuster.

Raad, Raymond, Jason Karlawish, and Paul S. Appelbaum. 2009. "The Capacity to Vote of Persons With Serious Mental Illness." *Psychiatric Services* 60(5): 624–628.

Raskin, Jamin B. 1993. "Legal Aliens, Local Citizens: The Historical, Constitutional and Theoretical Meanings of Alien Suffrage." *University of Pennsylvania Law Review* 141: 1391–1470.

Raskin, Jamin. 2004. "A Right-to-Vote Amendment for the U.S. Constitution: Confronting America's Structural Democracy Deficit." *Election Law Journal* 3(3): 559–573.

Ratcliffe, Daniel J. 2013. "The Role of Voters and Issues in Party Formation: Ohio, 1824." *The Journal of American History* 59(4): 847–870.

Rice, Tom W. and Jan L. Feldman. 1997. "Civic Culture and Democracy from Europe to America." *Journal of Politics* 59(4): 1143–1172.

Richey, Sean. 2005. "Who Votes Alone? The Impact of Voting by Mail on Political Discussion." *Australian Journal of Political Science* 40(3): 435–442.

Riker, William H. and Peter C. Ordeshook. 1968. "A Theory of the Calculus of Voting." *American Political Science Review* 62(1): 25–42.

Robert Putnam. 1993. *Making Democracy Work: Civic Traditions in Modern Italy*. Princeton: Princeton University Press.

Robertson, Andrew W. 2013. "Afterword: Reconceptualizing Jeffersonian Democracy." *Journal of the Early Republic* 33(Summer 2013): 317–334.

Rosberg, Gerald M. 1977. "Aliens and Equal Protection: Why Not the Right to Vote?" *Michigan Law Review* 75(5/6): 1092–1136.

Rosenstone, Steven J. and John Mark Hansen. 1993. *Mobilization, Participation, and Democracy in America*. New York: Macmillan Publishing Company.

Rubin, Aviel D. 2006. *Brave New Ballot: The Battle to Safeguard Democracy in the Age of Electronic Voting*. New York: Morgan Road Books.

Rusk, Jerrold D. 1970. "The Effect of the Australian Ballot on Split Ticket Voting: 1876–1908." *American Political Science Review* 64(4): 1876–1908.

Rusk, Jerrold D. 1974. "Comment: The American Electoral Universe: Speculation and Evidence." *American Political Science Review* 68(3): 1028–1049.

Rytina, Nancy. 2013. "Estimates of the Legal Permanent Resident Population in 2012." Department of Homeland Security, at http://www.dhs.gov/sites/default/files/publications/ois_lpr_pe_2012.pdf, last accessed February 13, 2015.

Saltman, Roy G. 2006. *The History and Politics of Voting Technology: In Quest of Integrity and Public Confidence*. New York: Palgrave Macmillan.

Samson, Frank L. and Lawrence D. Bobo. 2014. "Ethno-Racial Attitudes and Social Inequality" in J.D. McLeod et al. (eds.) *Handbook of the Social Psychology of Inequality*. DOI: 10.1007/978-94-017-9002-4_21.

Schattschneider, E.E. 1960. *The Semisovereign People: A Realist's View of Democracy in America*. New York: Holt, Rinehart and Winston.

Schur, Lisa and Meera Adya. 2012. "Sidelined or Mainstreamed? Political Participation and Attitudes of People with Disabilities in the United States." *Social Science Quarterly* 94(3): 811–839.

Schur, Lisa, Meera Adya and Douglas Kruse. 2013. "Disability, Voter Turnout, and Voting Difficulties in the 2012 Elections," Report to Research Alliance for Accessible Voting and U.S. Election Assistance Commission, Rutgers University, June 2013, at http://smlr.rutgers.edu/research-centers/disability-and-voter-turnout, last accessed May 1, 2015.

Searing, 1991. "Roles, Rules and Rationality in the New Institutionalism" *American Political Science Review* 85(4): 1239–1260.

Sherman, Alan T., Richard Carback, David Chaum, Jeremy Clark, Aleksander Essex, Paul S. Herrnson, Travis Mayberry, Stefan Popoveniuc, Ronald L. Rivest, Emily Shen, Bimal Sinha, and Poorvi Vora. 2010. "Scantegrity II Municipal Election at Takoma Park: The First E2E Binding Governmental Election with Ballot Privacy," at http://vote.caltech.edu/content/scantegrity-ii-municipal-election-takoma-park-first-e2e-binding-governmental-election-ballot, last accessed May 9, 2015.

Sherman, Jon. 2014. Saving Votes: An Easy Fix to the Problem of Wasting Provisional Ballots Cast Out of Precinct. Fair Elections Legal Network, at http://fairelectionsnetwork.com/sites/default/files/Provisional%20Ballot%20Rejection%20Memo%20FINAL.pdf, last accessed January 9, 2015.

Smith, Aaron. 2015. Smartphone Use in 2015, Pew Research Center, at http://www.pewinternet.org/2015/04/01/us-smartphone-use-in-2015/, last accessed May 4, 2015.

Southwell, Priscilla L. 2004. "Five Years Later: A Reassessment of Oregon's Vote By Mail Electoral Process." *PS: Political Science and Politics*, 1: 89–93.

Southwell, Priscilla L. and Justin I. Burchett. 2000. "The Effect of All-Mail Elections on Voter Turnout." *American Politics Research* 28(1): 72–79.

Stavinsky, Alan G. 1994. "The Changing Conception of Localism in U.S. Public Radio." *Journal of Broadcasting & Electronic Media* 38 (1):19–33.

Stein, Robert M. and Greg Vonnahme. 2008. "Engaging the Unengaged Voter: Vote Centers and Voter Turnout." *Journal of Politics.* 70: 1–11.

Stein, Robert M. and Greg Vonnahme. 2012. "Effect of Election Day Vote Centers on Voters Participation." *Election Law Journal* 11(3): 291–301.

Stein, Robert, Chris Owens, and Jan Leighley. 2003. "Electoral Reform, Party Mobilization and Voter Turnout." Unpublished manuscript, at http://www.nyu.edu/gsas/dept/politics/seminars/leighley.pdf, last accessed June 5, 2015.

Stephanopoulos, Nicholas. 2013. "The South After Shelby County." The University of Chicago Law School Public Law And Legal Theory Working Paper No. 451, at http://chicagounbound.uchicago.edu/cgi/viewcontent.cgi?article=1436&context=public_law_and_legal_theory, last accessed April 24, 2015.

Stewart, Charles III and Stephen Ansolabehere. 2013. "Waiting in Line to Vote." July 28, 2013, at https://www.supportthevoter.gov/files/2013/08/Waiting-in-Line-to-Vote-White-Paper-Stewart-Ansolabehere.pdf, last accessed May 1, 2015.

Tajfel, Henri. 1981. *Human Groups and Social Categories.* Cambridge: Cambridge University Press.

Tanielian, Terri, Lisa H. Jaycox, David M. Adamson, and Karen N. Metscher. 2008. "Introduction" in Terri Tanielian and Lisa H. Jaycox (eds.) *Invisible Wounds of War: Psychological and Cognitive Injuries, Their Consequences, and Services to Assist Recovery.* Santa Monica: Rand Corporation.

Tarr, G. Alan. 1994. "The Past and the Future of the New Judicial Federalism." *Publius: The Journal of Federalism* 24(2): 63–79.

Tate, Katherine. 1994. *From Protest to Politics: The New Black Voters in American Elections.* Cambridge: Harvard University Press.

Teixeira, Ruy A. 1987. *Why Americans Don't Vote: Turnout Decline in the United States, 1960–1984.* New York: Greenwood Press.

The Heritage Foundation. 2014. Does Your Vote Count? Ensuring Election Integrity and Making Sure Your Vote Counts, at http://thf_media.s3.amazonaws.com/2014/pdf/Doesyourvotecount.pdf, last accessed May 14, 2015.

The Pew Charitable Trusts. 2015. "New Survey Highlights the 2014 Voting Experience." (February 10, 2015), at http://www.pewtrusts.org/en/about/news-room/news/2015/02/09/new-survey-highlights-the-2014-voting-experience, last accessed April 28, 2015.

Thomassen, Jacques. 2014. *Elections and Democracy: Representation and Accountability.* Oxford: Oxford University Press.

Tokaji, Daniel P. 2006. "If It's Broke, Fit It: Improving Voting Rights Act Preclearance." *Howard Law Journal* 49(3): 785–842.

Tokaji, Daniel P. 2006. "The New Vote Denial: Where Election Reform Meets the New Voting Rights Act." *South Carolina Law Review* 57(4): 689–733.

Tokaji, Daniel P. 2007. "Leave It To the Lower Courts: On Judicial Intervention in Election Administration." *Ohio State Law Journal* 68: 1065–1095.

Tokaji, Daniel P. 2008. "Representation and Raceblindness: The Story of Shaw v. Reno." Chapter 14 in Rachel F. Moran and Devon W. Carbado (eds.) *Race Law Stories.* New York: Foundation Press.

Tokaji, Daniel P. 2014. "Responding to Shelby County: A Grand Election Bargain." *Harvard Law and Policy Review* 8: 71–108.

Tolbert, Caroline J., Daniel A. Smith and John C. Green. 2009. "Strategic Voting and Legislative Redistricting Reform: District and Statewide Representational Winners and Losers." *Political Research Quarterly* 62(1): 92–109.

Turner, Edward Raymond. 1916. "Women's Suffrage in New Jersey: 1790–1807." *Smith College Studies in History* 1(4): 165–187.

Tyler, Tom. 1990. *Why People Obey the Law*. New Haven: Yale University Press.

Tyson, Timothy B. and David S. Cecelski. 1998. "Introduction" in David. Cecelski and Timothy B. Tyson (eds.) *Democracy Betrayed: The Wilmington Race Riot of 1898 and Its Legacy*. Raleigh: University of North Carolina Press.

Uhlaner, Carole. 1989. "Rational Turnout: The Neglected Role of Groups." *American Journal of Political Science* 33(2): 390–422.

Umfleet, LeRae. 2006. 1898 Wilmington Race Riot Report of the 1898 Wilmington Race Riot Commission, accessed at http://www.history.ncdcr.gov/1898-wrrc/report/front-matter.pdf, last accessed February 3, 2015.

Valelly, Richard M. 2008. "Party, Coercion, and Inclusion: The Two Reconstructions of the South's Electoral Politics." *Politics & Society* 21(1): 37–67.

Valelly, Richard M. 2009. *The Two Reconstructions: The Struggle for Black Enfranchisement*. Chicago: University of Chicago Press.

Varsanyi, Monica W. 2005. "The Rise and Fall (and Rise?) of Non-citizen Voting: Immigration and the Shifting Scales of Citizenship and Suffrage in the United States." *Space and Polity*, 9(2): 113–134, DOI: 10.1080/13562570500304956.

Verba, Sidney, Kay Lehman Schlozman, and Henry E. Brady. 1995. *Voice and Equality: Civic Voluntarism in American Politics*. Cambridge: Harvard University Press.

Virtanen, Simo V. and Leonie Huddy. 1998. "Old Fashioned Racism and New Forms of Racial Prejudice." *Journal of Politics* 60(2): 311–332.

Von Spakovsky, Hans A. 2008. "The Threat of Non-Citizen Voting." The Heritage Foundation, Legal Memorandum #28, at http://www.heritage.org/research/reports/2008/07/the-threat-of-non-citizen-voting, last accessed February 15, 2015.

Wand, Jonathan N., Kenneth W. Shotts, Jasjet S. Sekhon, Walter R. Mebane Jr., Michael C. Herron, and Henry E. Brady. 2001. "The Butterfly Did It: The Aberrant Vote for Buchanan in Palm Beach County, Florida." *American Political Science Review* 95(4): 793–810.

Wang, Sam. 2013. "The Great Gerrymander of 2012." *The New York Times*, February 2, 2013, at http://www.nytimes.com/2013/02/03/opinion/sunday/the-great-gerrymander-of-2012.html?pagewanted=all&_r=0, last accessed June 14, 2013.

Wattenberg, Martin P., Ian McAllister and Anthony Salvanto. 2000. "How Voting Is Like Taking an SAT Test: An Analysis of American Voter Rolloff." *American Politics Research* 28(2): 234–250.

Webster, Gerald R. 2012. "Reflections on Current Criteria to Evaluate Redistricting Plans." *Political Geography* in press.

White, Ariel R., Noah L. Nathan, and Julie K. Faller. 2015. "What Do I Need to Vote? Bureaucratic Discretion and Discrimination by Local Election Officials." *American Political Science Review* 109(1): 129–142.

Wilentz, Sean. 2005. *The Rise of American Democracy: Jefferson to Lincoln*. New York: W.W. Norton and Company.

Wilson, David R. and Paul R. Brewer. 2013. "The Foundations of Public Opinion on Voter ID Laws: Political Predispositions, Racial Resentment and Information Effects." *Public Opinion Quarterly* 77(4): 962–984.

Wirth, Louis. 1938. "Urbanism as a Way of Life." *American Journal of Sociology* 44(July): 1–24.

Wolfinger, Raymond E. and Steven J. Rosenstone. 1980. *Who Votes?* New Haven: Yale University Press.

Woods, Neal D. 2009. "Promoting Participation? An Examination of Rulemaking Notification and Access Procedures." *Public Administration Review* 69(3): 518–530.

Yoshinaka, Antoine and Chad Murphy. 2011. "The Paradox of Redistricting: How Partisan Mapmakers Foster Competition but Disrupt Representation." *Political Research Quarterly* 64(2): 435–447.

Index

CPSIA information can be obtained
at www.ICGtesting.com
Printed in the USA
LVHW080355181120
671949LV00009B/185